The Fractured Schoolhouse

The Fractured Schoolhouse

Reexamining Education for a Free, Equal, and Harmonious Society

Neal P. McCluskey

ROWMAN & LITTLEFIELD
Lanham • Boulder • New York • London

Published by Rowman & Littlefield
An imprint of The Rowman & Littlefield Publishing Group, Inc.
4501 Forbes Boulevard, Suite 200, Lanham, Maryland 20706
www.rowman.com

86-90 Paul Street, London EC2A 4NE, United Kingdom

British Library Cataloguing in Publication Information Available

Library of Congress Cataloging-in-Publication Data
Names: McCluskey, Neal P., 1972– author.
Title: The fractured schoolhouse : reexamining education for a free, equal, and
    harmonious society / Neal P. McCluskey.
Description: Lanham, Maryland : Rowman & Littlefield, [2022] |
    Includes bibliographical references and index. |
Summary: "American public schooling was intended to shape and unify democratic
    citizens, but by its nature it forces divisive conflict. And democracy is not the goal
    of American government; liberty is. The Fractured Schoolhouse posits that freedom in
    education is not only consistent with liberty but is better suited to produce unity than
    public schooling"—Provided by publisher.
Identifiers: LCCN 2022001692 (print) | LCCN 2022001693 (ebook) |
    ISBN 9781475864243 (Cloth : acid-free paper) | ISBN 9781475864250 (Paperback :
    acid-free paper) | ISBN 9781475864267 (ePub)
Subjects: LCSH: Public schools—United States—Evaluation. | Democracy
    and education—United States. | School choice—Social aspects—United States. |
    Education—Political aspects—United States.
Classification: LCC LA217.2 .M3925 2022 (print) | LCC LA217.2 (ebook) | DDC
    371.010973—dc23/eng/20220310
LC record available at https://lccn.loc.gov/2022001692
LC ebook record available at https://lccn.loc.gov/2022001693

Contents

Acknowledgments

Many people have been of great assistance with the ideas in this book, which formed over several years of learning and thinking about how education systems interact with diversity and democracy. David Armor, my dissertation advisor at George Mason University, introduced me to the work of Gordon Allport and other key scholarship on social capital and intergroup contact. Alex Nowrasteh, Cato's Director of Immigration Studies, provided advice on chapters dealing with immigration and assimilation. And no doubt many people whose names I cannot remember pointed me to important work, or refined my thinking, in casual conversation.

Numerous Cato Center for Educational Freedom interns and research assistants—too many to list without fear of forgetting some—read the evolving manuscript for accuracy and intelligibility. Special thanks to former research associate Catherine Straus and intern Jolie Radunich, who commented on the nearly complete manuscript, and Cato books editor Jason Kuznicki, who offered probing thoughts. Cato Executive Vice President David Boaz also examined several chapters. Charles L. Glenn, perhaps the nation's top expert on the history of education in diverse communities, provided important insights, and his work on the hidden history of public schooling strife heavily informs this book. I also thank Tom Koerner at Rowman & Littlefield, who stuck with this project over many years, and Kira Hall at R&L, who shepherded the book, and me, through the publication process. Also, production editor Andrew Yoder. Finally, my wife Julia's editing has made me seem far less grammatically challenged than I am.

Any errors are, of course, mine.

Introduction

As I write this introduction, the country is suffering its greatest upheaval since at least the tumultuous 1960s. The most shocking manifestation of our division was the January 6, 2021, riot—some say *insurrection*—by supporters of then-president Donald Trump at the United States Capitol. It occurred as Congress was undertaking its constitutional duty to certify the 2020 presidential election, which Trump decried as fraudulent. One would struggle to envision an event more searingly symbolic of a breakdown of American unity and democratic norms than a mob smashing windows, storming doors, and running roughshod through the Capitol, especially on that day.

Of course, the riot was almost certainly a culmination of many things that had been prying apart long-present fissures. The COVID-19 pandemic, which hit home in March 2020, provoked widespread fear, lockdowns, and a culture clash over the wearing of protective masks. Meanwhile, cities and towns across the nation were seeing Black Lives Matter protests sometimes mixed with violence, the destruction of Confederate and other monuments, and widespread renaming of schools dedicated to racists and segregationists.

The greatest impetus for the latter was the murder of George Floyd, a black man, under the knee of white Minneapolis police officer Derek Chauvin. But Floyd's death was just the latest shocking, racially charged event that many saw as symptomatic of a nation riven with racism from its earliest days. Indeed, the *New York Times*' 1619 Project—published in 2019 to mark the 400th anniversary of the arrival of the first enslaved Africans in America—argued precisely that, and became a major political battleground.

At the same time, some Americans had taken to "canceling" anyone with an opinion that they deemed unacceptable. Seemingly any thought that did not toe a racially, philosophically, or politically correct line activated mobs that demanded the offender's banishment from social media, employment, and more. Even a letter calling for greater viewpoint tolerance signed by left-wing luminaries Noam Chomsky, Gloria Steinem, and Katha Pollitt elicited rebukes from mobs. And all this occurred in the fourth year of the Trump administration, which typified the ugliness with tweets right out of the Oval Office that to many felt insulting and inflammatory.

While it is almost cliché to say that this feels like the most divided time in U.S. history—surely the Civil War must hold that title—it defies intuition to think we are not close.

But that should be impossible.

If we look at the promises made by advocates of public schooling—"free" schools for all paid for and run by government—from their earliest days to today, such a state of separation and hostility should not exist. Public schools, we are told, will foster virtue in all children, bring all Americans together in harmony, and create an idyllic society. Yet here we are, engulfed by conflict and anger.

Have we just not had enough public schooling? No.

The "common schooling" movement began in the late 1830s and grew steadily from there. Since 1918, every state has had compulsory school attendance laws. And since 1889, the earliest year with federal data on public and private school enrollment, public schools have accounted for between 86 and 93 percent of school enrollment.[1] Yet we are deeply fractured.

It is not for want of good intentions. Most public schooling advocates no doubt desire a system that will create harmony. But as we shall see, the system they champion is derived from faulty—even superficial—thinking about how to do that. It is based on a simplistic, force-them-together-and-they-will-stick assumption, which flies in the face of reality: diverse people want and need different things—different math instruction, discipline policies, worldviews, and more—and pushing them into the same district or school building does not change that.

Perhaps even more important than its failure to unify, the basic nature of public schooling also crushes the bedrock good of American political life: liberty, or people freely deciding for themselves how they will live. Indeed, that may be a major reason it fails to unify.

This book consists of seven chapters that tackle the crucial facts and theoretical constructs surrounding public schooling, and make clear that the system has not and *cannot* unify diverse people. The book also examines the supposedly special—but rarely well-defined—relationship between education and democracy. Finally, it furnishes theory and evidence pointing to the way to achieve the harmonizing goals of public schooling while simultaneously upholding liberty: educational freedom, often reduced rhetorically to "school choice."

Chapter 1 examines how the United States, a country often thought synonymous with individualism, adopted an education system that might seem more appropriate for an authoritarian nation. It looks at the evolution of American thought—and *feeling*—about education, from a laissez faire colonial period to a modern day when most people may believe that public schooling is the only possible way to deliver mass education. A more subconscious level of thinking may also be at work: an underlying sense that public schooling is an institution that is somehow necessary to a democratic and unified United States.

The next chapter blankets American education history, assessing the degree to which public schooling advocates' promises of unity and equality have been fulfilled. As the chapter lays out, those promises have proven largely empty; indeed, worse than just failing to bring peace, public schooling has often stoked social warfare and marginalized numerous groups. Whether through forced segregation of African Americans and other marginalized groups, insulting immigrant assimilation schemes, or tuition for a "good" public school being the price of a home in a wealthy neighborhood, history shows repeated public schooling failure to bring Americans together, while trampling on liberty and equality under the law.

Chapter 3 gets into the theories behind the goals and structures of an education system. Is it about reproducing the status quo? Transforming it? Simply imparting marketable skills? The chapter also introduces the theory that makes the most logical sense for unifying diverse people, and lays the groundwork for understanding why, in education, school choice may be crucial.

The next two chapters look at one of the most common justifications for public schooling: it is essential to democracy. It is an assertion that is rarely unpacked—it is typically stated as if self-evident—but it demands much closer analysis than it gets.

Chapter 4 examines what different theorists have meant when they have referred to "democracy." It also looks at how different conceptualizations interact with education, and breaks approaches to democracy and education into six schools of thought. Chapter 5 establishes that regardless how one understands democracy, liberty is *the* bedrock American value, and while different formulations of the nexus between education and democracy are more or less threatening to liberty, none are ultimately consistent with a free and equal society.

Chapter 6 dives deep into the evidence on how bridges are built among separated groups. It then focuses on empirical evidence concerning physical—and, more important, psychological—integration brought about by several approaches to education delivery. The emphasis is on bridging divides, especially racial, America's deepest and most painful cleavage, and the one we have seen the most concerted—and studied—efforts to close.

The final chapter ties everything together, explaining that public schooling has not unified diverse people and, on the occasions it has brought diverse people into one system, it has fostered conflict and legal inequality while sacrificing liberty. It then focuses on choice as the key to peace and unity in education. It does not overpromise—school choice will not erect millions of bridges, and they will not go up immediately—but by allowing people to freely interact, it will create the conditions, at least within education, to slowly and sustainably unite.

NOTE

1. Digest of Education Statistics, "Enrollment in elementary, secondary, and degree-granting postsecondary institutions, by level and control of institution: Selected years, 1869–70 through fall 2029," https://nces.ed.gov/programs/digest/d20/tables/dt20_105.30.asp.

Chapter 1

Why Do We Have Government Schooling?

In 1925, in violation of Tennessee's new Butler Act, teacher John Thomas Scopes elected not to teach "the story of the Divine Creation of man as taught in the Bible" and taught "instead that man has descended from a lower order of animals." What ensued from this act of defiance was what some dubbed the "Trial of the Century," a conflict that not only enthralled the entire country, but pitted broad swaths of Americans against each other in the starkest of terms.

The trial was such a spectacular happening that it was eventually moved outside of the Rhea County courthouse, lest the sheer size of the crowd trying to get into the proceedings collapse the building's floor. Outdoors, the rhetorical lightning bolts flung by the two sides—conservative Christians represented by William Jennings Bryan, urbane liberals by Clarence Darrow—could singe the ears and hearts of even more people. No one was safe.

For Bryan, the contest was about nothing less than protecting faith itself. "These gentlemen . . . did not come here to try this case," he decried. "They came here to try revealed religion. I am here to defend it." For Darrow, it was a battle as stark as enlightenment versus superstition. "We have the purpose of preventing bigots and ignoramuses from controlling the education of the United States and you know it, and that is all," he thundered.[1]

Darrow did not just address his remarks to the court or people of Tennessee, by the way. He addressed them to the entire country.[2]

What is it about public schools? Why does a nation thought to be immersed in individual liberty, almost radical self-reliance, and what some derisively call "cowboy capitalism," have an education system that could, without a major stretch, be defined as socialist? Why does it have a system in which everyone pays taxes to support schools established by government, typically run by government, and which enroll about 90 percent of all school-aged

1

children? Why does it have an elementary and secondary education system that, depending on how you slice it, offers less freedom than many countries that Americans typically think of as socialist?

While those other countries often require that all or almost all schools follow a national curriculum, Argentina, Belgium, Denmark, the Netherlands, Sweden, and more allow citizens to choose among schools with public financing. The norm in many European countries is families choosing a Protestant, Roman Catholic, or nonsectarian school. Indeed, the United Nations Universal Declaration of Human Rights states that "parents have a prior right to choose the kind of education that shall be given to their children."[3] This has been reinforced by the Parliamentary Assembly of the Council of Europe and the European Court of Human Rights.[4]

This chapter examines the reasons that have been offered for instituting and maintaining what seems to be a most un-American education system. One in which government determines where, how, and what children will learn. Essentially, how their very minds will be formed.

THE MANY ARGUMENTS FOR
GOVERNMENT SCHOOLS

How did the education system of a country founded in "life, liberty, and the pursuit of happiness" become dominated by government? What was the trajectory, and what rationale drove it? The next chapter tackles the history of American education in greater depth, but to start this discussion it is necessary to examine a bit how education was handled not just before there were American states, but before there were even American colonies, and why. That starts with England, from whence the main culture and institutions of the early United States grew.

In sixteenth and seventeenth-century England education was laissez faire, thought to be the proper jurisdiction of families and churches, not government. Formal education had primarily been the realm of clerics through most of England's history, and it was not until roughly the latter sixteenth century that even nobles began to pursue much formal schooling.[5] Most ordinary education was focused on practical skills, often through apprenticeships or just daily work. There was also significant religious instruction, with churches tending to bear major responsibility for education. But even the learning people undertook on their own was often religious in nature.

Lawrence Cremin, in his three-volume history of American education, lays out in detail the family-centric, religiously motivated education of colonial Americans, and its roots in England. He notes that even when King Henry

VIII commented on education, he made clear that responsibility lay with families and clergy:

> [T]he role of the family as systematic educator was both emphasized and enlarged by Tudor social policy. On the religious side, the Tudors reaffirmed the traditional responsibility of the Christian family for the elementary and spiritual instruction of youth. Thus, the Royal Injunctions of Henry VIII (1536) charged parsons, vicars, and other curates diligently to "admonish the fathers and mothers, masters and governors of youth, being under their care, to teach, or cause to be taught, their children and servants, even from their infancy, their Pater Noster, the Articles of our Faith, and the Ten Commandments, in their mother tongue: and the same so taught, shall cause the said youth oft to repeat and understand."[6]

The primacy of the family in educating children was also emphasized by the highly influential philosopher John Locke, who proclaimed that "to inform the Mind, and govern the Actions of their yet ignorant Nonage, till Reason shall take its place, and ease them of that Trouble, is what the Children want, and the Parents are bound to."[7]

There is appreciable evidence that the English, including American colonists, of their own volition pursued guidance on education and child rearing. Enabled by the invention of the printing press in 1450, and the subsequent expansion of reading material and literacy itself, numerous books on child rearing and education, generally religious in nature, proliferated on both sides of the Atlantic. Titles included *The Poor Man's Family Book* by Richard Baxter and *The Pilgrim's Progress* by John Bunyan, both of which were used for the raising of children.[8]

The first English settlers in the New World, the Puritans of New England, brought a tradition of education controlled by the foundational institutions of family and church, and, to a much lesser extent, schools. (The successful expedition to Jamestown, Virginia, predated the Pilgrims, but was motivated more by commercial gain than a desire to establish a new society in the New World.) That education was primarily the purview of churches and families was the widespread belief in colonial New England for some time. But what many historians and analysts see as the germ of public schooling did eventually arise in colonial Massachusetts.

As Puritans transported themselves from long-settled Europe to the largely open New World, it was inevitable that old social structures would be difficult, if not impossible, to replicate. For practical purposes, the vast wilderness offered limitless room to spread out, and the extended families that often made English towns synonymous with family units—and enabled oversight of the children and moral rectitude of the community—scattered. Families

separated into smaller units as members occupied their own lands and established their own livelihoods. The result was a perceived weakening of institutions such as church dominion, and a governmental reaction.[9]

In 1647, Massachusetts Bay authorities enacted the "Old Deluder Satan"
Act. It was a bid to ensure that the diffuse populace could read and understand the scriptures, and hence escape the machinations of "that old deluder,
Satan." It mandated that all towns of 50 to 99 households maintain someone
to teach children, and all of 100 or more maintain a grammar school.[10]

This seemingly seminal act in establishing public schooling was most
directly motivated by religion, but to put a sociological bent on it, it was
more broadly about "social reproduction." That term will be dealt with more
extensively in subsequent chapters, but it essentially means education is supposed to perpetuate current values and social structures. That said, the act is
described as *seemingly* seminal for a reason: while it may at first appear to be
a definitive break from the family-and-church-centered, laissez faire educational tradition of England, it was not.

It is first important to note that in the Massachusetts Bay Colony the civil
and religious authorities were one and the same, so the act established essential, *Puritan* control. Second, education was not necessarily free to families.
The act stated that for teachers of children in smaller towns "wages shall be
paid either by the parents or masters of such children, or by the inhabitants in
general." No funding directions were given for larger towns, suggesting that
any common building could be used as a grammar school and the teacher
could be paid in the same manner as in smaller villages. Third, failure to
uphold the law eventually became rampant. Potential reasons ranged from
disinterest in classical education, to too many competing demands—defense,
food, etc.—crowding schooling out.[11] Finally, while colonies such as Virginia
and New York had laws requiring that children receive some education, and
Connecticut had a statute similar to "Old Deluder," most colonial education
was as it had been in *old* England: ensconced in civil—*voluntary*—society.

It was into this decentralized, religious educational culture that two major
strains of public schooling thought slowly gained adherents, primarily among
elites, as America transitioned from colonies to united states. They were that
education should be controlled and provided by government to (1) educate
the people so that they could wisely exercise sovereign power, and (2) form
young minds so that they would hold uniform opinions on matters and values
thought central to American society.

EDUCATION TO EMPOWER SOVEREIGN PEOPLE

Two of the most prominent Founders, Thomas Jefferson and John Adams, were clearly in the "informed citizens" camp. They argued that education was essential to prepare people to participate in government, and that some education should be provided at public expense to make it universal. (Universal, at least, for white children.)

Jefferson is the better known for his embrace of public schooling, having in 1779 introduced for Virginia his "Bill for More General Diffusion of Knowledge," which called for each county to be divided into "hundreds," and for each hundred to contain a school that would educate all "free" children within its boundaries for three years, at no expense to the scholars' families. All students would learn reading, mathematics, and "Grecian, Roman, English, and American history."[12] From there, a few of the top-performing boys would be appointed to higher levels of schooling at public expense—"raked from the rubbish," as Jefferson described the first culling[13]—eventually culminating in a tiny few being educated gratis at what was then the state's primary institution of higher education, the College of William & Mary.

The purpose of the bill was to educate citizens, especially in history, so that "they may be enabled to know ambition under all its shapes, and prompt to exert their natural powers to defeat its purposes." The measure would also ensure that the ablest citizens could be fully developed regardless of their financial circumstances, and hence "become useful instruments for the public."[14] Jefferson hoped to equip all citizens with the basic knowledge needed to counter those who would use government for their own ends, and to eventually elevate the "natural aristocracy."[15]

Adams's rationale for expanding education through the public purse was similar to Jefferson's, though he seems not to have given as much thought to the subject. Indeed, in an 1814 letter to Jefferson, Adams acknowledged that he had not had close to the time he would have liked to ruminate on education. "If I venture to give you any thoughts at all," he averred, "they must be very crude."[16]

In a letter to British political reformer John Jebb, Adams argued that education would enable the people to handle their democratic power. He also believed that:

the Whole People must take [upon] themselves the Education of the Whole People and must be willing to bear the expences of it. There should not be a district of one Mile square without a school in it, not founded by a charitable individual but maintained at the expense of the People themselves.[17]

Adams believed, as did Jefferson, that Americans needed education so that they would not rely, dangerously, on other men to rule them.

On a higher level, as president, George Washington extolled the virtues of a national university. One of his goals, like Jefferson's and Adams's, was to educate the leaders of a Republic in "the science of government." In his final address to Congress, Washington asked about that science: "In a Republic, what species of knowledge can be equally important and what duty more pressing on its legislature than to patronize a plan for communicating it to those who are to be the future guardians of the Liberty of the Country?"[18]

Washington's thinking, similar to Jefferson's and Adams's about equipping the people for self-governance, also fell in with the next major group of early public schooling enthusiasts: those who wanted to render the people more homogeneous and, hence, unified. As Washington also stated in his final message to Congress, "Amongst the motives" of a national university is "the assimilation of the principles, opinions and manners of our Country men . . . The more homogeneous our Citizens can be made in these particulars, the greatest will be our prospect of permanent Union."

In particular, the unity Washington sought to foster was among people of the new country's different regions—north and south, east and west—which Washington presciently feared would cleave the union. Assembling geographically diverse future leaders at a national university, Washington hoped, would impress upon them their many similarities and mutual reliance. He wrote to Alexander Hamilton, "Young men from different parts of the United States would be assembled together, & would by degrees discover that there was not that cause for those jealousies & prejudices which one part of the union had imbibed against another part."[19]

ENGINEERING UNITY

While Washington wished to employ government-provided education to promote homogeneity and unity, his main proposal (on a personal level he helped fund lower-level schools,[20] and wrote occasionally about advancing knowledge broadly[21]) was at an advanced level and through one institution, not an entire system. Some of his contemporaries—and some celebrated advocates of public schooling in later years—promoted a comprehensive, and eventually obligatory, public schooling system. For these theorists, uniform norms and thought had to be forced on children, not subtly encouraged.

Perhaps the most adamant of the Founders when it came to schooling for uniformity was Benjamin Rush, a prominent Philadelphian who had, among other things, been surgeon general of the Continental Army. Rush believed that publicly funded education was essential to the new republic, both for building bonds among its people and teaching Christian virtue he thought essential to liberty. Wrote Rush, "Our schools of learning, by producing one general and uniform system of education, will render the mass of the people more homogeneous and thereby fit them more easily for uniform and peaceable government."[22]

Rush felt not only that education should make minds "homogeneous," but echoing Aristotle's call for people to be taught that they belong to their city, that schooling should teach children that they belong to the state. "Our country includes family, friends, and property, and should be preferred to them all," he wrote. "Let our pupil be taught that he does not belong to himself, but that he is public property."[23] Rush's plan was similar to Jefferson's, calling for schools in all towns consisting of at least 100 families, and rising like a pyramid with a state university at the pinnacle.[24]

Writing at roughly the same time as Rush were Samuel Harrison Smith and Samuel Knox, who shared a 1797 American Philosophical Society (APS) prize for the best essay proposing a national system of education. The APS was founded by Benjamin Franklin, among others, and was an intercolonial, and eventually interstate, society of men interested in learning about and disseminating information on scientific and philosophical questions and phenomena. Given that hue, and a tendency of all people to think, at least occasionally, that their ideas are so enlightened they should be imposed on everyone, it was perhaps natural that the APS would seek plans "for instituting and conducting public schools in this country."[25]

Proposing a pyramidal system of education like Jefferson's, Smith argued that the key to a successful republic was an enlightened and virtuous citizenry, and to achieve that widespread knowledge was necessary. Knowledge would change people's orientation from selfishness to regard for others and would equip them for profitable, comfortable lives. Those attributes would also create a harmonious society. In particular, Smith wanted children to be instructed in history so that they could see that selfishness fuels the horrors of war, and in so doing "restrain . . . the indulgence of furious passion" in them.[26]

Smith saw the ends of public education as securing liberty, like Jefferson, and creating harmony, like Rush. Unlike Rush, Smith did not think harmony came from creating identical thoughts, but by equipping people to think for themselves. He did, though, see a need for compulsion similar to Rush. Smith argued that it was crucial that students be removed from their homes for schooling, and that private education—which he treated as synonymous with home schooling—was a danger. He thought it necessary to remove the child from the exclusive control of the family to inspire "a spirit of independent reflection and conduct."[27]

With that in mind, Smith was explicit:

> That it is the duty of a nation to superintend and even to coerce the education of children and that high considerations of expediency not only justify but dictate the establishment of a system which shall place under a control, independent of and superior to parental authority, the education of children.

In a way perhaps only somewhat less clear—but far more concrete—than Rush, Smith argued that children belong to the state.

Samuel Knox delved much more into the details of how a system rising from primary schools for all to a national university would work than did Smith. The detail of his plan was so fine that he described the rise of the pews in primary schools and specific placement of a botanical garden at the national university. His reasons for advancing a national system of public education, however, were familiar: to create an enlightened populace, made so especially by obtaining academic, rather than just practical, knowledge, and harmonizing the scattered, disparate Americans, just as Washington desired.

Wrote Knox:

> A considerable local diversity in improvement, whether with respect to morals or literature, must be the consequence of such a wide extent of territory inhabited by citizens blending together almost all the various manners of every country in Europe. Nothing, then, surely, might be supposed to have a better effect towards harmonizing the whole in these important views than an *uniform system of national education.*[28]

Knox called not just for a national schooling system, but even a uniform system of producing schoolbooks. That said, his focus did not appear to be on creating identical thought or attachment to the state, as with Rush, or separation from families, as with Smith, but enlightenment, which Knox seemed certain could come broadly only through a national system of public schools.

Finally, we come to Noah Webster, probably the most famous of the early United States' education thinkers, in large part because he is the progenitor of the dictionaries many of us use to this day.

Webster, like many of his elite contemporaries, sought publicly provided education to "implant in the minds of American youth the principles of virtue and of liberty," though he also hoped to impart some of the skills they would need in their economic lives, as opposed to advocating a classical curriculum.[29] In particular, he desired a system that would foster an attachment to the new United States. Much of Webster's essay "On the Education of Youth in America" is an appeal not to send children abroad for education, even if it were superior to what was available at home, lest those children grow more attached to their place of study than their own country. In the same spirit he encouraged young men to travel across the United States, learning from "the citizens of different states . . . each others' characters and circumstances, that all jealousies should be removed, that mutual respect and confidence should succeed and a harmony of views and interests be cultivated by a friendly intercourse."[30]

Webster's goal in putting together his famous dictionary and speller was also to create Americans, via a uniform American, rather than English, language. The exhortation at the conclusion of "On the Education of Youth in America" is clear about Webster's intent:

> Americans, unshackle your minds and act like independent beings. You have been children long enough, subject to the control and subservient to the interest of a haughty parent. You have now an interest of your own to augment and defend: you have an empire to raise and support by your exertions and a national character to establish and extend by your wisdom and virtues.[31]

THE NEXT GENERATION

Rush, Washington, Webster, and others so far discussed were all writing before there was public schooling, certainly on a national level, in America. In contrast, Horace Mann, often referred to as the "Father of the Common School," played a huge part, as his patriarchal appellation attests, in establishing public schooling. Propounding on education in such volume one wonders if he slept more than a couple of hours a night, in his 12 years serving as the first Secretary of the Massachusetts Board of Education, Mann shared the unity and enlightenment expectations of previous writers, but promised numerous additional benefits.

In his final report to the board in 1848, Mann proclaimed the awesome effect common schools would have in a nation with sovereign power vested in the people:

> Never will wisdom preside in the halls of legislation, and its profound utterances be recorded on the pages of the statute-book, until common schools—or some other agency of equal power not yet discovered—shall create a more far-seeing intelligence, and a purer morality, than has ever existed among communities of men.[32]

This was *the* message for Mann and many other public schooling advocates: Public schooling was necessary to empower all people to discern good from bad, right from wrong, and focus on the betterment of society. Free schools were "indispensable to the continuance of a republican government," Mann proclaimed, because only they were "capable of diffusing" widespread "intelligence."[33]

Importantly, Mann did not think such a national infusion of enlightenment would come simply by teaching reading, writing, and arithmetic—the
ol' "three Rs." No, it would require imbuing children with selflessness and,
echoing Benjamin Rush, molding the young so that they were "fitted for
society as well as for themselves."[34] The focus on virtue was in the same
vein as Aristotle's belief that people of a city, young and old, must be educated especially for "living in peace and being at leisure," and understanding
"noble" actions.[35]

In addition to teaching students that they are a part of society and must
always consider the welfare of others, Mann argued that attending common
schools would build affection among children that would last as adults. As he
proclaimed in his first report to the board in 1837:

> It is on this common platform, that a general acquaintanceship should be formed
> between the children of the same neighborhood. It is here that the affinities of
> a common nature should unite them together so as to give the advantages of
> pre-occupancy and a stable possession of fraternal feelings, against the alienat-
> ing competitions of subsequent life.[36]

In addition to arguing that common schooling would unite society by fostering contact among children, Mann made an economic argument: educated
workers are more conscientious, productive, and innovative than uneducated.
Anticipating modern debates and anxieties, Mann connected economic
effects to social unity, arguing that expanding education would diminish
resentment-breeding income inequality. He wrote that education "prevents
being poor," and by eliminating poverty would enlarge "the cultivated class
or caste" and "open a wider area over which the social feelings will expand."[37]

Mann, at the very least, sounded as if he believed common schooling
would have extraordinary transformative, enlightening power. And it would
need Herculean potency, because as optimistic as Mann was about public
schooling, he appeared pessimistic about the average person. Based on his
ruminations about parents in particular, Mann seemed convinced that many,
well, *common* people were either well intentioned but dangerously ignorant,
or rotten. In other words, common schooling was not about perfecting something already good, but overhauling people who were intellectually, and often
morally, dilapidated.

Mann's concern about parents was illuminated in litanies on their almost
countless deficiencies. To put it mildly, leaving education to parents would
too often lead to education not being completed, or being done wrong.
Indeed, Mann concluded, often out of love parents did things patently—and
shockingly—wrong:

Nature supplies the love; but she does not supply the knowledge. The love is spontaneous; the knowledge is to be acquired by study and toil, by the most attentive observation and the profoundest reflection. Here, then, lies the fatal error:—parents rest contented with the feeling of love; they do not devote themselves to the acquisition of that knowledge which is necessary to guide it.[38]

Parents' shiftless love, Mann opined, could almost literally lead to suffocating a child with affection. Mann explained that on cold nights a loving mother "will visit the closet-like bed-chamber of her darling, calk up every crevice and cranny, smother him with as many integuments as incase an Egyptian mummy, close the door of his apartment, and thus inflict on him a consumption,—born of love."[39] Or, Mann wrote, a matriarch "will consult the infinite desires of a child's appetite, instead of the finite powers of his stomach, and thus pamper him, until he languishes into a life of suffering and imbecility, or becomes stupefied and besotted by one of sensual indulgence."[40]

Parental bungling was not confined to children's physical well-being, but also their spiritual and moral health. Here, especially, is where the common schools must intervene:

All children have foolish desires, freaks, caprices, appetites, which they have no power or skill to gratify; but the foolish parent supplies all the needed skill, time, money, to gratify them; and thus the greater talent and resources of the parent foster the propensities of the child into excess and predominance. The parental love which was designed by Heaven to be the guardian angel of the child, is thus transformed into a cruel minister of evil.[41]

The common schools were needed to take children, especially from love-drunk parents, and break them of their dissolute, selfish natures. That, in turn, would empower them to live well both for themselves and for society. They would be freed from their base instincts, and thus rendered fit for a state—and nation—built on the sovereignty of the people.

Historians John Meyer, David Tyack, Joane Nagel, and Audri Gordon have suggested that a sort of "nation building" along the lines of what Mann wanted, though with a far more evangelical Protestant bent than the Unitarian Mann would have embraced, fueled public schooling in much of the nineteenth century north and west. It was primarily rural areas that drove the system, where the generally conservative, Protestant populace tended to believe that education should be employed to combat ignorance, sin, political subordination, and sloth, and in so doing create a national, American mindset. It would also, some believed, lay the groundwork for the enlightened millennium that would precede the second coming of Christ.

Write Meyer et al:

To liberate . . . individuals and to link them by education and salvation to a millennial America seemed within the reach of a responsible citizenry. "Educate the rising generation mentally, morally, physically, just as it should be done," a Yankee Republican senator exhorted his colleagues, "and this nation and this world would reach the millennium within one hundred years."[42]

The spread of this powerful mindset largely preceded widespread compulsory schooling.

Last, at least chronologically, among the public schooling crusaders who emphasized the power to foster unity was the famous progressive John Dewey. Among many endeavors, Dewey established the University of Chicago Laboratory School, a test tube for his theories about how schools—ultimately within a system of government schooling—could maximize unity without ignoring children's basic humanity.

Like many thinkers discussed in this chapter, Dewey—who was most active between roughly 1890 and 1930—believed that universal, free schooling was a crucial unifying advancement, ending the longstanding notion of education as something only for elites. But providing something called "education" to all people was not sufficient to overcome divisions, especially by class. Such divisions, Dewey concluded, were reinforced by a system in which elites received education geared toward "leisure"—creative mental pursuits aimed to "reward intelligence"—while most others were educated for "labor" aimed at receiving a wage.[43]

Dewey thought that this bifurcation maintained class separation, while creating a dangerous and illogical dichotomy between what people do and their moral obligations to others. It was to eradicate such divisions that Dewey argued education was crucial, but it had to be education in which diverse students worked together in largely self-driven pursuits. Such student-centered teamwork, Dewey theorized, would foster contact among children of diverse backgrounds. It would also foster a sense that one's work is not about a wage, but the work's inherent value to the person undertaking it and others around him. It was this social outlook that Dewey believed would enlighten children, not by teaching them Christian or other moral codes, but by making them feel a duty to society.

Wrote Dewey in *Democracy and Education*:

[T]he great danger which threatens school work is the absence of conditions which make possible a permeating social spirit; this is the great enemy of effective moral training. For this spirit can be actively present only when certain conditions are met. . . . The plea which has been made for education through continued constructive activities in this book rests upon the fact they afford an opportunity for a social atmosphere. In place of a school set apart from life as a place for learning lessons, we have a miniature social group in which study and growth are incidents of present shared experience. Playgrounds, shops, workrooms, laboratories not only direct the natural active tendencies of youth, but they involve intercourse, communications, and cooperation,—all extending the perceptions of connections.[44]

Dewey believed, like many predecessors, that education must be universal and government provided. But he also held that morality and enlightenment could not be forced into children, but instilled only by leaving children largely free to direct their own learning.

"DEMOCRACY" TRUMPS FREEDOM

Dewey was writing just as the philosophical justification for public schooling was changing. Indeed, to some extent he was both a response to, and perpetuator of, "progressive" dominance in education thinking. Progressives, broadly, believed that scientific thinking—formulating hypotheses, testing them, revising them based on test results, testing again—could be brought to bear on social and political problems. In education, this manifested itself in two groups that education historian David Tyack has labeled "pedagogical" and "administrative" progressives.

The former were thinkers such as Dewey who embraced child-centered learning, based on the idea that children are natural learners and the most effective way to educate them is to embrace their instinctive inquisitiveness. This notion was at loggerheads with administrative progressives, who, inspired by the corporate form and factories, applied "scientific" management to education systems. Administrative progressivism boasted that elites—the wealthy, or university-educated experts—had the knowledge and ability to engineer the best societal outcomes. It also assumed that average people could not understand expert analyses, and would not produce expert-prescribed outcomes on their own. The result was growing bureaucratic domination of increasingly centralized districts, and the wielding of new "scientific" tools to make educational decisions. These included IQ testing and tracking of students into (usually) vocational learning or (rarely) academic programs.

Perhaps no thought leader of the time typified confidence in the power of science more than Ellwood P. Cubberley, an Indianan who served a stint as the schools' superintendent in turn-of-the-century San Diego, and spent most of his career as a professor at Stanford University. He was an outspoken advocate for public schooling and was perhaps most distinguished for his effort to elucidate education history. In that effort, Cubberley made clear what he believed was the proper construction and role of education: state-dominated, to train people for their lives as citizens. As he wrote in *The History of*

Education, which traced schooling from the Greeks to the time immediately after World War I:

> Suffice it here to say that from mere teaching institutions, engaged in imparting a little religious instruction and some knowledge of the tools of learning, the school, in all the leading nations, has to-day been transformed into an institution for advancing the national welfare. The leading purpose now is to train for political and social efficiency in the more democratic types of governments being instituted among peoples, and to impart to the young those industrial and social experiences once taught in the home, the trades, and on the farm, but which the coming of the factory system and city life have otherwise deprived them of otherwise knowing.[45]

In tracing history, and in keeping with the era's science-triumphant ethos, Cubberley enunciated a clear theme: history suffered from a stupefying dearth of scientific thought and a dominance of mystical, religious mindsets. It was only when science was allowed to triumph—a victory enabled by, and contributing to, the ascendancy of state-run schooling—that humanity emerged from darkness. Discussing the transitional eighteenth century, Cubberley expressed how he saw education evolving from backward and superstitious to modern and *progressive*:

> The new spirit and interests and attitudes which came to characterize the eighteenth century in the more progressive western nations meant the ultimate overthrow of the tyranny of mediaeval supernatural theology, the evolution of a new theory as to moral action which should be independent of theology, the freeing of the new scientific spirit from the fetters of church control, the substituting of new philosophical and scientific and economic interests for the old theological problems which had for so long dominated human thinking, the substitution of natural political organization for the older ecclesiastical foundations of the State, the destruction of what remained of the old feudal political system, the freeing of the serf and the evolution of the citizen, and the rise of the modern society interested in problems of national welfare—government in the interest of the governed, commerce, industry, science, economics, education, and social welfare.[46]

Cubberley saw the state seizing control of education as a good thing, liberating it from mysticism and, ultimately, serving democracy. But what did Cubberley mean by "democracy"? The nexus of education and democracy will be tackled in depth in chapter four, but for Cubberley, the answer seemed to be a popularly elected government that incongruously recognized individual liberty but had overriding involvement in people's lives, usually to engineer the optimal distribution of social and economic goods.

At the same time Cubberley wrote of the centrality of state schools in creating "social efficiency," he concluded that "the extension of the suffrage to
new classes gave a clear political motive for the school, and to train young
people to read and write and know the constitutional bases of liberty became
a political necessity."[47] Cubberley also argued that government schools would
unite diverse peoples by ending the balkanization of religion-based schooling
and assimilating the immigrants that streamed into America. The latter was a
crucial issue in Cubberley's time of peak industrialization, immigration, and
world war.

The root paradox in Cubberley's thought, like that in Benjamin Rush's
and others, before him, was that while the purpose of education was in part
to teach students "the constitutional basis of liberty" it was also to *suppress*
individualism and the Lockean conception of individual rights. Summarized
Cubberley:

> The great needs of the modern world call for the general diffusion among the
> masses of mankind the intellectual and spiritual and political gains of the centu-
> ries. . . . Among the more important of these are the religious spirit, coupled with
> full religious liberty and tolerance; a clear recognition of the rights of minori-
> ties, so long as they do not impair the advancement of the general welfare; the
> general diffusion of a knowledge of the more common truths and applications
> of science, particularly as they relate to personal hygiene, sanitation, agricul-
> ture, and modern industrial processes; the general education of all, not only in
> the tools of knowledge, but in those fundamental principles of self-government
> which lie at the basis of democratic life; training in character, self-control, and
> in the ability to assume and carry responsibility; the instilling into a constantly
> widening circle of mankind the importance of fidelity to duty, truth, honor, and
> virtue; the emphasis of the many duties and responsibilities which encompass all
> in the complex modern world, rather than the eighteenth-century individualistic
> conception of political and personal rights; the clear distinction between liberty
> and license; and the conception of liberty guided by law. In addition each man
> and woman should be educated for personal efficiency in some vocation or form
> of service in which each can best realize his personal possibilities, and at the
> same time render the largest service to that society of which he forms a part."[48]

Cubberley's "great needs" were, at best, a collection of centimeter-close
contradictions, at worst a manifesto for oppression, perhaps best captured
by his invocation of "rights of minorities, *so long as they do not impair the
advancement of the general welfare.*" Education was to prepare people for
self-government, but only within whatever box the state saw fit to put them.

Cubberley also did not see the education system as primarily a means
of upward mobility—an elevator from the gutter to the penthouse—as
others have presented it. That public schooling should pinpoint "personal

possibilities" in the interest of "service to . . . society" is quite similar to his somewhat infamous line, written in 1909, that schools "should give up the exceedingly democratic idea that all are equal and that our society is devoid of classes," and they should educate according to the class into which children are likely to go.[49] "The employee tends to remain an employee," he wrote, and "the wage earner tends to remain a wage earner."[50]

Today, that public schooling is essential to "democracy," and democracy should override individual concerns, is commonplace among public schooling defenders. The most direct in enunciating this case is political scientist Amy Gutmann, whose book *Democratic Education* touts public schooling's role in "conscious social reproduction," an idea mentioned at the beginning of this chapter. Gutmann holds that the school system is a mechanism society uses to inculcate in the newest generation what they will need to know to live in the society they are entering, and uphold social norms and institutions.[51]

Government control is also, to some extent, about protecting liberty by suppressing intolerance. Gutmann posits that families, if in charge of education, would instill repressive values. She especially singles out religion:

> To save their children from future pain, especially the pain of eternal damnation, parents have historically shielded their children from diverse associations, convinced them that all other ways of life are sinful, and implicitly fostered (if not explicitly taught them) disrespect for people who are different.[52]

Gutmann goes so far as to argue that the education system in a "democratic" government is well within its rights to impose teachings on minority groups that dislike, or even abhor, those teachings, as long as those groups have had some kind of say in formulating the policy. That say may be as minor as an opportunity to share their thoughts at a school board meeting:

> If the challenge is directed to the teaching of values that directly conflict with those of some citizens, then the response to dissenting adults can take the following form: "The values we are teaching are the product of a collective decision to which you were party. Insofar as that decision deprives no one of the opportunity to participate in future decisions, its outcome is legitimate, even if it is not correct."[53]

Democracy not only trumps liberty, it tramples it: As long as the process lets everyone make a peep, almost any outcome is just. Gutmann offers two provisos: A democratically made decision is not acceptable if it (1) "stifles rational deliberation," meaning, essentially, it curbs decision-making based on the freedom of all to express their beliefs, and (2) it discriminates by not educating "all educable children." Gutmann would allow spheres below government—families, religious groups—some educational role, but would require all people to pay for public schools to make families look beyond those groups and "share the rights and obligations of citizenship with people who do not share our complete conception of the good life."[54]

Such practicing of "deliberative democracy" is supposed to draw people together by requiring those who disagree to confront one another. As Gutmann and Dennis Thompson write in *Why Deliberative Democracy*:

> Deliberative democrats do not expect deliberation always or even usually to yield agreement. How citizens deal with the disagreement that is endemic in political life should therefore be a central question in any democracy. Practicing the economy of moral disagreement promotes the value of mutual respect. . . . By economizing on their disagreements, citizens and their representatives can continue to work together to find common ground.[55]

This is an important function of public schools for historian and public schooling advocate Diane Ravitch, who warns that "as we lose neighborhood public schools, we lose the one local institution where people congregate and mobilize to solve local problems, where individuals learn to speak up and debate and engage in democratic give-and-take with their neighbors."[56] Similarly, Deborah Meier—school founder and public schooling defender— writes in her book *In Schools We Trust*, "It is in schools that we learn the art of living together as citizens." Indeed, she says public schools are beneficial when they attack basic rights because "it's within such schools that we need to learn to resist what we see as improper encroachments on our rights, and to organize and expand what we believe to be our entitlements."[57]

WHAT DOES THE PUBLIC THINK?

There is a clear line of thinking from early in our national history through the present day that public schooling—not just education of the public, but schooling *controlled by government*—is a uniquely important, if not indispensable, institution. The reasoning behind this, however, varies, and two seemingly opposed goals are often intertwined.

For some thinkers, the purpose of public schooling is to promote individual liberty. This is to be done, largely, by forging children into alert, active citizens in the governmental system thought best able to protect their freedom: democracy. For others, the goal is to shape children so they are not threats in a government system that is supposed to reflect the desires of "the people." What they seem to want is to neutralize the threat of radically thinking adults by rendering people at least somewhat identical during childhood. They must be instilled with common views about the role of the citizen; shared moral values; and a sense that everyone, regardless of race, creed, or color, is essentially the same.

The first view, the active-citizens model, is typified by Jefferson's view that broad education is needed for the populace to detect dangerous power-seekers. The extreme form of the other view is Rush's assertion that public schools are needed to "render the mass of the people more homogeneous and thereby fit them more easily for uniform and peaceable government."

But how prominent is the connection between social cohesion, democracy, and public schooling in the modern American mind? To what extent does the belief that public schooling is necessary for unity and democracy manifest itself in broad support for government schooling? How about a conviction that such education is necessary to protect liberty?

It is not easy to answer these questions, but there are some survey results that suggest that the belief that public schools are essential to the nation, perhaps in the service of engineering or preserving cohesion, is widely present, if not consciously or definitively so.

Americans certainly tend to like their local public schools. Consistent with many years of results, for instance, the 2019 Phi Delta Kappa survey of Americans' attitudes concerning education found that 44 percent of respondents graded the public schools in their communities an A or a B, and 76 percent of public school parents gave their child's school such grades.[58] This does not, however, translate into approval of the performance of American public schooling overall—only 19 percent gave that an A or B, again consistent with a long-standing trend.[59]

Popular affection for the "democratic" ideal of public schooling articulated by formative thinkers could well manifest itself in widespread love of local schools, the level at which oft-romanticized democratic control is supposed to occur. Public schooling advocate and scholar Diane Ravitch, and scholars such as Kenneth R. Howe and David E. Meens, think the school district embodies true democratic education, because districts are most directly influenced by the communities they are supposed to serve.[60]

That said, as is discussed in great depth later in the book, we do not commonly reside in diverse communities. And if we tend to live with people like ourselves, giving high grades to one's local schools may not reflect support of public schools as conveners of diverse people, but places in which children of very similar backgrounds congregate. So the question remains: Is there compelling evidence that the public embraces public schooling as an institution that is essential to the fabric of pluralist, democratic, united society?

There is some such evidence, but assessments of the public's feelings on the social and democratic missions of public schooling are not nearly as numerous as, say, surveys about specific school policies and academic outcomes. That alone may indicate that the public is not particularly interested in the social cohesion and citizen-creation purposes of public schooling that justified its creation and expansion.

The 2016 Phi Delta Kappa poll directly addressed the social mission of public schools, asking what "the main goal of public school education" should be: preparing students "academically," for "work," or "to be good citizens"? The clear winner was "academically," with 45 percent of respondents prioritizing it. Preparing students to be good citizens barely slipped into second, beating "work" 26 to 25 percent.[61] Of course, preparing for a career and financial viability are big goals, so maybe they just swamped the more abstract—but still important—"citizenship."

When respondents were able to assess preparing "good citizens" along with several other desired outcomes, forming citizens did well, with 82 percent of respondents saying it was "extremely," or "very" important, but that was in line with most other outcomes from which respondents could choose. It outpaced teaching "students to work successfully in groups" but appreciably lagged "help students develop good work habits."[62] In both questions respondents were given preparing "good citizens" as an outcome from which to choose, and it is unknown how it would have fared in an open-response question requiring that people volunteer it.

A 2012 survey of parents by the Thomas B. Fordham Institute suggested that public schools' unifying mission may have receded in Americans' minds as federal law had fixated on math and reading scores, and "workforce development," since at least the 2002 enactment of the No Child Left Behind Act. Robust math and reading instruction, and instilling good study skills, were by far parents' top desires. "Instruction in citizenship, democracy, and leadership" and fostering "a love of country/patriotism" were relatively low.[63] Exposing kids to diversity, and preparing them to work with diverse groups, also fell deep on priority lists, a reality that also held for public, private, and charter school parents.

That said, one cohort of parents—about 24 percent of those surveyed—placed preparation of citizens much higher than other respondents, a group the pollsters labeled "Jeffersonians." In addition, about 22 percent placed learning "how to work with people from diverse backgrounds" disproportionately high, a subset they termed "multiculturalists." So there was at least a nucleus of parents who elevated preparing future citizens and enabling them to work effectively with diverse people.

2012 may have also been a nadir. A 2017 survey of 18- to 34-year-olds found 31 percent placed preparing students to "be good citizens" as "the main goal of a public school education," versus 39 percent academic preparation, and 29 percent preparing students "for work."[64] A 2021 survey saw 43 percent of adults agree it is "extremely important" for schools to teach kids in grades K–8 "how to be good citizens," and 47 percent said the same for high schoolers. The top concern for K—8 was "core academic subjects," with 56 percent of respondents deeming it "extremely important," and for high school 58 percent cited "skills for future employment."[65]

There is, then, an explicit belief among at least some people today that public schools should foster social cohesion and create democratic citizens, consistent with the main focus of public schooling theorists historically. Perhaps among members of the public there is also a broad, but unconscious, sense that public schools are essential because of their social, rather than academic, functions. Maybe many people do not *explicitly* identify public schools as having a key unifying or democracy-preserving role, but they *feel* that they do.

This is possibly captured in 2001 polling by political scientist Terry Moe, who detected what he called a "public school ideology . . . a normative attachment to the public schools."[66] Moe perceived this in parents' responses to statements pitting public against private schools.

One statement was, "I believe in public education, and I wouldn't feel right putting my kids in private or parochial school." 43 percent of parents who had only sent their children to public schools agreed with that, as did 31 percent of parents who had used both public *and private schools*. That such large percentages of parents—including many who had used private institutions—not only supported public schooling, but felt that using private schools would not be "right," suggests a strong emotional response.

Another statement, this time asked of parents and non-parents, drives the point further home. 41 percent of non-parents, 40 percent of parents who had only used public schools, and 28 percent of parents who had used both public and private institutions agreed that "the more children attend public schools, rather than private or parochial schools, the better it is for American society." Again, large percentages of parents, but also non-parents, saw not just education, but *public schooling*, as crucial to the country. And the implication is not that students would be uneducated absent public schools. The statement presents private and parochial schools, not nothing, as the alternatives. It is probing beliefs about *where* education takes place.

Perhaps many Americans simply think public schooling is academically superior . . . or not. A third statement to which respondents were asked to react was, "The public schools deserve our support even if they are performing poorly." 67 percent of non-parents agreed, as did 64 percent of public-only parents, and 68 percent of parents who had used both public and private schools. Even private-school-only parents split 49–49, with 3 percent answering, "don't know." This suggests that support, at least to some extent, should not hinge on academic effectiveness.

CONCLUSION

How did a nation "conceived in liberty," to borrow from Abraham Lincoln, find itself with an education system dominated by government schooling? The answer seems to be "slowly," with an evolving conception of what education—ultimately framed as synonymous with government-run schooling—is supposed to do. From a tradition grounded in voluntary, civil society, the goal appeared to evolve from protecting liberty by enlightening the people—the goal of Jefferson and even Mann—to controlling society through government coercion, as Rush, Cubberley, and Gutmann encouraged.

Today, these sorts of non-academic, social aims may reside largely in the recesses of the collective heart, but evidence suggests that sometimes overtly, other times subtly, Americans still believe that public schooling is a necessary institution for forming citizens and fostering cohesion. And these are important goals; most Americans want social harmony and support government by and for the people.

Here's the problem: Aiming at a goal and hitting it are two different things, as any skeet shooter, bowler, or socks-to-the-hamper hoopster can tell you. And missing can sometimes have disastrous consequences, from failing to strike the charging bear, to sending a favorite lamp crashing to the floor. The next chapter tackles whether public schools have achieved their unifying goal, truly serving as "the forges of our citizenship and the bedrock of our democracy," as Benjamin Barber has put it.[67] Or have they actually further cleaved social divisions while quashing the liberty that democracy is supposed to serve?

NOTES

1. "Days Six and Seven: Transcript of Scopes Trial, Friday July 17 and Monday July 20, 1925," The Clarence Darrow Digital Collection, University of Minnesota Law Library, http://darrow.law.umn.edu/documents/Scopes%206th%20&%20 7th%20days.pdf, 288.

2. H. L. Mencken, "Coverage of The Scopes Trial by H. L. Mencken," https://archive. org/stream/CoverageOfTheScopesTrialByH.l.Mencken/ScopesTrialMencken.txt.

3. United Nations, "The Universal Declaration of Human Rights," article 26, section 3 https://www.un.org/en/about-us/universal-declaration-of-human-rights.

4. International Organization for the Right to Education and Freedom of Education and Novae Terrae Foundation, "Freedom of Education Index Worldwide Report 2016 on Freedom of Education," 6–14, https://www.oidel.org/doc/FEI_complet2.pdf.

5. J. H. Hexter, "The Education of the Aristocracy in the Renaissance," *The Journal of Modern History* 22, no. 1 (March 1950): 1–20.

6. Lawrence A. Cremin, *American Education: The Colonial Experience 1607–1783* (New York: Harper Torchbooks, 1970), 119.

7. John Locke, *Two Treatises of Government*, ed. Peter Laslett (New York: Cambridge University Press, 1994), 306.

8. Cremin, *The Colonial Experience*, 49–50.

9. Bernard Bailyn, *Education in the Forming of American Society* (New York: W. W. Norton and Company, 1960).

10. "The Old Deluder Satan Act (1647)," https://www.mass.gov/files/documents/2016/08/ob/deludersatan.pdf.

11. Jon Teaford, "The Transformation of Massachusetts Education," in *The Social History of American Education*, eds. B. Edward McClellan and William J. Reese (Urbana, IL: University of Illinois Press, 1988), 25–28.

12. Thomas Jefferson, "A Bill for the More General Diffusion of Knowledge," in *Jefferson: Writings*, comp. Merrill D. Peterson (New York: Literary Classics of the U.S., 1984), 365–373.

13. Jefferson, "Query XIV," *Jefferson: Writings*, 274.

14. Jefferson, "A Bill for the More General Diffusion of Knowledge," 365.

15. Thomas Jefferson, "The Assent of the Mind: Jefferson to Adams, October 28, 1813," in *The Adams–Jefferson Letters: The Complete Correspondence between Thomas Jefferson and Abigail and John Adams*, ed. Lester J. Cappon (Chapel Hill, NC: The University of North Carolina Press, 1987), 387–392.

16. John Adams, "Most Honourable to Human Nature: Adams to Jefferson, July 16, 1814," in *The Adams–Jefferson Letters: The Complete Correspondence between Thomas Jefferson and Abigail and John Adams*, ed. *Lester J. Cappon*, 438.

17. John Adams, "John Adams to John Jebb, September 10, 1785," Founders Online, https://founders.archives.gov/documents/Adams/06-17-02-0232.

18. Washington, "Eighth Annual Message," *Washington: Writings*, 983.

19. Washington, "To Alexander Hamilton," *Washington: Writings*, 960–61.

20. Washington, "To William Pierce," *Washington: Writings*, 898; "Last Will and Testament," 1024–1027.

21. Washington, "First Annual Message to Congress," *Washington: Writings*, 750.

22. Benjamin Rush, "Thoughts upon the Mode of Education Proper in a Republic," in *Essays on Education in the Early Republic*, ed. Frederick Rudolph (Cambridge, MA: The Belknap Press of Harvard University Press, 1965), 9.

23. Rush, *Essays on Education in the Early Republic*, 13–14.

24. Rush, "Plan for the Establishment of Public Schools," *Essays on Education in the Early Republic*, 3–8.

25. Lawrence A. Cremin, *American Education: The National Experience, 1783–1876* (New York: Harper Colophon Books, 1980), 122.

26. Samuel Harrison Smith, "Remarks on Education," *Essays on Education in the Early Republic*, 196.

27. Smith, "Remarks on Education," 207.

28. Samuel Knox, "An Essay on the Best System of Liberal Education, Adapted to the Genius of the Government of the United States," *Essays on Education in the Early Republic*, 311.

29. Noah Webster, "On the Education of Youth in America," in Frederick Rudolph, ed., *Essays on Education in the Early Republic* (Cambridge, MA: The Belknap Press of Harvard University Press, 1965), 45.

30. Webster, "On the Education of Youth in America," 76.

31. Webster, "On the Education of Youth in America," 77.

32. Horace Mann, "Report for 1848," in *Life and Works of Horace Mann*, ed. Mary Mann (Boston: Horace B. Fuller, 1868), 695.

33. Mann, "Report for 1846," in *Life and Works of Horace Mann*, 531.

34. Mann, "Report for 1845," in *Life and Works of Horace Mann*, 422.

35. *The Politics of Aristotle*, trans. Peter L. Phillips Simpson (Chapel Hill, NC: The University of North Carolina Press, 1997), 142.

36. Horace Mann, "First Annual Report," in *Lectures, and Annual Reports, on Education*, ed. Mary Mann (Boston: Lee and Shepard, 1872), 417–418.

37. Mann, "Report for 1848," 669–670.

38. Horace Mann, "Lecture IV: What God Does, And What He Leaves for Man to Do, in the Work of Education," *Life and Works of Horace Mann*, 212.

39. Mann, "Lecture IV: What God Does, And What He Leaves for Man to Do, in the Work of Education," 213.

40. Mann, "Lecture IV: What God Does, And What He Leaves for Man to Do, in the Work of Education," 213.

41. Mann, "Lecture IV: What God Does, And What He Leaves for Man to Do, in the Work of Education," 225.

42. John W. Meyer, et al., "Public Education as Nation-Building in America: Enrollments and Bureaucratization in the American States: 1870–1930," *American Journal of Sociology* 85 (1979): 601. See also Carl F. Kaestle, *Pillars of the Republic: Common Schools and American Society, 1780–1860* (New York: Hill and Wang, 1983), 75–103.

43. John Dewey, *Education and Democracy*, 273–285.

44. Dewey, *Education and Democracy*, 390.

45. Ellwood P. Cubberley, *The History of Education* (New York: Kessinger Publishing, 1920), 474.

46. Cubberley, *History of Education*, 303.

47. Cubberley, *History of Education*, 474.

48. Cubberley, *History of Education*, 537.

49. Ellwood P. Cubberley, *Changing Conceptions of Education* (Boston, MA: Houghton Mifflin Company), 57.

50. Cubberley, *Changing Conceptions of Education,* 10.

51. Gutmann, *Democratic Education*, 289

52. Gutmann, *Democratic Education*, 31.

53. Gutmann, *Democratic Education*, 39.

54. Gutmann, *Democratic Education*, 44–47.

55. Amy Gutmann and Dennis Thompson, *Why Deliberative Democracy* (Princeton, NJ: Princeton Paperbacks, 2004), 7.

56. Diane Ravitch, *The Death and Life of the Great American School System: How Testing and Choice are Undermining Education* (New York, NY: Basic Books, 2010), 356.

57. Deborah Meier, *In Schools We Trust: Creating Communities of Learning in An Era of Testing and Standardization* (Boston, MA: Beacon Press, 2002), 176–177.

58. Phi Delta Kappa, "How would you grade the public schools?" *The 2019 PDK Poll of the public's attitudes toward the public schools*, September 2019, https://pdkpoll.org/results/how-would-you-grade-the-schools.

59. Phi Delta Kapp.

60. Ravitch, 356; Kenneth R. Howe and David E. Meens, "Democracy Left Behind: How Recent Education Reforms Undermine Local Governance and Democratic Education," National Education Policy Center, October 2012.

61. Phi Delta Kappa, "The 48th Annual PDK Poll of the Public's Attitudes Toward the Public Schools."

62. Phi Delta Kappa, K10.

63. Dara Zeehandelaar and Amber M. Winkler, "What Parents Want: Education Preferences and Trade-offs," Thomas B. Fordham Institute, August 2013.

64. GenForward, "GenForward July 2017 Toplines," August 2017, http://genforwardsurvey.com/assets/uploads/2017/09/GenForward-July-Toplines-_-Education.pdf.

65. EdChoice, "Public Opinion Tracker," July 7, 2021, https://edchoice.morningconsultintelligence.com/assets/124032.pdf.

66. Terry M. Moe, *Schools, Vouchers, and the American Public* (Washington, DC: Brookings Institution Press, 2001), 86–91.

67. Benjamin R. Barber, "Public Schooling: Education for Democracy," in *The Public Purpose of Education and Schooling*, eds. John I. Goodlad and Timothy J. McMannon (San Francisco, CA: Jossey-Bass, 1997), 22.

Chapter 2

Reality Begs to Differ: Little Unity, Wrenching Conflict

Sixth-grade students in the Dover-Sherborn Regional School District in Massachusetts were assigned to read So Far from the Bamboo Grove, *a semi-autobiographical novel about a Japanese family fleeing Korea at the conclusion of World War II. Decades of brutal Japanese occupation of the Korean peninsula had made the Japanese hugely reviled—and marked targets. The novel's main protagonist, an 11-year-old girl, witnesses atrocities such as murder and rape against Japanese people, including children, and relates those horrors in the story.*

The reading shook many people, and 13 parents called for its removal from the curriculum. They objected to its graphic content, and what some saw as ahistorical demonization of Koreans, especially Korean men, whom they felt were portrayed as monsters. "You'll notice throughout the book these acts are committed by Korean men—it is a pretty disturbing connotation of a group of people," father Henry Jaung told a Boston Globe *reporter. "The first impression you imprint in a child's mind is typically very hard to erase."*

But was not grappling with the young child's experience enlightening for readers who would eventually have to deal with ugly truths about the real world? The district had been teaching the book for 13 years, and as one mother, Karen Masterson, related to the Dover-Sherborn Regional School Committee, working through So Far from the Bamboo Grove *had been one of her children's "best educational experiences," one that "ignited a love of reading" in her daughter. Meanwhile, author Yoko Kawashima Watkins said that her goal was not to denigrate Koreans. She just wanted to tell a story of survival.*

The conflict smoldered for months. But it did, eventually, foster some fleeting unity: both the governments of North and South Korea condemned the assignment.[1]

Instinctively, it makes sense: Put diverse children and communities under one schooling roof, teach all kids the same norms, values, and perhaps literature and interpretations of history, and you will achieve harmony. Do that in service of democracy and you will also reinforce the system of government designed to protect the sovereignty of the people, and the one thought most friendly to liberty.

You need, however, go no further than the old saw, "in *theory* communism works . . ." to know that what may seem wise in the abstract often fails in practice. The history of American education, and other countries, strongly suggests that what one might call the Lego Theory of Social Cohesion—push them together and they will stick—does not, itself, hold together. Indeed, the evidence is considerable that public schools have served as combat-sparking, net social *dividers*. As legal scholar Stephen Arons put it, "As the majoritarian assumption took hold, public education policy was transformed into a battleground for determining orthodoxy in a heterogeneous culture."[2]

Despite triumphal assertions about the seminal role of public schooling in unifying Americans and advancing democracy, unity within public schooling has often been a mirage, and broader social cohesion may have occurred *in spite of* common schooling. As Clive Belfield and Henry Levin of the National Center for the Study of Privatization in Education have noted, "it is difficult to find empirical research that substantiates the importance of common schooling in promoting social order."[3] Why? As education scholar Christopher J. Lucas has written, sooner or later public schools have to deal with the reality of people holding diverse values and beliefs:

> If the values taught in the school have to compete with others fostered elsewhere, the difficulty for educators is obvious. Nor is it simply a question of how to inculcate certain values in preference to others. The issue is also one of institutional choice: the school must adjudicate the conflicting demands made upon it and retain public support for its programs, all the while determining *which* mores, standards, values, and ideologies it can endorse.[4]

Peacefully and fairly adjudicating conflicting demands, especially when cherished values have been at stake, has often proven a Herculean task.

To examine public schooling's role in fostering social harmony, it may be useful to break American educational history into two blocks. Prior to 1837, the year Horace Mann began his crusading tenure as the first Secretary of the Massachusetts Board of Education, and after. In particular, examining whether the period before widespread public schooling featured mass illiteracy and ignorance, leading to disunity and autocracy, and whether the period after saw an eruption of learning, government by the people, and unity.

Of course, evolutionary change does not suddenly happen on a specific date. American educational history incorporates myriad trends and thoughts, actions and inactions, that have ebbed and flowed in often unclear currents. Rarely has anyone been able to wake up, brew their morning coffee, read their news, and declare, "It's education paradigm shift day!" Still, few steeped in education history would likely disagree that Horace Mann's secretarial tenure was pivotal.

Note that the goal is not to revisit the ground covered in the previous chapter, which traced somewhat briefly the evolution of the thinking driving public schooling. It is to examine the concrete evidence of how *necessary*, and then *successful*, the public schooling experiment has been. The following revisits some names and ideas, but only to give public schooling's record the rigorous examination it deserves.

BEFORE COMMON SCHOOLS

One thing it seems historians and analysts from any perspective can agree on is that in seventeenth-century England education was at most loosely connected to government, its provision a matter mainly reserved for civil society. As historian Lawrence Cremin has put it, the English colonists "were heir to Renaissance traditions stressing the centrality of the household as the primary agency of human association and education."[5] Similarly, progressive Ellwood Cubberley lamented of reform efforts in the 1850s and 1860s that "so deeply ingrained . . . was the English conception of education as a private and voluntary and religious affair and no business of the State . . . that the arguments for national action encountered tremendous opposition from the Conservative elements, and often were opposed even by Liberals."[6]

It was family- and community-based education that British settlers brought to America, and while it underwent alterations in New England, it remained the colonial norm. The middle Atlantic colonies, the most diverse culturally and religiously, had numerous schools largely grounded in individual religious and ethnic communities. In colonial Pennsylvania and New York, laws required that families provide children basic education—literacy and religion, mainly—but other middle colonies did not even adopt that. In the South an even lighter wisp of government was felt, though Virginia enacted a statute in 1705 requiring that masters of children apprenticing with them provide their charges some literacy.[7]

Even in the colonies of New England, where the old England tradition of private education was most appreciably altered, the change occurred unevenly and proved unsustainable. At first all eight towns meeting the "Old Deluder Satan Act" population thresholds for grammar schools complied with the law, while it is estimated that only about one-third of smaller settlements retained a teacher.[8] Within a few decades compliance greatly eroded from even that.

Historians are at odds over why, exactly, things fell apart, with possibilities varying from a need to move precious resources from education to colonial defense, to a determination that grammar schools' Latin-intensive, classical curriculum was superfluous to many pioneering colonists. Consistent with the latter, historian Jon Teaford has catalogued that marked drops in students attending, and towns maintaining, grammar schools were accompanied by big enrollment increases in private schools focused on practical instruction such as writing and bookkeeping.[9]

Despite this disintegration, when public schooling advocates attempt to identify the beginning of their favored institution, they often point to the 1642 Massachusetts law compelling education, and especially the 1647 "Old Deluder." As Cubberley wrote, "It can be safely asserted, in the light of later developments, that the two laws of 1642 and 1647 represent the foundations upon which our American state public-school systems have been built."[10]

By the start of the Revolutionary War, colonial authorities no longer even tried to confront towns that failed to provide grammar schools, and by the 1830s, Mann lamented that the system had become but a shadow of the "Old Deluder" ideal. In his 1846 annual report he bemoaned, "It is common to say that the act of 1647 *laid the foundation* of our present system of free schools; but the truth is . . . it laid a far broader foundation than has since been built upon, and reared a far higher superstructure than has since been sustained." Mann especially decried the demise of the grammar schools, only a few of which were operating. "The contrast between our ancestors and ourselves in this respect is most humiliating," he mourned.[11]

Continuing his lamentation, Mann expressed deep regret that other states had not even come close to replicating the system that Massachusetts once had. And what would be the effect of failing to maintain public schools? Doom for government by and for the people, Mann argued, because free schooling is the only institution "capable of diffusing" the "general intelligence . . . indispensable to the continuance of a republican government."[12]

The demise of republican government for want of public schools was a curious thing to pronounce considering that prior to 1846, when Mann wrote those words, the colonies, which had all had republican governments, banded together to form an independent country with a republican national government and a guarantee of republican government for all states. Were Mann right not just about the erosion of common schooling in Massachusetts, but the dearth of public schooling in the rest of the colonies-turned-states, it would be logically impossible to deem free schools "indispensable" to republican government. Yet deem he did.

Was Mann right about the nonexistence of government-supplied free schooling in the states outside of New England? Generally, yes, though in 1795 New York State supplied funds for the "encouragement" of schooling, which it maintained until 1812 when it passed legislation establishing common schools. Pennsylvania's 1776 constitution called for a school in each county, but not for all children.

A break from the pre-Mann norm, at least on paper, occurred in western territories, where the federal government under the Land Ordinance of 1785 stipulated that the proceeds of the sale of one-thirty-sixth of each township be dedicated to funding public schools. Perhaps as a result—we cannot know with certainty what territories and states would have done in the absence of the ordinance—Ohio's 1802 constitution required equal access for the poor to any school funded under the ordinance. Indiana's 1816 constitution established permanent funding for public schools, and Michigan did likewise in 1835.

The stipulation "at least on paper" is important. No matter what the laws said, the money raised for schooling was often diverted to other uses, mismanaged, or insufficient for the operation of common schools.[13] As Cubberley wrote, "Regardless of the national land grants for education made to the new States, [or] the provisions of the different state constitutions . . . it can hardly be said that the American people had developed an educational consciousness . . . before about 1820."[14]

While the ordinance was ineffectual, early Americans most certainly had an "educational consciousness." Indeed, the evidence is compelling that education was abundant in the colonies and early United States. Americans' "educational consciousness" just was not manifested as Cubberley wanted: in "a democratic system of public schools."[15]

Education in reading and writing was commonplace before public schooling. Historian Albert Fishlow, using U.S. Census data, estimated that as of 1840 "more than 90 percentage of white adults" had achieved at least a minimal level of literacy—determined by a head of family reporting the percent of people in the home over 20 who were illiterate—which was a rate likely equaled only by Scotland and Germany among Europeans, and exceeding England and France. Fishlow concluded, "What therefore seems to be the case is that popular education successfully preceded an extensive system of publicly supported and controlled schools."[16]

Efforts to look farther back in American history strongly suggest that schooling was occurring in the absence of major government provision. In New England, reports historian Bernard Bailyn, numerous schools were funded by private bequests, which only changed when it was determined that more support would be needed than could be obtained privately, in large part because the investment that would typically yield the greatest returns in the Old World—land—was the one thing in superabundance in the colonies. Even then, while some funding came from taxation, even more came from people voluntarily choosing to support the schools that might in the past have lived off endowments.[17]

Outside of New England, schooling was also occurring, typically without any government assistance. In the ethnically and religiously diverse middle colonies, schooling was widespread but largely private, run by religious denominations, though sometimes open to all regardless of religion. Eventually, especially as port towns such as New York and Philadelphia grew in size and importance, for-profit schools offered education in commercially useful skills.[18]

In the South, less formal schooling occurred largely due to its more diffuse population, making schools less sustainable. Nonetheless, wealthy benefactors sometimes established endowed schools meant to be free to students, and "old field" schools were erected on plots with soil exhausted from tobacco cultivation.[19] Meanwhile, port towns such as Charleston and Savannah saw growth in for-profit schools similar to that of New York and Philadephia.[20]

A good indicator of broad learning without, necessarily, expansive schooling—and certainly without expansive *public* schooling—was book and newspaper reading. The colonial and early national periods saw a profusion of newspapers and wildly popular books, items that would only become ubiquitous if a substantial share of people was able to read them. Of course, illiterate Americans could, and did, have others read to them, but the number of newspapers and other periodicals, as well as direct research on literacy levels, strongly suggests that there were not just a few readers and a whole lot of listeners.

Cubberley himself argued that the phenomenal growth of newspapers— nonexistent in England before 1662—"did much to compensate for the lack of a general system of schools for the people."[21] Cremin furnishes statistics showing newspapers were more readily available in 1775 America than England.[22] According to Cremin's data, 37 newspapers served 2,464,000 colonists (about one paper per 67,000 people). England and Wales had 67 newspapers for 7,244,000 people (one per 108,000 people).

Books and political pamphlets also proliferated in the seventeenth and eighteenth centuries, and they were often aimed at what public schooling advocates such as Rush, Mann, and others said required government-run schooling: shaping and promoting enlightenment and a common culture.

Much of the popular writing in the nation's formative centuries was focused on morality, and its broad appeal helped to create a common colonial culture. John Bunyan's *The Pilgrim's Progress,* depicting Christian piety battling temptations from sloth to vanity, was very widely read. It was joined by many other exhortatory, enlightening, and popular books. Of course, Bible reading was essential for most Americans up to and through the common school movement, and Horace Mann, as we shall see, went to great pains to assure the people of Massachusetts that it would remain so: "The Bible is in our common schools by common consent."[23]

By the time of the Revolution, political pamphlets such as Thomas Paine's *Common Sense*, John Dickinson's *Farmer's Letters*, and before that *Cato's Letters* from England were major prods of public opinion. An estimated 500,000 copies of *Common Sense* were sold in colonial America, with its population of only about 2.5 million.[24] The Declaration of Independence, which not only announced the nation's separation from England but laid out the new country's philosophical foundations, was widely distributed around the brand new United States, both in public readings and, by order of Congress, in newspapers. In total, thirty American newspapers published it.[25]

After the Revolution, which had an obvious nation-unifying effect, came another seminal event: drafting and adoption of the Constitution. This was accompanied by newspaper and tract writing on all sides of the question, including the *Federalist Papers* by John Jay, James Madison, and Alexander Hamilton, and anti-federalist writings under such pen names as Brutus, Cato, and Centinel. The *Federalist Papers* were 85 articles printed in New York newspapers under the pseudonym Publius, as supporters of the proposed Constitution worked to sway that state to approve the proposed national government. Anti-federalist writings appeared in numerous newspapers, first mainly in New York and Philadelphia, then throughout the country.

Perhaps the most telling story about the ability of free society to unify through the written word is that of Noah Webster's spellers and other peda-gogical publications. Webster was without question interested in establishing public schools,[26] arguing that they would inculcate sound moral values, pre-pare people for professions, and literally Americanize the people of the new United States. Included in the latter goal was a desire to see all American chil-dren educated in America, by Americans, and to create a distinctly American culture, including uniquely American ways of speaking and spelling.

When it came to speaking and spelling, Webster succeeded marvelously, but not via public schooling. No, by publication of his famous dictionary, and even more so, his "blue-backed" spellers, which Americans hoarded not because government compelled them to, but because they wanted to.

The first edition of Webster's speller was published in 1783, and by 1801 roughly 1.5 million copies had been sold. By 1829 approximately 20 million copies had been sold.[27] To put that in perspective, in 1830 the entire U.S. population was only 12.9 million—the speller must have been ubiquitous.[28] Webster's dictionary, first published in 1801, changed American English to forms still used, including removing the "u" from British spellings of words such as "colour," and the "k" from words such as "musick."[29] As historians

Wayne Urban and Jennings Wagoner have concluded, "There is little doubt that his [Webster's] texts had a more profound impact on the development of American education than his theoretical schemes."[30]

Moving beyond the power of the written word, many other unifying forces were at work before public schooling. Electing George Washington president of the United States was a huge spur to patriotism, as his accolade-filled trip from Mount Vernon to the temporary capital in New York City attested. Washington encountered ecstatic well-wishers at every turn, and as Philadelphia's *Federal Gazette* put it in covering the parade accompanying his arrival, "What a pleasing reflection to every patriotic mind, thus to see our citizens again united in their reliance on this great man who is, a second time, called upon to be the savior of his country!"[31]

Or consider the evolution of Pennsylvania's German population. As Cremin notes, despite great fear among English Pennsylvanians of Germans becoming so numerous they would dominate the colony, German communities increasingly made common cause with English-speaking Pennsylvanians due to common threats and mutual self-interest. An effort to create schools to bring together German and English Pennsylvanians failed miserably as Germans rejected what appeared to be overt and insulting efforts to Anglicize them, but they eventually allied with each other in combatting attacks from Native Americans and, later, British rule.

Meanwhile, improved communications were bringing all the colonies closer together, and, as a port town, Philadelphia became increasingly cosmopolitan, incentivizing many once-isolated groups to intermingle. Religious revivals illustrated to many Protestant Germans that they were not all that different from the Protestant English. So while they often maintained their own language, Germans integrated in society and the body politic.[32]

Writing in the early 1830s Alexis de Tocqueville, while admiring the existing public schools of Massachusetts, concluded from his travels that the key to American patriotism and unity was *not* having government "help." He wrote:

> In the United States the interests of the country are everywhere kept in view; they are an object of solicitude to the people of the whole Union, and every citizen is as warmly attached to them as if they were his own. He takes pride in the glory of his nation; he boasts of its success, to which he conceives himself to have contributed; and he rejoices in the general prosperity by which he profits. . . . In America, then, it may be said that no one renders obedience to man, but to justice and to law. . . . When a private individual meditates an undertaking, however directly connected it may be with the welfare of society, he never thinks of soliciting the co-operation of the government; he publishes his plan, offers to execute it, courts the assistance of other individuals, and struggles manfully against all obstacles.[33]

COMMON SCHOOLS

Looking at America before the spread of common schooling, it is impossible to say that education was scarce, or that democratic institutions and common culture were unable to rise. The period furnishes no compelling evidence that widespread public schooling is *necessary* for unity and government by the people.

Examining history after establishment of common schooling enables the answering of different questions: Is government-furnished schooling helpful for promoting harmony and democratic government—not to mention liberty and equality under the law—or might it be antithetical to those things? From 1837 on, how instrumental or deleterious was public schooling in shaping national unity and promoting democracy?

The evidence after 1837 is no more consistent with the pro–public schooling narrative than before. Public schooling often fostered conflict—which is divisive, not unifying—that would have been avoidable had all people not been required to fund a single system of government schools. And where there was no conflict, it was largely because the schools were serving homogeneous communities, not bringing together diverse peoples.

The divisions that government schooling exacerbated as it pushed more and more people into one venue were foreshadowed by its earliest champions, including Webster, Rush, and Franklin, and different religious communities of Massachusetts. They were part of the pre–common schooling era, of course, but their tensions illustrate the eternal nature of disputes that were painfully magnified by common schooling. It is easy to say "everyone should get the same education," but settling on specifics—where education happens, with whom, what is taught—can be a fraught process.

Why Education?

Perhaps the most enduring debate has been the most basic: What is the purpose of education? Is it cultivating enlightenment by exploring grand ideas and enduring truths, or furnishing concrete, practical skills and knowledge that will be useful in one's daily life? It is a debate still burning today—liberal arts college or business school, workforce development or well-rounded citizens?—and it was contested in colonial America. Indeed, it was contested at least as far back as the time of Aristotle.

In America, Benjamin Franklin laid out plans for education focused on practical skills and knowledge such as geometry, English grammar, and geography. As he wrote in *Proposals Relating to the Education of Youth in Pensilvania*, students should "learn those Things that are likely to be most useful and most *ornamental*. Regard being had to the several Professions for which they are intended."[34] The citations in the proposal—far longer than the proposal itself—drove home the emphasis on the practical, especially regarding languages.

Rather than the traditional emphasis on Greek and Latin, English would be taught. Included in a lengthy quotation from John Locke was the exhortation, "Would not a *Chinese*, who took Notice of this Way of Breeding, be apt to imagine, that all our young Gentlemen were designed to be Teachers and Professors of the dead Languages of foreign Countries, and not to be Men of Business in their own." Indeed, outside of his towering political work, Franklin was renowned as a scientist with fewer than two years of formal schooling, and for the popular, profitable instruction he provided the public in *Poor Richard's Almanack*.

Contrasted to Franklin and others who eschewed the teaching of classical subjects were men such as Samuel Knox, one of the co-winners of the 1797 American Philosophical Society national education system design contest. Knox doggedly defended the teaching of "dead languages," contending that "it is only from the study of these and other languages that the improvement of our own language can be promoted by attending to the principles of universal grammar and the consequent enlargement of the mind from such literary views."[35]

Religion

A much more deep-seated and fundamentally personal conflict in the early Common School era, as is about to become painfully clear, that had precedent among the Founders was the proper place of religion in education. Like the classical curriculum, battle lines were being drawn as advocates sketched out potential common school religious programs. The conflagration became far more intense—deadly, even—after common schools had been established.

Early public schooling enthusiasts Benjamin Rush and Noah Webster quarreled over the place of the Bible in academic instruction. Webster opposed using the Bible as a "schoolbook," arguing that mundane use built contempt for scripture. "Will not the familiarity, contracted by a careless disrespectful reading of the sacred volume, weaken the influence of the precepts upon the heart" he asked. "No person has less sensibility than the surgeon who has been accustomed to the amputation of limbs. No person thinks less of death than the soldier who has frequently walked over the carcasses of his slain comrades."[36]

Rush rejected Webster's stance. Saying that reading from the good book gave children "the means of acquiring happiness both here and hereafter,"

Rush feared that objecting "to the practice of having it read in schools because it tends to destroy our veneration for it" would visit disaster on society. The Bible, he warned, would eventually be pushed out of all but "the offices of magistrates and in courts of justice."[37]

This basically friendly tiff was but a slight foretaste of the religious donnybrooks that would erupt from the earliest days of the Common School era to today. Far worse than friendly disagreements about threats to biblical reverence, at stake in most battles was whose religion the government schools would inculcate, and whose would be sidelined or even denigrated. And such battles began in Horace Mann's Massachusetts *before* the major influx of Roman Catholics, the religious minority that most people would likely associate with religious strife in America. The first clashes were among Protestants.

Intra-Protestant Battles

Mann committed a substantial chunk of his final annual report to the state school board to defending against accusations he was maneuvering to excise the Bible from the schools. And he was not presumed to be motivated, as was the case with Webster, by a desire to see the Bible retain an exalted place. No, the accusation was leveled at least in part because Mann was a Unitarian, and more orthodox Protestants feared he was attempting to strip from the schools disputed doctrines many felt were central, but Unitarians did not hold. As the historian Charles Glenn, Jr. wrote in *The Myth of the Common School*, objectors:

> insisted that what was presented was in fact a false religion, worse than no mention of religion at all, since it took no account of sin as a corruption of human nature cutting man off from God and from his own happiness, or of God's plan of salvation through Jesus Christ. By retaining only those aspects of Christianity with which Unitarians agreed, the proposed religious teaching was in fact identical with Unitarian teaching.[38]

To combat what they saw as dangerous proposals promulgated by Mann, and an education system careening toward state control, many Massachusetts legislators in 1840 sought to disband the newly created board of education. As a legislative committee reported in 1840, many found the idea of state educational direction, of any religious bent, menacing. The moment authority was given to the state, the committee warned, the people of Massachusetts would say "farewell to religious liberty, for there would be but one church; farewell to political freedom, for nothing but the name of a republic would survive such a catastrophe."[39]

The board also had a heavily Unitarian majority, which drew the rebuke of one of the three non-Unitarians. Episcopalian Edward Newton decried as ripping out the substance of religion the board's eschewing, on the grounds adopting them would be too "sectarian," of any disputed Christian doctrine. "The idea of a religion to be *permitted* to be taught in the schools, in which all are at present agreed, is a mockery," Newton wrote. "There is not a point in the *Christian* scheme, deemed important, and of a *doctrinal* character, that is not disputed or disallowed by some."[40]

Perhaps Mann's most fervent nemesis was Matthew Hale Smith, a minister who had moved from Unitarianism to Calvinism. In an ongoing debate with Mann, Smith wrote:

> Certain views that you entertain, you call religion, or "piety." These you allow to be taught in schools. . . . Those which clash with your particular views, you reject as "dogmatic theology" or "sectarianism." By what authority do you settle those grave and important questions for every town and school district in Massachusetts?[41]

Mann could not actually dictate that his version of Christianity be used in schools—his position was vested with no legislative authority—but his influence was great, and as leader of the State Board of Education he had, at a minimum, a pretty high soapbox.

So unhappy were some Old School Presbyterians with common schools that, as early as 1812, conservative Presbyterians in Connecticut sought to create their own schools. It became a more energized movement in the 1840s, as these Presbyterians sought a share of public funding for their own, parochial institutions. One reason for their efforts: As the report on parochial schooling to the 1846 denominational General Assembly explained, complete education was simply not considered possible absent the "doctrines of grace."[42] Religion was integral to Old School Presbyterian education, and specific doctrines were integral to their religion.

Mann's plan simply could not accommodate denominational orthodoxy. He wrote:

> That our public schools are not theological seminaries, is admitted. That they are debarred by law from inculcating the peculiar and distinctive doctrines of any one religious denomination amongst us, is claimed; and that they are also prohibited from ever teaching that what they do teach is the whole of religion, or all that is essential to religion or to salvation, is equally certain. But our system earnestly inculcates all Christian morals; it founds its morals on the basis of religion; it welcomes the religion of the Bible; and in receiving the Bible, it allows it to do what it is allowed to do in no other system,—*to speak for itself.*

But here it stops, not because it claims to have compassed all truth, but because it disclaims to act as an umpire between hostile religious opinions.[43]

Some asserted that Mann intended to exclude disputed Christian doctrines in order to render the schools de facto Unitarian. That is possible. Much more likely, though, is that Mann realized that to attain sufficient political support to make common schooling truly *common*, the schools needed to alienate as few citizens as possible. And less alienation would come by an absence of disputed theological doctrines than their presence. By the same logic, Mann offered lowest-common-denominator curricula to allay fears of political bias:

those articles in the creed of republicanism which are accepted by all, believed in by all, and which form the common basis of our political faith, shall be taught to all. But when the teacher . . . arrives at a controverted text, he is either to read it without comment or remark; or, at most, he is only to say that the passage is the subject of disputation, and that the schoolroom is neither the tribunal to adjudicate, nor the forum to discuss it.[44]

Ironically, a key contention of common schooling advocates was that their system would inoculate society against religious conflicts, not spur them. In his first annual report, Mann wrote that a private system would replicate England's sad state, in which "Churchmen and Dissenters . . . maintain separate schools, in which children are taught . . . to wield the sword of polemics with fatal dexterity; and where the gospel, instead of being a temple of peace, is converted into an armory of deadly weapons, for social, interminable warfare." Mann saw but "one preventive" to avoid such endless conflict: "the elevation of the Common Schools."[45] This echoed Samuel Harrison Smith's essay, which asserted that the "great result" of common schooling "will be harmony" as it spread rational thought. "Discord and strife," in contrast, "have always proceeded from, or risen upon, ignorance and passion."[46]

Catholics

Not many years after Mann's report, Horace Bushnell, a liberal Congregationalist minister who hoped to see newly arriving Roman Catholics accommodated in the common schools, wrote broadly that "Common schools are nurseries thus of a free republic, private schools of factions, cabals, agrarian laws and contests of force." He continued, "No bitterness is so bitter, no seed of factions so rank, no division so irreconcilable, as that which grows out of religious distinction, sharpened to religious animosities, and softened by no terms of intercourse; the more bitter when it begins with childhood."[47]

It was the rapid growth of Roman Catholics that moved the central common school conflict from a bout between orthodox Protestants and Unitarians to one between Roman Catholics and Protestants broadly. But even after that, intra-Protestant differences periodically reared their aggrieved heads, and Edward Newton anticipated what the flexing of Catholic muscle would do to common schools, which Mann said had to be free of sectarian content but also would always include the Bible. Starting with a quotation from Mann, Newton explained:

> It is a principle of action in the Board of Education, that no book for reading or instruction shall be used in our schools, or form any part of our school district libraries, that contains any doctrine or precept in theology or divinity that any member of the Board shall take exception to." The Board is said to embrace all religious denominations; it does, I believe, save and except the papist, who, very soon, will demand admittance, and, on their principle of action, must be admitted. What then? *He*, the papist, may, and will, except to the received translation of the Bible; and when he does, the Bible must be excluded from our schools, or the established principle of action in the Board abandoned.[48]

Roman Catholics use a different version of the Bible than most Protestants, including more books and requiring the blessing of the Church.

Mann answered Newton that were the schools to reflect people's religion the state would be confronted with institutions run by sects that Mann, presumably reflecting popular sentiment, portrayed as kooks. Referring to the "papist" threat, he wrote:

> Allow our schools to become nurseries of proselytism—battle-grounds where each contending sect shall fight for the propagation of its own faith,—and how long would it be, before we should have schools for the Come-outers, for the Millerites, and the Mormonites? How long, before one portion of the children would be sent to school in their "ascension robes," and before another portion, instead of the Bible, would carry a Catechism, whose first doctrine would be that "God is the Lord, and Joseph Smith is his Prophet?"[49]

"Democratic" schools for all could accept no sectarianism, but "father" Horace Mann could find some sects to mock. The Mormons were a popular target, with their embrace of polygamy and the church's hierarchical control. Indeed, in 1885 Reverend Josiah Strong, then secretary of the Evangelical Alliance for the United States, favorably reported that Senator George Frisbie Hoar of Massachusetts had proposed that a commission take over the finances of the Mormon church in the Utah Territory, and "apply to the purposes of supporting common schools . . . [any] funds which have been collected contrary to law."[50] Government would literally take from a minority religion to pay for public schools.

Without question, though, Roman Catholics presented the biggest problem for the common schools. Probably no development in its history, save perhaps the dissolution of the Roman Empire, convulsed Europe more than the Reformation, which divided Christianity into Roman Catholic and Protestant factions. There had been a split among eastern and Roman churches centuries before that, but the Reformation set millions of people within countries and principalities against each other, and launched centuries of bloody internal and external conflicts and oppression in Europe.

Escaping this suffering was a major reason that many Europeans came to America. But because many Europeans sought refuge in the New World, and because England, too, had been wrenched by centuries of religious animus, America could not escape the hatreds that so pained Europe. So while sectarian tensions existed among American Protestants, they paled in comparison to those between Catholics and Protestants. And public schooling, far from bridging the yawning divisions, often seemed to widen them further.

The colonial Massachusetts law to which many public schooling advocates point as the genesis of their beloved institution—the Old Deluder Satan Act—was overt about its Protestantism, referring to the Devil having "kept men from the knowledge of the Scriptures, as in former times by keeping them in an unknown tongue." It was an unmistakable shot at the Catholic Church, which had declared its Latin translation of the Bible as "authentic," and had long forbidden certain translations into the languages spoken by common people.[51]

Indeed, while the Pilgrims had left England to escape disputes with, and persecutions by, the Church of England, much of their split was grounded in Puritan conviction that the Anglican Church, in its liturgy and structure, was too Catholic. Meanwhile, British Protestants were very familiar with John Foxe's *The Acts and Monuments of the Christian Church*—better known as *Foxe's Book or Martyrs*—which portrayed Protestants as chosen by God, the Roman Catholic Church as in league with the Devil, and England as a special nation in Christian history.[52] By 1684 it was likely the second highest-circulating book in England, after the Bible itself.[53]

Until roughly 1840, while resistance to "Popery" was a consistent theme among many Protestant Americans, the Catholic Church was no immediate threat. Maryland had been established as a refuge for Catholics, having been given to the Catholic George Calvert, Lord Baltimore, by King Charles I. From the outset it included both Catholic and Protestant settlers, but with the Glorious Revolution of 1688, which brought William of Orange to the throne, practicing Catholicism was outlawed in Maryland, and Catholic citizens were barred from public office. Catholics were also a tiny group, accounting for no more than 1 percent of the U.S. population in 1790, or about 35,000 people.[54]

Something big happened in the 1840s to change that status quo. Responding to the potato blight of 1845, and long-oppressive British rule, Catholics from Ireland immigrated in huge numbers, ballooning the Catholic population from roughly 650,000 in 1840 to 1,600,000 in 1850.[55] By 1850 Catholics were the country's largest denomination, though still small relative to all Protestants.[56] Irish refugees concentrated in New England and middle states such as New York and New Jersey and their influx elevated opposition to the Catholic Church from mainly theological, or a vestige of Old World politics, to, in many people's eyes, a political priority.

Mann knew that his audience was primarily Protestant, stating in his last annual report that "Christianity has no other authoritative expounder" than the Bible.[57] That was *sola scriptura*: The Bible alone is the earthly authority on Christian matters, a conclusion that the Roman Catholic Church—which sees itself as the Jesus-ordained final earthly authority—rejected. That said, people other than Mann, or co-common school crusader Henry Barnard, were much more worried about Catholics. Indeed, in 1865 Barnard sided with Catholics in a dispute over whose version of the Bible could be read in Hartford, Connecticut, schools.[58]

Among the loudest sirens was Lyman Beecher, a Connecticut-born Presbyterian minister and father of *Uncle Tom's Cabin* author Harriett Beecher Stowe and abolitionist Henry Ward Beecher. He presented his fears in *A Plea for the West*, a compilation of sermons delivered as head of Lane Seminary in Cincinnati, Ohio, then a gateway to the frontier. Beecher declared the country's future was in the West, but faced a grave threat: Catholicism connected to education. He said, "The conflict which is to decide the destiny of the West, will be a conflict of institutions for the education of her sons, for purposes of superstition, or evangelical light; of despotism, or liberty."[59]

Beecher had numerous theological differences with the Catholic Church, but his primary concern was that Catholics, in his mind, tended to be ignorant, chiefly because their church wanted them so. He feared that their ignorance would render them pawns of monarchical Catholic powers, or of the politically grasping Church itself. Reflecting, perhaps intentionally, James Madison's fear of a minority faction exerting great power, Beecher intoned:

> No government is more complex and difficult of preservation than a republic, and in no political associations do little adverse causes produce more disastrous results. Of all the influences, none is more pernicious than a corps of men acting systematically and perseveringly for its own ends upon a community unapprized of their doings, and undisciplined to meet and counteract them. A tenth part of the suffrage of the nation, thus condensed and wielded by the Catholic powers

of Europe, might decide our elections, perplex our policy, inflame and divide the nation, break the bond of our union, and throw down our free institutions. The voice of history also warns us, that no sinister influence has ever intruded itself into politics, so virulent and disastrous as that of an ambitious ecclesiastical influence, or which demands, now and always, keener vigilance or a more active resistance.[60]

The key to fending off this grave threat, argued Beecher, was Catholic assimilation, including attendance at common schools:

I have no fear of the Catholics, considered simply as a religious denomination, and unallied to the church and state establishments of the European governments hostile to republican institutions.

Let the Catholics mingle with us as Americans and come with their children under the full action of our common schools and republican institutions, and the various powers of assimilation, and we are prepared cheerfully to abide the consequences. If in these circumstances the Protestant religion cannot stand before the Catholic, let it go down, and we will sound no alarm, and ask no aid, and make no complaint. It is no ecclesiastical quarrel to which we would call the attention of the American nation.[61]

A considerable concern for Beecher was that Catholics were establishing schools more quickly than Protestants, and were doing so in part with money from Europe. The schools often educated more Protestant than Catholic children, leading, Beecher feared, to conversions. Such enrollment was the case at the Ursuline Convent in Charlestown, Massachusetts, a girls school destroyed after a sermon by Beecher, though whether it incited the attack is unknown. Rumors of abuse at the school had been circulating for some time and came to a head on the night of August 11, 1834, when a crowd of mainly poor laborers who lived below the hilltop-mounted convent demanded to interrogate the nuns, and, the nuns refusing, razed the convent.[62]

Beecher produced no meaningful evidence of Catholic plotting to take down the United States—most Catholic European powers probably paid little attention to the weak new country across the Atlantic—but his concerns were not utterly baseless. The Catholic Church had been a political force in Europe for centuries, and to think it might try to influence American politics was not crazy. Meanwhile, Catholics could not separate their religion from the institutional church—it was integral to their religion—and act "simply as a religious denomination" like Baptists or Presbyterians.

What about the "various powers of assimilation" that Beecher lauded? They, too, could be problematic for Catholics, without any Catholic plotting being afoot. Those powers would likely be employed to tell Catholics that, among other things, they should interpret scripture for themselves, something forbidden in the eyes of the Church. Or perhaps to go ahead and eat meat on Fridays, or sing Protestant hymns.

To many Americans, the nation was inherently Protestant; one could no more truly be an American if not Protestant than water if not wet. The schools, therefore, also had to be Protestant. As Horace Bushnell stated:

> We began our history . . . as Protestant communities; and, in those especially of New England, we have had the common school as a fundamental institution from the first—in our view a Protestant institution—associated with all our religious convictions, opinions, and the public sentiment of a Protestant society. We are still, as Americans, a Protestant people.[63]

The hottest common schooling conflagrations between Catholics and Protestants, not surprisingly, involved the Bible, as well as a tendency in pedagogical materials to scold and prick Catholicism.[64] At the Fourth Roman Catholic Provincial Council, held in Baltimore in 1840, the gathered bishops enunciated their concerns about the burgeoning common schools:

> Since it is evident that the nature of public education in many of these Provinces is so developed that it serves heresy, as well as that the minds of Catholic children are little by little imbued with the false principles of the sects, we admonish pastors that they must see to the Christian and Catholic education of Catholic children with all the zeal they have, and diligently watch that no Protestant version of the Bible be used, nor hymns of the sects be sung, nor prayers be recited. Therefore it must be watched that no books or exercises of this kind be introduced with discrimination of faith and piety.[65]

Tensions peaked in New York City between 1840 and 1842, when Catholics, led by Bishop John Hughes, sought a share of state funding, which was all going to the de facto Protestant New York Public School Society. Before the city's Common Council, Society members argued that state funding for Catholic schools would entangle state and religion. Hughes replied that the results of the society's position were "either the consciences of Catholics must be crushed and their objections resisted, or the Public School system must be destroyed."[66] Catholics were not the first to ask for money—in the 1820s the council cut off a Baptist school, and in 1832 denied a Methodist Episcopal request[67]—but they were the only large group for which Protestant instruction, even lowest common denominator, was absolutely unacceptable.

In 1840, New York governor William Seward suggested that immigrants should have schools that provided instruction in their own languages and faiths. This inspired Catholics to petition for a share of public education funding, as did a Scotch Presbyterian church and two Jewish congregations.[68] The

Common Council denied the request in 1841, and the city's Catholics took their case to the state legislature.

A legislative effort to break the Public School Society's monopoly, also in 1841, would have divided the city into districts able to fund any schools they wished. Consideration of the bill, after a long critique from Society board member Hiram Ketchum, was postponed on a last-second vote that surprised bill supporters and angered Catholics. It spurred denunciations of Ketchum by Hughes, Hughes by Presbyterian minister William Brownlee, and brawls between Protestants and Catholics over speeches by Brownlee.[69]

In 1842, the state passed the Maclay law, which created elected, ward-level school boards and a central New York City Board of Education, as opposed to funding the Public School Society. The latter was a win for Catholics who had inveighed against the Society and its state-money monopoly, but the measure also forbade funding for any school "in which any religious sectarian doctrine shall be taught."[70] Soon after the bill was passed came election day, which saw nativists and Catholics clash in the streets, and Bishop Hughes's house stoned.

Importantly, in practice "non-sectarian" meant that lowest-common-denominator Protestantism was okay, furnishing little relief for Roman Catholics. Indeed, the first Board of Education leaned heavily against Catholics, instituting daily Bible reading restricted to Protestant versions of the Bible, and with no notes or commentary—including Church interpretation—allowed.[71] And lest the schools interpret the Maclay law as forbidding use of the Bible, in 1844 it was amended to state that no district could exclude Bible reading in schools.

Catholic and Protestant clashes over the common schools were not restricted to New York City, nor did the situation there ignite the most searing violence. That distinction belongs to Philadelphia in 1844, where, by the end of two waves of days-long, street-level warfare, an estimated tens of people had died, hundreds had been wounded, and property damage estimated at hundreds of millions of dollars had been inflicted. Indeed, cannons were turned against soldiers called upon to restore peace as Protestant and Catholic mobs battled, and homes and churches were torched.[72]

What match ignited war in the City of Brotherly Love? The Good Book, again.

From the mid-1830s until the riots, publicly funded schools in Philadelphia and surrounding communities had included Bible reading, almost exclusively from the Protestant King James version, and in many cases lessons incorporated material critical of the Catholic Church. At the time Irish immigration was burgeoning and as Catholics gained strength, their bishop, Francis Kenrick, petitioned to have the schools allow their students to read from the

Catholic Douay version of the Bible. He also attacked the schools for being de facto Protestant.

Kenrick warned in the June 1841 *Catholic Herald* that even if the schools were not controlled by a specific Protestant sect, the system "will necessarily be Protestant in its character. It is founded on a Protestant principle, it is managed chiefly by Protestants, and the books, even if free from direct invective against Catholics, which is not often the case, are all of a Protestant complexion."[73] Kenrick did not want to compel anyone to feign belief, so his ultimate goal was to create Catholic schools to teach Catholic children, not control the public schools.[74] But that was not yet close to attainable, so he sought to at least make the public schools tolerable.

In 1843, the city's Board of Controllers issued two resolutions in response to Catholic pleadings, declaring that no child could be forced to undertake Bible readings to which their parents objected, but if they did, the readings could not be accompanied by commentary. It seemed intended to aggravate both Catholics, who believed religion was essential to education but needed Church-approved biblical interpretations, and Protestants, who saw the ruling as a step toward removing the Bible from "their" schools. Meanwhile, in the actions of Kenrick and Hughes Protestants perceived what Beecher had warned about: scheming Catholic hierarchy.[75] This precipitated creation of two nativist groups in Philadelphia, the American Protestant Association and the American Republican Association, to oppose Catholic influence.

The situation came to a head in 1844, when a Catholic school board member was accused of ordering a teacher to stop reading from a Protestant Bible. Violence erupted in Kensington, a community immediately outside of Philadelphia in which working-class Protestants and Catholics lived in close proximity. As nativists held a rally for the schools, they were met by Catholics armed with clubs who demanded they disperse. Three days later, another Protestant gathering resulted in brawling, shots fired, and finally urban combat resulting in several deaths, including that of 18-year-old George Shiffler, who was hailed as a martyr for the Protestant cause.

For days fighting raged, and several Catholic churches and homes were burned and pillaged. Many Protestants and Catholics alike wrote "Native American" on their homes in hopes they would be spared.[76] Only the arrival of thousands of soldiers, marines, and sailors restored order, and not before numerous houses and Catholic churches had been destroyed.

Even then, peace was only temporary.

On July 5, following an Independence Day celebration featuring numerous banners proclaiming the exalted place of the Bible in American life, warfare broke out again, this time in the largely Protestant neighborhood of Southwark, where Catholics armed themselves to defend St. Philip's Church. Accurate rumors of weapons at the church, and later-disproven tales of Catholics beating some Protestant July 4th revelers, launched the new hostilities. The St. Philip's defenders voluntarily disarmed after a mob and magistrates arrived, but the next day a throng of Protestants tore the church apart. More warfare commenced, and again peace was not restored until the governor had mobilized thousands of troops.

The common schools, intended to be furnaces to forge unity, had instead ignited a powder keg.

The physical ferocity of the Catholic–Protestant schooling war never again reached the point it did in Philadelphia. In part, this was because Catholics slowly created their own system of schools, which at its 1965 peak enrolled roughly 12 percent of all schoolchildren.[77] But an absence of street-level combat does not mean animosity and tension did not remain.

In 1859, Boston was the site of weeks of conflict when a Catholic student refused to read the Protestant version of the Ten Commandments. The version contains some different wording and ordering. The boy was whipped, and several other Catholic students refused to recite the commandments, resulting in numerous school expulsions.[78]

A similar situation occurred in Ellsworth, Maine, when several students were cast out of school for refusing to read from the King James Bible, and a Catholic priest was tarred and feathered for opening a school to accommodate the exiled children.[79] Eventually, Maine's supreme court ruled that the expulsion was legal because the Bible was not used to teach "the theological doctrines of any religion, or of any religious sect." It was, though, used to inculcate moral values.[80]

In Cincinnati, Ohio, and Detroit, Michigan, policies allowing students to choose which version of the Bible they would use also created heated debate.[81] Cincinnati's policy, however, was interrupted by the "Bible War" of 1869, when the city's school board voted to exclude the Bible entirely. That contest saw Lyman Beecher's son Henry argue that Catholic and Jewish objections to Bible reading were *valid*, with such readings constituting religious compulsion. Many non-Catholics joined against forced Protestant Bible reading, and in 1873 the Ohio Supreme Court upheld Cincinnati's decision, finding that Bible reading violated freedom of conscience, and rejecting the idea that the country was intentionally and necessarily Christian.[82]

In 1880s Boston, a public school teacher taught that the Catholic Church's granting of indulgences was giving payees license to sin, to which the pastor of Gate of Heaven Catholic Church took great exception. Fr. Theodore Metcalf lodged a complaint against the teacher and the textbook cited, *Swinton's Outline of the World's History, Ancient, Medieval and Modern*. A countercomplaint was lodged against Catholic schools for using texts biased toward the Church. After several months, the board banished the textbook and moved the teacher to another subject. That precipitated a school board election featuring rank anti-Catholicism, including the recommendation that any Protestant employer of Catholic servants threaten with termination any employee who did not intend to vote for anti-Catholic candidates.[83]

The battle over Catholic—indeed, *all* private education—reached its apogee in the U.S. Supreme Court's 1925 *Pierce v. Society of Sisters* decision. The case tackled an anti-Catholic, Ku Klux Klan–backed referendum in Oregon that made public schools the only institutions in which families could satisfy compulsory education mandates. Catholics opposed it, as did many other religious and secular private schoolers. The Society of Sisters of the Holy Names of Jesus and Mary and the Hill Military Academy fought all the way to the Supreme Court, which in striking the law down famously stated that a child is not a "mere creature of the state."[84]

Neutralizing the existential threat to private schooling ensured that the Catholic alternative to public schooling could survive. Catholics could continue to escape a system which, rather than building unity between Catholics and Protestants, too often tried to dominate Catholics. But Catholic schools would still have to compete against "free" public schools for which all Catholics had to pay taxes, rendering Catholics essentially second-class citizens.

Presence and Defense of Religion

A consequence of seemingly endless Protestant-Catholic tussles, intra-Protestant battles over the place and character of religion and the Bible, and growing populations of Jews, atheists, and other non-Christians was that religion of any stripe in the public schools became increasingly contentious. In the 1960s, the U.S. Supreme Court eradicated any official connection between public schools and religion, but not without major brawls over potential places for religion and the shape of moral instruction. And traditional religion has not just capitulated, but fought on to remain in the public schools.

Questioning any presence of religion in public schools started as early as 1860, with, for instance, *Harper's New Monthly Magazine* critiquing Bible use.[85] Criticism escalated in 1875, when President Ulysses S. Grant proposed that common schools be encouraged in all states, but seemingly free of all religion. Importantly, Grant used "sectarian"—often code for "Catholic"—for what should be forbidden, but at least the wording was neutral.[86]

Debate escalated with a federal constitutional amendment, proposed by Maine Senator James G. Blaine, to prohibit public funds raised for public schools from being controlled by "religious sects or denominations." Again, this was likely aimed against Catholics, but at least had the veneer of secularism.[87] The conflict continued for decades, as Protestants, Catholics, Jews, atheists, and more struggled with conflicting desires for religious education, basic moral formation, and beliefs that the United States was an intentionally Protestant country.[88]

The height of the war between religion and secularism was the Scopes "monkey trial," a 1925 legal/religious/philosophical/entertainment spectacle that riveted the country and was captured in Jerome Lawrence and Robert Edwin Lee's famous play, *Inherit the Wind*. The proximate cause of the trial was teacher John Thomas Scopes teaching evolution in his Dayton, Tennessee, classroom, violating a state law against eschewing "the story of the Divine Creation of man as taught in the Bible, and to teach instead that man has descended from a lower order of animals."[89]

That said, the real purpose of the trial was not to determine guilt. Scopes had intentionally violated the law. His goal for the sensational proceedings was to publicly try the law, creationism, and the beliefs of millions of Americans.

What proceedings they were, pitting religious man against secular, urban against rural, democrat against civil libertarian. Revival tents were all about the courthouse grounds, vendors hawked everything from hot dogs to toy monkeys, live chimps—including one named Jo Mendi who wore a three-piece suit—entertained onlookers, and courthouse crowds were so large Judge John Raulston held the last part of the trial outdoors, lest the weight of the spectators collapse the courthouse floor. Finally, reporters came from across the country, and commentators, perhaps most famously H. L. Mencken, fired off broadsides against their religious and social opponents.

The trial's climax was the testimony of creationist and three-time Democratic presidential candidate William Jennings Bryan, who had been serving on the prosecution but was called to the stand by the defense. Bryan faced intense questioning about his religious beliefs from agnostic American Civil Liberties Union counsel Clarence Darrow, including interrogatives about how long it took God to create the Earth, the Great Flood, and other biblical happenings. It was a testy exchange on both sides as creationism versus evolution came to a head on the proceedings' biblically ironic seventh day.

Bryan on several occasions objected to attempts by district attorney Tom Stewart—with whom he was working on the prosecution—to end the questioning. Said Bryan in response to Stewart's first attempt, "These gentlemen . . . did not come here to try this case. They came here to try revealed religion. I am here to defend it, and they can ask me any question they please."[90] Bryan also accused Darrow of insulting the people of Tennessee by callng them "yokels."

When it came to venom, Darrow gave as good as he got. Perhaps better, laying into Bryan when he suggested that Darrow held Tennesseans in contempt. He responded that Bryan's answers insulted "every man of science and learning in the world because he does not believe in your fool religion."

The vitriol peaked after the last of Stewart's efforts to end Bryan's grilling, in which Stewart interrupted to ask the purpose of the questioning. Darrow replied, "We have the purpose of preventing bigots and ignoramuses from controlling the education of the United States and you know it, and that is all."[91] This did not even play out in front of the jury, which was retired, but the assembled masses and media laughed and applauded as the venom ran on.

In almost a historical footnote, Scopes was convicted, as he no doubt knew he would be. The conviction, however, was tossed on a technicality: Judge Raulston, not the jury, had set Scopes's $100 fine, in violation of state law.

While Scopes may have been the peak, conflict over religion in the schools went on. Many of the debates were taken up, and evolved, in U.S. Supreme Court cases. After *Pierce*, perhaps the most jarring were two cases exploring the extent to which public schools could force students to say things and perform acts that violated their religious beliefs. *Minersville School District v. Gobitis* and *West Virginia State Board of Education v. Barnette* both pitted Jehovah's Witnesses against compelled saluting of the American flag. The Witnesses believed the salute violated the Biblical injunction against bowing down to or serving a "graven image."

In *Gobitis*, the court ruled 8 to 1 against a family whose children refused to salute the flag, with Justice Felix Frankfurter writing an opinion that essentially declared that a state or district could compel children to violate their consciences if doing so was in service of national unity and "order." Without those things, Frankfurter argued, individual liberty could not be defended. In destroy-the-village-to-save-it fashion, the decision wholly subordinated liberty to the state, though it technically turned on the belief that the court owed deference to state legislatures.

Frankfurter's opinion read like the sum of all libertarian fears. He argued that religious rights could be trampled because "the ultimate foundation of a free society is the binding tie of cohesive sentiment." He declared that it is key that "public school children share a common experience at those periods of development when their minds are supposedly receptive to its assimilation." Finally, he acknowledged that "what the school authorities are really asserting is the right to awaken in the child's mind considerations as to the significance of the flag contrary to those implanted by the parent."

By crushing liberty, the court said government was protecting it: "The preciousness of the family relation, the authority and independence of which give dignity to parenthood, indeed the enjoyment of freedom, presuppose the kind of ordered society which is summarized by our flag." The court also concluded that when it came to efforts to promote "national cohesion . . . we are dealing with an interest inferior to none in the hierarchy of legal values.

National unity is the basis of national security."[92] It was apiece with Benjamin Rush's charge to teach the child "that he does not belong to himself, but that he is public property."

The *Gobitis* dissent, by lonely Justice Harlan F. Stone, defended religious rights against the power of the state, correctly proclaiming that "the very essence" of liberty "is the freedom of the individual from compulsion as to what he shall think and what he shall say, at least where the compulsion is to bear false witness to his religion." Stone went on to note that invoking "the public good" has too often been a pretext to crush the liberties of "politically helpless minorities."

Stone was not on the winning side that day. But he would be soon. Just three years later, in *West Virginia State Board of Education v. Barnette*, the court reversed *Gobitis*, with three justices who had ruled against religious objectors now supporting their right to not salute the flag, as well as new members of the Court.

Why the about-face? For one thing, the *Gobitis* decision, coinciding with the onset of World War II, loosed an ugly backlash against the Witnesses, including mobs burning down meetinghouses and forcing Witness children to drink castor oil and parade through town. The salute also required a raised arm that, the decision noted, provoked "objections . . . as 'being too much like Hitler's.'" Basically, the war changed how Americans acted and felt, such that even Frankfurter, who dissented in *Barnette*, tempered his thoughts from *Gobitis*, shying away from coerced unity and focusing on deference to legislatures.

Perhaps most incisive was a statement by Justice Robert H. Jackson, who had replaced now–Chief Justice lone *Gobitis* dissenter Stone on the court: "As governmental pressure toward unity becomes greater, so strife becomes more bitter as to whose unity it shall be." That had been illustrated by a century of public schooling warfare. But it was not the most famous part of the opinion. That was Jackson's declaration: "If there is any fixed star in our constitutional constellation, it is that no official, high or petty, can prescribe what shall be orthodox in politics, nationalism, religion, or other matters of opinion, or force citizens to confess by word or act their faith therein."

Barnette helped to limit how much children could be compelled to violate their religious principles for state-set secular ends. Meanwhile, efforts to at least accommodate religion in the public schools continued.

A powerful compromise movement in the 1930s and 1940s was to remove devotional instruction from public schools' formal activities and build in "released time" during which students could receive religious instruction. Essentially, students would get religious instruction from non–public school teachers during school time. As articulated by Evangelical Lutheran minister and released-time champion George U. Wenner, the goal was to render the public schools truly secular while allowing educationally essential religion a fair allocation of weekday time.

Wenner appealed to most of American history, in which education was religiously oriented and controlled. "Does America owe so little to the religious life of the nation that she cannot afford two hours for its perpetuation," he wrote. "We ought not to say surrender, we ought to say restore. For, viewed historically, it is only a partial restoration of the time which originally belonged to churches, but which under conditions that have been indicated, has been taken away from her [the Church]."[93]

Released time was unable to sidestep the church-state morass. As historian Jonathan Zimmerman has explained, it ignited intra-religious debates about what was taught, with liberal and conservative Protestants suspicious of one another. As a 1943 article in the periodical *United Evangelical Action* warned:

> If there is religious education on released time the questions of the origin of the race, the deity of Christ, the infallibility, authenticity and authority of the Bible cannot be avoided. If the teaching of Protestant children is left to leadership selected by the average federation or council of churches the effect will be disastrous to faith. . . . The evangelicals of the nation have a responsibility to impress the boards of education with the fact that so-called Protestantism is divided into *two entirely and irrevocably diverse groups* [italics added].[94]

Similarly, Jews saw tensions between religiously liberal and conservative factions exacerbated by the content of the instruction, while many Jews were of differing minds about released time itself. At least for a short period each week, it segregated them based on religion.

Released time during the school day, subject to oversight by district officials, was struck down by the U.S. Supreme Court in *McCollum v. Board of Education* in 1948. The ruling held that the program in Champaign, Illinois, violated the Constitution's First and Fourteenth Amendments by promoting religion and discriminating against children who did not attend religious classes and, hence, received no instruction when others were released. Justice Frankfurter wrote that the entanglement between church and state was too great.

Students were not just released early, allowing those who wanted religious education to get it and those who wanted something else to do as they pleased. No, the classes were during the normal school day and "conducted in the regular classrooms of the public schools by teachers of religion paid for by the churches and appointed by them, but '. . . subject to the approval and supervision of the Superintendent.'" This violated the "wall of separation" between church and state. "Separation means separation, not something else," Frankfurter wrote.[95]

In his decision, Frankfurter waxed poetic, saying public schooling was "designed to serve as perhaps the most powerful agency for promoting cohesion among a heterogeneous democratic people," and "the public school is at once the symbol of our democracy and the most pervasive means for promoting our common destiny." It was a whitewashed conclusion atop a hagiographic retelling of education history that assumed "nonsectarian" truly meant "nonreligious" as far back as Mann, and ignored huge religious imbroglios. And religion, as shall soon be seen, was but one of many planes on which public schooling failed to unify.

Grounded much more deeply in reality was the opinion of Justice Jackson, who trenchantly observed that education and religion could never be separated by an impenetrable wall, at least if education was to have any real meaning. On the matter at hand, he thought that the Champaign program went too far, but that local districts must have latitude to navigate the minefield of educating diverse people. Noting that the country had an estimated 256 "separate and substantial religious bodies," Jackson wrote:

> If we are to eliminate everything that is objectionable to any one of these warring sects or inconsistent with any of their doctrines, we will leave public education in shreds. . . . Music without sacred music, architecture minus the cathedral, or painting without the scriptural themes would be eccentric or incomplete, even from a secular point of view. . . . Even such a "science" as biology raises the issue between evolution and creation as an explanation for our presence of this planet. Certainly a course in English literature that omitted the Bible and other powerful uses of our mother tongue for religious ends would be pretty barren. And I should suppose it is a proper, if not an indispensable, part of preparation for a worldly life to know the roles that religion and religions have played in the tragic story of mankind.

Jackson was trying to cope with the reality of government schooling—it *had* to deal with religion—but he, admittedly, did not have the answer for how individual rights and common schools could coexist. The best he could offer was to give local districts latitude to "adopt different customs which will give emphasis to different values and will induce different experiments." Still, he conceded, "no matter what practice prevails, there will be many discontented and possibly belligerent minorities."

In 1952, the Supreme Court again assessed the constitutionality of released time, examining a New York City program in which students were let go for religious instruction outside of the school, and churches reported whether students attended. Students whose parents chose not to participate remained in school but received no academic instruction. In *Zorach v. Clausen* the court upheld the program, reasoning that it neither provided religious instruction in public buildings nor involved expenditure of public funds, and hence did not violate church-state separation.

Justice William O. Douglas wrote the majority opinion. The court's stance was summed up in Douglas's statement that by providing released time for instruction not subsidized by government, the state merely "respects the religious nature of our people and accommodates the public service to their spiritual needs. To hold that it may not would be to find in the Constitution a requirement that the government show a callous indifference to religious groups."[96]

The problem was that the program did not simply accommodate religion; public schools bent toward it, releasing children for religious instruction and retaining those who did not seek it. As Justice Jackson explained in his dissent, "simply shortening everyone's school day would facilitate voluntary and optional attendance at Church classes," but New York City's program did more. Jackson wrote why:

> The greater effectiveness of this system over voluntary attendance after school hours is due to the truant officer who, if the youngster fails to go to the Church school, dogs him back to the public school room. Here, schooling is more or less suspended during the "released time" so the nonreligious attendants will not forge ahead of the churchgoing absentees. But it serves as a temporary jail for a pupil who will not go to Church.

While on the wrong legal side of *Zorach*—the government was putting its thumb on the side of religion—Justice Douglas made a crucial point, saying that having no accommodation "would be preferring those who believe in no religion over those who do believe." He was correct, just as Protestant opponents of Horace Mann were correct in asserting that keeping only what all Christians could agree on rendered schools de facto Unitarian. Along similar lines, removing religion rendered the public schools de facto atheist, or at least agnostic.

As John Ireland, archbishop of St. Paul, Minnesota, told a National Education Association gathering in 1890, "Secularists and unbelievers will interpose their rights. I allow them their rights. I will not impose upon them my religion which is Christianity. But let them not impose upon me and my fellow-Christians their religion which is secularism."[97]

Judges, bishops, and others were seeing that public schooling and religious equality *were irreconcilable*, with all people paying for government schools that *could not be simultaneously religious and nonreligious*. Indeed, just as Justice Douglas wrote that *not* allowing released time would be unfair to religious children, Justice Black noted that *allowing* it meant that "the religious follower and the atheist are no longer to be judicially regarded as entitled to equal justice under law."

Since *Zorach*, released time has persisted in some places, but enrollment has dropped from its 1947 peak of about 2 million students in 2,200 communities to somewhere in the vicinity of 250,000 to 600,000 students today.[98] Mormons are heavy users of released time, and there is a major program in New York City, but it is otherwise rare. The decline was perhaps due to the precarious legal position on which released time teetered, but it may also have been a consequence of many Christians vowing to keep religion explicitly in public schools.

Even as legal battles were being fought over mandatory flag saluting and released time, many public schools retained prayers and Bible reading during instructional hours (though typically with students able to excuse themselves). But the possibility of any prayer or Bible reading being inoffensive to everyone became increasingly remote as the nation became more religiously diverse and districts grew in size. By the early 1960s, the matter of prayer in school had reached the Supreme Court in *Engel v. Vitale* and *Abington School District v. Schempp*.

Capturing the nation's ever-more detailed religious mosaic was the diversity of plaintiffs and testimony in *Schempp*, which had been combined with *Murray v. Curlett et al.* The *Schempp* appellee was a Unitarian family that objected to recitation of Bible verses and the Lord's Prayer at Abington Senior High School in Abington, Pennsylvania. In the companion case, atheist Madalyn Murray and her son William objected to similar exercises in Baltimore City. In its decision, the court cited the testimony of a Jew, Dr. Solomon Grayzel, who said that not only was the Christian Bible fundamentally different from Jewish scriptures, saying Jesus was the son of God was "practically blasphemous." He also noted that parts of the New Testament portrayed Jews negatively.[99]

Both *Engel* and *Schempp* challenged school prayer as a violation of the First Amendment's prohibition against government-established religion, with *Engel* more clear-cut because it attacked recitation of a prayer that invoked "Almighty God" and was composed and approved by the New York Board of Regents.[100] In that case, the court had little trouble deciding that, impermissibly, "New York's state prayer officially establishes the religious beliefs embodied in the Regents' prayer." The vote was 6–1, with Justice Frankfurter having been forced into retirement by a stroke and Justice Byron White not participating.

In dissent, Justice Potter Stewart mainly cited other ways in which government mixed with religion, including opening sessions of the court itself, which commence with a crier proclaiming, "God save the United States and this Honorable Court." He also raised a concern that would feature more prominently in concurring opinions in *Schempp*: whether prohibiting the recitation of prayer would discriminate *against* religious children. "For we deal here not with the establishment of a state church," he wrote, "but with whether school children who want to begin their day by joining in prayer must be prohibited from doing so."

While the always untenable idea of public schools furnishing religious instruction had become even more endangered by the 1970s, many Americans absolutely wanted prayer in their schools. And they did not relent easily. As reported by historian Jonathan Zimmerman, millions of Americans organized in the wake of *Engle* and *Schempp* to keep prayer in the schools, and work-arounds such as moments of silence were tried.[101]

Telling about the evolution of American religion was that much support for prayer in schools came from Roman Catholics. It was not interesting that Catholics supported prayer—the Church had always said religion was integral to education—but that they were joining forces with conservative Protestants, long their political and theological nemeses. It was perhaps classic enemy-of-my-enemy: while they had long been weak forces in American life, atheism and agnosticism were ascending, while conservative Christians, as well as conservative Jews, were banding together.

Growing allegiances among conservative Catholics and Protestants were a strong signal that Catholics had integrated into "mainstream" American life. Meanwhile, once-powerful denominations that had staunchly defended public schools saw big turns against them. For instance, in the 1880s Baptist leaders took strong stands against Catholics and Lutherans who opposed Wisconsin and Illinois laws de facto requiring students to attend public schools that taught only in English.[102] (Many Catholic and Lutheran schools taught in German.) By 2004, Southern Baptists were considering official resolutions calling for a public school "Exodus."

The effort to keep prayer in public schools hit its political apogee in the 1980s, a major battle zone in the era's culture wars. The presidential election of Ronald Reagan was the most visible sign of conservative social power. The Gipper amassed support from traditional Republicans and blue-collar "Reagan Democrats" who yearned for a muscular foreign policy and traditional values. The strength of Reagan's coalition also delivered Republicans the Senate majority for the first time since 1952.

Prayer in public schools had been a plank of the GOP platform since 1972. Reagan was fully in tune with that. Indeed, Terrel Bell, Reagan's first secretary of education, lamented that when Reagan spoke at the unveiling of *A Nation at Risk*—a federal jeremiad about the woeful academic state of America's schools—Reagan instead focused "on the need for students to be free to pray in school, telling that this was a fundamental right that must be restored."[103]

Despite Reagan's popularity and the strength of the conservative coalition, "official" prayer did not return to public schools. But prayer controversies continue to this day, including over coaches praying with their teams, school board meetings commencing with prayer, and student-led prayers during morning announcements. As of May 2021, the Cato Institute's Public Schooling Battle Map—an interactive database of values- and identity-based conflicts in the country's non-charter public schools, collected for roughly 15 years—contained more than 60 battles over prayer.[104]

Today, after numerous U.S. Supreme Court rulings, the legal balance on religion and the public schools seems to be this: No district employee may participate in prayer or other religious activity with students in school, but students may pray or form religious clubs as long as they do not interfere with the orderly working of the school, and are provided on an equal footing with non-religious activities. A hazier area concerns "official" student speech, such as valedictory addresses, which takes place at events all students are de facto compelled to attend, but also present the views of individual students. Every year disputes make headlines, with student remarks getting official approval; students ditching approved scripts to deliver a prayer, or thank God for their success; and all hell—or the atheist equivalent thereof—breaking loose.

Religion has been arguably the broadest and deepest ground for conflict and division in public schooling history. It remains a huge bone of contention today, with the Public Schooling Battle Map containing nearly 360 religious conflicts as of May 2021, in almost every state of the union. But it is not even close to being the only battleground.

Values

Public schooling has also been riven with battles over values. "Values" are, of course, potentially related to religion, but for many people moral values can be separate from religious beliefs, and sometimes religious beliefs can be couched in nonreligious terms. These can include battles over the content and timing of sex education, or what bathrooms and locker rooms transgender students can access. In such throwdowns, norms can have religious bases but also secular, with some parents, for instance, objecting that sixth-grade instruction on contraception violates Catholic rules, but others that it is not age appropriate.

Another instance, like the Philadelphia Bible Riots, of violence spurred by public schools were the "Textbook Wars" of Kanawha County, West Virginia, a district containing the urban state capital of Charleston and rural communities. In 1974, the county school board adopted 325 textbooks and related material for use in district language arts classes. Board member Alice Moore challenged many for content she perceived as un-American, anti-Christian, or just poor English.

Among the titles to which Moore and eventually thousands of others objected was *The Autobiography of Malcolm X*, which includes, "All praise is due to Allah that I moved to Boston when I did. If I hadn't, I'd probably still be a brainwashed black Christian." There was also a textbook tackling Sigmund Freud's idea that children have a sexual attraction to the opposite sex parent. The list of unacceptable content went on.[105]

Within a few months of the curriculum's original adoption, protestors had gathered over 12,000 signatures objecting to it, but the board voted to obtain most of the books. This incensed the largely rural, conservative faction, and when the next school year opened a boycott led to a roughly 20 percent enrollment reduction, and demonstrations joined by a sympathetic strike of coal miners in West Virginia and eastern Kentucky. The board tried to defuse the situation by briefly closing schools, removing the books temporarily, and appointing a review committee.

The board's expedients did little to mollify anti-textbook forces, whose boycott continued. They did, though, inspire 1,200 students at George Washington High School to walk out to protest *removal* of the books. Eventually the tension sparked violence, including the bombing of schools and the Board of Education. It was not until the board approved guidelines put forth by Moore for future adoptions, including prohibitions on purchasing books teaching racial hatred, encouraging sedition, or containing offensive language, that the conflict subsided.

A National Education Association autopsy of the bitter struggle concluded:

> The Kanawha County Public School System has the responsibility for providing a "quality" education to students who come from two culturally polarized communities—communities that may be only miles apart in distance, but which are light-years apart in values, beliefs, and in what they consider to be a "quality" education.[106]

For teachers, propagation of values, often operationalized as conducting oneself in accordance with community standards, was long heavily applied. Teachers could be, and often were, let go for all sorts of private activities and orientations, from drinking at a bar, to adultery, to being of any non-hetero-sexual orientation. Teachers were understandably believed to be role models for students—exemplars—and parents did not want their ideas of right behavior transgressed. This emphasis on teacher rectitude did not start to significantly erode until the 1970s, as society and law began to focus more on individual rights.[107]

Values battles can encompass many things, including sex education, reading assignments, and curricular decisions. As of May 2021, Cato's map contained 239 "moral values" battles, a bit of a catchall for disputes over "right" action, such as corporal punishment (cruel, or necessary to instill discipline?) and sex education. Reading material battles involve such repeated flash points as Toni Morrison's *The Bluest Eye* (inappropriate sexual content or social justice?). There have also been many fights over recognition of LGBTQ student support clubs (inclusive or promoting bad behavior?). Add all such battles to "moral values," and the map contained 611 values fights.

Immigrants

While tensions between Catholics and Protestants had religious and political bases, they were also tightly intertwined with worries about mass immigration—Catholics were almost all of immigrant stock—that created a parched tinderbox often ignited by public schooling. Frankly, it should have been obvious that public schooling, which many saw as the tip of the "Americanizing" spear for ethnicities very different from the Anglo-Saxon mold, would produce great acrimony. And not just that: great resistance as well.

Contemplating immigration from all parts of the globe, Ellwood P. Cubberley wrote:

> No such great movement of peoples was ever known before in history, and the assimilative power of the American nation has not been equal to the task. The World War revealed the extent of the failure to nationalize the foreigner who has been permitted to come, and brought the question of "Americanization" to the front as one of the most pressing problems connected with American national education. With the world in flux racially as it now is, the problem of the assimilation of non-native peoples is one which the schools of every nation which offers political and economic opportunity to other peoples must face. This has called for the organization of special classes in the schools, evening and adult instruction, community-center work, nationalization programs, compulsory attendance of children, state oversight of private and religious schools, and other forms of educational undertakings undreamed of in the days when the State first took over the schools from the Church the better to promote literacy and citizenship.[108]

Cubberley's thinking about immigration was intertwined with race. In 1909, he wrote of non-"Anglo-Teutonic" immigrants:

> Everywhere these people tend to settle in groups of settlements, and to set up here their national manners, customs, and observances. Our task is to break up these groups of settlements, to assimilate and amalgamate these people as a part

of our American race, and to implant in their children, so far as can be done, the Anglo-Saxon conception of righteousness, law and order, and to awaken in them a reverence for our democratic institutions and for those things in our national life which we as a people hold to be of abiding worth.[109]

Public schools, as Cubberley prescribed, were employed as assimilation machines.[110] The primary problem they encountered was that forcing people to not just give up, but often disdain, their ethnic and cultural identities was often neither a simple nor welcomed undertaking. Like their religion, many people will not simply surrender their cherished histories, cultures, or identities for the sake of educational peace. If anything, immigrant groups often adapted their culture, language, and ethnic identity in *spite* of the education system.

Naturally, ethnic and cultural differences tended to become especially glaring during periods of intense immigration, which the nation saw especially in the 1840s and 1850s and 1880s and 1890s. In the earlier period the main arrivals were Irish and Germans in the East, but also, as part of the gold rush, Chinese in California, which became a state in 1850. In the last decades of the nineteenth century, heading into the twentieth, the complexion of the major immigrant groups was different—literally and figuratively—with throngs of Italians, Eastern Europeans, and Russians flooding the nation's ports, as well as Irish, Germans, British, Asians, and Mexicans.[111]

Many of the new arrivals lacked sufficient funds to go any farther than their ports of entry; hence, they packed into neighborhoods not far from where they had dropped anchor. They also settled into such places, as will be discussed, because assimilation is much easier when eased into. These settlements became ghettos—crowded blocks of linguistically, culturally, and ethnically similar peoples.

Not surprisingly, these areas of hyperconcentrated foreign tongues, cultures, and poverty caused American elites the most alarm, and fueled the public-school-as-assimilator drive of the late nineteenth and early twentieth centuries. This contrasts with the nexus of immigration and schooling in the 1840s and 1850s. There was concern then about assimilation of the foreign born, but more, as we saw with Lyman Beecher, fear of direct foreign influence over the country. And whether common schools should even exist was still an open question, with supporters mainly focused on fostering citizenship and virtue among existing Americans than immigrants.

By the 1880s public schooling was firmly established, though even by 1890 in only about half of states was attendance compulsory.[112] In that latter period the central goals of the system were to Americanize immigrants; lift education out of filthy politics; and impose efficient, scientific control on education. Of course, the latter went hand in hand with the former; the districts that seemed most befouled by graft-ridden political control were often small, ethnically homogeneous urban districts.

As one New York State senator put it, the children needed to fall "under the influence of educated, refined, intelligent men and women, so they will be elevated and lifted out of the swamp into which they were born and brought up."[113] More broadly, a committee of the Graduate School of Education at the University of Nebraska fretted in 1919, "How can we have national spirit in a commonwealth where there is an infusion of the language and blood of many nations unless there is a very strong effort made to socialize the different elements and weld them into a unified whole?"[114]

The difficulty was human nature: large swaths of immigrants were not going to just eject everything about their culture, ethnic identity, or whatever else the schools told their children was not "American" enough. Many chafed under Americanization efforts and rebelled as best they could. As we know, a great deal of the warfare between immigrants and natives was fought on the soil of religion, which did so much to define people and cultures. Similarly, native language is intimately connected to one's identity. And both overlap heavily with national origin.

Often immigrants, having far less ability to publish their thoughts than promoters of Americanization, expressed their discontent by avoiding taxes or keeping their children out of school.[115] This was common especially among immigrants from southern Italy, who were highly suspicious of government, which in their Old World experience had often been corrupt and capricious. But sometimes immigrants' objections were delivered more overtly.

Historian David Tyack recounts a revolt in a Texas history class attended by Mexican newcomer Guadalupe Toro Valdez in 1919. A recitation about Sam Houston defeating Mexican soldiers and taking Mexican possessions ended in students defacing a portrait of Houston and ripping pages on the offending events from textbooks.[116] In 1904, when the New York City Board of Education sought to move 1,500 Jewish students from a bursting-at-the-seams Lower East Side school, parents were outraged. The chairman of a gathering to combat the move said that the community had "stood for a good many municipal evils. . . . But we will not stand for this."[117] Among many things, the families feared their children would miss morning prayers and afternoon religious instruction, and encounter hostility in non-Jewish neighborhoods.

Perhaps the widest conflicts were over Wisconsin's "Bennett Law" and similar legislation in Illinois, mandating that most school instruction be provided in English, and hurting private schools by stipulating that every child attend school "in the city, town or district in which he resides."[118] An official declaration against the law from representatives of German Protestant churches focused on the law's curbing religious freedom. It highlighted, among many concerns, that "we can not celebrate church-holidays, that occur on a school-day during the compulsory period, with our children, with our pastors and teachers, without incurring a penalty."[119]

The platform adopted by the 1890 Anti-Bennett State Convention was clear about the feelings of many German immigrants, stating that those assembled "opposed . . . all measures tending to oppress the immigrated citizens, or to suppress their native tongue."[120] Lutheran parochial school apologist Christian Koerner asserted that German was no more "foreign" than English. "Having been spoken for centuries by a not inconsiderable number of the population of the Old Colonies and of the revolutionary heroes, and at present by millions of the inhabitants of the States and Territories—it is no more a *foreign* language than the English language."[121]

The law was revoked in 1891, following acrimonious statewide and national debate, and a drubbing of the Bennett-supporting Republican Party in the 1890 elections.

Assimilation forces frequently pitted young against old, sometimes intentionally, almost always inevitably. If children were being taught that there was something deficient about the dress, diet, language, or other characteristics of their parents, how could anything but rifts—and gashed feelings—result? Tyack illustrates this with the following story:

> From his own experience as an immigrant from Aviliano to New York, Leonardo Covello knew how painful forced assimilation could be to children and parents alike. He recalled the evening when he first brought home his report card for his father to sign. "What is this?" asked his father, "Leonardo Covello! What happened to the *i* in Coviello . . . from Leonardo to Leonard I can follow . . . a perfectly natural process. In America anything can happen and does happen. But you don't change a family name." The son explained that the teacher found Covello easier to say, and he wanted it that way too. When his mother joined her husband in protest, Leonard made the reply that was all too familiar to immigrant parents: "Mama you don't understand." "Will you stop saying that!" she replied. "I don't understand. I don't understand. What is there to understand? Now that you have become Americanized you understand everything and I understand nothing." Covello and his friends did their best to keep their mothers away from school, for they were ashamed of their shawls and Italian speech. Hearing nothing of Italy or Italians in school, except for Columbus, he "soon got the idea that 'Italian' meant something inferior."[122]

Ethnic Finns experienced similar shame and strife. As Louis Adamec related in his 1937 book, *From Many Lands*, which examined the plights of immigrant families, because of Americanization efforts "a great number of the American-born sons and daughters of Finnish immigrants were ashamed of their parents."[123] Their families were smeared as "backward" and "inferior," and "the result was conflict in the home. Boys and girls wanted to change their names, refused to learn Finnish, and did not want to know anything about Finland."

Even after immigrants assimilated there were conflicts over nationalities. They were especially intense in response to World War I. Reacting to suspicion of anyone whose family hailed from the country's enemies, especially Germany, numerous groups vied to have their contributions to the United States highlighted in the schools. Irish groups claimed that 13 Declaration of Independence signers, 7 Constitutional Convention members, and a third of the Continental Army had been of Irish descent. Germans highlighted the contributions of their ancestors in fighting slavery, and the British in the Revolution. Italians and Norwegians bickered over whether Christopher Columbus or Leif Eriksson discovered America.[124] And again the German language was attacked, with instruction removed, and sometimes outlawed.[125]

By the 1980s and 1990s "multiculturalism" was the primary battleground, though it was just one theater in culture wars raging over everything from abortion to taxpayer-funded art. In 1994, federally commissioned guidelines for teaching U.S. history ignited a backlash that ended with the U.S. Senate condemning the standards by a 99 to 1 vote. The lone dissenter was a member who thought the condemnation not condemnatory enough. Former chair of the National Endowment for the Humanities Lynne Cheney railed in the *Wall Street Journal*:

> The authors tend to save their unqualified admiration for people, places and events that are politically correct. The first era, "Three Worlds Meet (Beginnings to 1620)," covers societies in the Americas, Western Europe and West Africa that began to interact significantly after 1450. To understand West Africa, students are encouraged to "analyze the achievements and grandeur of Mansa Musa's court, and the social customs and wealth of the kingdom of Mali."

> Such celebratory prose is rare when the document gets to American history itself. In the U.S. context, the kind of wealth that Mansa Musa commanded is not considered a good thing. When the subject of John D. Rockefeller comes up, students are instructed to conduct a trial in which he is accused of "knowingly and willfully participat[ing] in unethical and amoral business practices designed to undermine traditions of fair open competition for personal and private aggrandizement in direct violation of the common welfare."

> African and Native American societies, like all societies, had their failings, but one would hardly know it from National Standards. Students are encouraged to consider Aztec "architecture, skills, labor systems, and agriculture." But not the practice of human sacrifice.[126]

On the other side were those who thought the standards were fair, and the objectors politically motivated. "The controversy is not really about kids becoming better historical thinkers," wrote authors Gary Nash and Ross Dunn. "It's about that perennial topic of public contention—political correctness and multiculturalism. It won't take long for teachers to see that they—and the public—are being misled for political advantage."[127]

Multicultural battles continue today. Cato's battle map documented more than 293 conflicts over race or ethnicity as of May 2021, and almost no state has been immune over the last decade or so. Of course, some states have far more ethnically and racially diverse populations than others. And many conflicts, such as over history curricula, can include racial and ethnic elements even if they are not primarily about identity.

In the mid-2000s, the Tucson school district became a battle zone over its ethnic studies department, and La Raza Studies program in particular. Meaning studies of "the race," the program sought to inculcate pride in Hispanic students. But it upset many Arizonans, including former state superintendents Tom Horne and John Huppenthal, who found an instructional program tailored to a specific ethnic group repugnant. They also objected to U.S history classes that taught that large swaths of the southwestern United States had been illegally taken from Mexico, and appeared to favor revolutionaries such as Che Guevara and Emiliano Zapata.

The fight over the ethnic studies program, which took place in the context of a desegregation order dating back to 1978 that *required* it, captured a basic disagreement. In the words of Horne, Raza Studies fostered balkanizing "ethnic chauvinism" and separatism. Defenders contended that it helped instill pride and self-esteem in students whose ethnic groups were marginalized in WASP-centric curricula. They also asserted that it countered the well-known problem of history being written by the "winners."[128]

An exchange between Anna Graves, a Mexican immigrant who became a U.S. citizen, and state Rep. Peter Rios, in a hearing about an ethnic studies bill, captured the zero-sum clash. "I absolute [*sic*] deplore people who come from another country and do not want anything to do with the culture, the language or anything to do with the government," Graves said. Rios replied that the program was necessary to teach Hispanic students their culture, and "some . . . have to pick up some of this positive self-image building at the school because they're not getting it at home, they're not getting it in the barrios of the neighborhood."[129]

The well-being of minority children and communities was directly pitted against social cohesion.

In 2010, the state passed a law prohibiting instruction that would advocate overthrowing the U.S. government, promote resentment of races or classes of people, or "advocate ethnic solidarity instead of the treatment of pupils as individuals."[130] In October of that year 11 ethnic studies teachers sued to block the law in federal court, alleging that it was racially biased and would curb their speech rights. Still, the state moved to punish the Tucson district if it did not eliminate the ethnic studies department, inspiring widespread protests and civil disobedience, including students chaining themselves together and shutting down school board meetings.

The state prevailed in federal appeals court, except Judge A. Wallace Tashima struck down the prohibition on teaching classes designed for particular ethnic groups. The district took that to allow the reintroduction of several texts it had removed, including Rodolfo Acuña's *Occupied America: A History of Chicanos* and Paulo Freire's *Pedagogy of the Oppressed*. State superintendent John Huppenthal felt that violated the law and he tried to punish the district, also citing material for African American students. The tide turned again in December 2017, when Judge Tashima ruled that the state's action had been driven by "racial animus," and was illegal.

Native Americans

Native Americans, the farthest group from immigrants, have also been subjects of aggressive—sometimes brutal—Americanization efforts. Even before the common schooling era, a primary goal of many education undertakings was to assimilate Native Americans, instilling in them European ways and, especially, Christian religion. The East India Company established a school for that purpose in Virginia, and the original 1650 Harvard charter committed the school to "the education of the English and Indian Youth of this Country in knowledge and godliness."

Unlike most government schooling, efforts to assimilate Native Americans were driven more by the federal government than states or districts. And from roughly the late 1870s to the early 1920s they were the harshest of assimilation campaigns, with children shipped to boarding schools often far from their homes, sometimes under police compulsion, eventually under threat of lost federal assistance to families the U.S. government had boxed onto reservations.[131] As Carlisle Indian Industrial School founder Richard Henry Pratt expressed in a statement often shortened to "kill the Indian, save the man," the goal was to eliminate:

> the reservation wild man . . . in his most hideous costume of feathers, paint, moccasins, blanket, leggings, and scalp lock, and to display his savagery, by hair lifting war-whoops. . . . It is this nature in our red brother that is better dead than alive, and when we agree with the oft-repeated sentiment that the only good Indian is a dead one, we mean this characteristic of the Indian. Carlisle's mission is to kill THIS Indian, as we build up the better man."[132]

To commit this "murder," boarding schools such as Carlisle militarized Americanization. Students' hair was shorn upon arrival, eliciting lamentations from children for whom cutting hair was an act of mourning. Victorian-era clothing was required, speech in native languages was forbidden, and students were broken into companies and marched from place to place. The children even woke to reveille and ended their days with taps.

Some children attempted to escape, but capture carried harsh penalties. At the Chemawa Indian School in Salem, Oregon, there were 46 "desertions" in 1921, and 70 in 1922. According to an interviewed student, when two female escapees were caught, "They tied their legs up, tied their hands behind their backs, put them in the middle of the hallway so that if they fell, fell asleep or something, the matron would hear them and she'd get out there and whip them and make them stand up again."[133] That said, some students and families appreciated the instruction provided by the schools; some Native Americans wanted to assimilate into the dominant culture.

By the 1920s, the expense of the Indian schools was seen as too great, and "killing" fell out of pedagogical and sociological favor. Indians moved primarily into reservations and regular public schools over the ensuing decades. But even with many Native American students in reservation schools, and constituting less than 1 percent of students nationwide, conflicts still rear their heads in modern public schools.

Perhaps most common are disputes over Native American mascots. Many states and districts have battled over whether such mascots are proud community and Native American monuments, or demeaning caricatures. Other conflicts involve dress codes requiring that students have short hair, or forbidding them from wearing important tribal symbols. There's also *The Absolutely True Diary of a Part-time Indian*, by Sherman Alexie, to which parents often object when it is on school reading lists or in libraries, for, among other things, its portrayal of Native Americans. In 2014 it sat atop the American Library Association's "most challenged" list.[134]

African Americans

The greatest injustice and deepest, most jagged scar on American history has been the treatment of African Americans. While other groups suffered prejudice and sometimes educational exclusion, none did so on the scale or with the seemingly interminable, malignant constancy of African Americans. First, they had to fight just to get into the public schools that, by our mythology, served and unified all. Then many had to fight—and are *still* fighting—to get what they actually wanted out of the schools.

Recall that in many states it was long illegal to provide blacks just with reading instruction, much less equal access to common schools. The fear was that enlightened slaves would see the base servility of their positions and demand something better. Slave revolts, including uprisings in South Carolina in 1800, 1816, and 1822, and in Virginia in 1800 and 1831, inflamed this fear.[135]

South Carolina made teaching a slave to read or write a crime in 1740, and Virginia did so in 1819.[136] Georgia passed such a law in 1829.[137] Other states and territories enacted statutes that made slaves assembling for the purpose of education illegal. Such rules were common parts of "slave codes," and sometimes incorporated freedmen in their prohibitions.

In the North, while instructing African Americans was legal, accessing schools, especially integrated, was a constant challenge, with black families often relegated to separate schools.[138] Indeed, segregation was quite common in northern states. Even "Athens of America" Boston did not desegregate until 1855, and only after lengthy political and legal battles that originated the "separate but equal" doctrine that would solidify Jim Crow 40 years later.[139]

After emancipation, strict legal prohibitions against educating African Americans disappeared. But the struggle to access education did not. While the arrival of northern armies often brought efforts to create schools for freed slaves, and readmission to the union often required states to establish common schools, equal access to education was not achieved. Blacks were typically educated with other blacks, and their schools were funded at a fraction of white schools. Even worse, those public schools often instilled inferiority, and prepared students for jobs that white society would not let them fill, at least if they competed with whites.

"The result, then, is that the Negroes thus mis-educated are of no service to themselves and none to the white man," wrote black, Harvard-trained historian Carter G. Woodson. He continued:

> The white man does not need the Negroes' professional commercial or industrial assistance . . . . The "highly educated" Negroes, moreover, do not need the Negro professional or commercial classes because Negroes have been taught that whites can serve them more efficiently in these spheres.[140]

Woodson also decried schools teaching almost exclusively European and white American culture and history, implying that Africa had contributed little to the world. He laid out what he would add to end inferiority by omission:

> In our own particular history we would not dim one bit the luster of any star in our firmament. We would not learn less of George Washington, "First in War, First in Peace and First in the Hearts of his Countrymen"; but we would learn something also of the three thousand Negro soldiers of the American Revolution who helped to make this "Father of our Country" possible. We would not neglect to appreciate the unusual contribution of Thomas Jefferson to freedom

and democracy; but we would invite attention also to two of his outstanding contemporaries, Phillis Wheatley, the writer of interesting verse, and Benjamin Banneker, the mathematician, astronomer, and advocate of a world peace plan set forth in 1793 with the vital principles of Woodrow Wilson's League of Nations.[141]

The list went on.

W. E. B. Du Bois, who taught for a summer in a black, rural Tennessee school, was also exasperated. "To-day it has been only by the most strenuous efforts on the part of thinking men of the South that the Negro's share of the school fund has not been cut down to a pittance," he wrote in *Souls of Black Folk*. "What in the name of reason does this nation expect of a people, poorly trained and hardpressed in severe economic competition, without political rights, and with ludicrously inadequate common-school facilities?"[142]

Du Bois also opposed the heavily industrial bent of African American education, which he saw creating a permanent underclass and blocking full realization of black humanity. This put Du Bois at odds with Booker T. Washington, who believed blacks must focus on useful, in-demand skills, making themselves economically indispensable and setting the groundwork for integration. Of course, this conflict—practical education versus enlightenment—was just one skirmish in a seemingly eternal fight, though with stakes much higher for long-oppressed African Americans than many other groups.

There was another major rift among African Americans that remains today: while many wanted to integrate with whites, some preferred all black institutions. Du Bois himself changed on this, ultimately concluding that black students would be better off with black teachers, a position at odds with the National Association for the Advancement of Colored People that Du Bois helped found, and from which he eventually resigned over the matter.[143] Du Bois would have preferred integration, but despaired of such schools ever being free of "unsympathetic teachers, with hostile public opinion, and no teaching of truth concerning black folk."[144]

Similar was the view on integration of black Muslim leader Malcolm X. Shabazz, who attended integrated schools, saw segregation as bad, but believed separation was realistic. "*Segregation* is when your life and liberty are controlled, regulated, by *someone else*," he argued. "[S]egregation is that which is forced upon inferiors by superiors. But *separation* is that which is done voluntarily, by two equals—for the good of both!"[145] Marginalizing public schools, with few African Americans on school boards and curricula that neglected black history, were cited in the federal Kerner Report as a cause of devastating race riots in the 1960s.[146]

Many African Americans chafed at the notion implicit in school integration that black children needed to be in close proximity to whites to learn. Others felt a deep loss with the demise of schools controlled by, and therefore fully serving, African Americans. Said one Wilmington, North Carolina, woman about the integration of her formerly all-black alma mater, "We were in a cocoon bathed in a warm fluid, where we were expected to excel." But when the school was desegregated and turned into a black and white middle school, "We went from our own land to being tourists in someone else's. It never did come together."[147] In 1968, Horace Tate, long-time head of the Black Georgia Teachers and Education Association, referred to the way integration was happening—African American schools and educators taken over and pushed out by whites—as "outergration."[148]

A study of "Crossover High School," a pseudonym for a high school in Memphis, Tennessee that was integrated by moving black students into it, reported the same sense of loss. Said one African American student who would have gone to "Feeder High School," a formerly all-black school, "I don't know why they closed our school, it was good. It is just another way white folks have of messin' us over."[149] A former Feeder teacher lamented, "People in the community would call me when they saw children cutting class and I would go out into the street and bring them back to school. You don't get that kind of cooperation anymore."[150]

Having little control of the schools that taught their children lit one of the hottest conflagrations in New York City public schooling history, engulfing blacks, Puerto Ricans, and Jewish unionists through the 1960s. Many poor African Americans and Puerto Ricans determined that they did not control the schools meant to serve their children and communities, but were instead subject to the power of city bureaucrats who neither listened to nor cared about them. When the United Federation of Teachers struck for a second time over the Ocean Hill–Brownsville subdistrict dismissing numerous teachers—an action Ocean Hill leaders saw as exerting control over *their* schools—ugliness ensued. As Diane Ravitch describes it:

> The racial and religious antagonisms which had simmered in the schools for several years burst to the surface during the second strike. Picketing teachers claimed that they were subjected to antiwhite, anti-Semitic invective. Governing board partisans charged the teacher picketers with using antiblack invective. Tension increased each day. Parents were angry because the schools were closed; blacks were angry because a small, black school board was being stepped on by a powerful union; union members were angry because it appeared that the mayor was union-busting; Jews were angry because Jewish teachers were pushed out of their jobs without cause while the Board of Education complacently tolerated outbursts of anti-Semitism at its public meetings.[151]

Residents' concerns were easily understood: Why should African Americans, or Hispanics, have to fight bureaucracies, or unions, to make decisions for their children? It was the problem of public schooling in microcosm: Why should government get to override what any parent thinks is best for their children? By what right are people stripped of their self-governance?

Directly related to these foundational questions, mandatory busing to integrate public schools led to conflict on par with the Philadelphia Bible Riots and Kanawha County textbook war, including bus bombings, violent demonstrations, and student brawls. And many African Americans did not see busing as beneficent. In 1972, the National Black Political Convention resolved that busing was "a bankrupt, suicidal method of desegregating schools, based on the false notion that black children are unable to learn unless they are in the same setting as white children."[152] The Crossover study found a large group of African American children "were not as much anti-white as anti-assimilation. . . . Whites and school desegregation were fine as long as assimilation was not the goal. They were adamantly for a form of cultural pluralism."[153]

We continue to see African Americans struggling to get the education they want for their children, sometimes overtly trying to wrest control of the public schools they attend. In 2005, African American Nebraska state senator Ernie Chambers (D-Omaha) amended education legislation to split the Omaha district along racial lines: black, Hispanic, and white. Said Chambers, "My intent is not to have an exclusionary system, but [one that] we, meaning black people, whose children make up the vast majority of the student population, would control."[154] The division was eventually enacted, but rescinded before it took effect.

One of the two lawsuits wrapped into the U.S. Supreme Court case *Parents Involved in Community Schools v. Seattle School District No. 1* (2007) took on a school assignment policy in Jefferson County, Kentucky, that used a school's racial makeup as a factor in determining which students could attend. A student whose presence would upset a desired racial balance would not be admitted. African Americans Dionne Hopson and Ja'Mekia Stoner wanted desperately to attend Central High School—historically, Louisville's black high school—but were denied because they would have thrown off the balance.

Hopson and Stoner's plight eventually led to several lawsuits against the district which wended their way to the Supreme Court. In a plurality opinion, the court struck down policies that used a student's race as a mechanistic factor in assignments. (Districts could still use approaches such as drawing attendance zones likely to produce diverse student bodies.)[155] As Carman Weathers, a Louisville activist, put it, "We were never allowed to assimilate on our terms. We were assimilated on somebody else's terms."[156]

African Americans' inability to control the schools their children attend has repeatedly led to conflicts. This may have peaked with the Ebonics furor of the 1990s, a brouhaha over the Oakland, California, school district recognizing a distinctly African American way of speaking as an official language that could be used in at least some instruction. While this troubled many whites and blacks—civil rights activist Jesse Jackson and former Reagan education secretary William Bennett rebuked it—many blacks felt affirmed. As one Oaklander put it: "We need to stand on our own two feet. . . . I defy anyone of another race to tell us how to speak."[157]

Similarly, in 2013 Chicago Public Schools adopted a controversial African and African American studies program that taught, among other controversial ideas, that Greek culture was derivative of black Egyptian culture. Superintendent Barbara Byrd-Bennett said the program "will enrich the understanding and appreciation of African and African-American history and culture to help build stronger and more cohesive student communities."[158] Many people objected to the plan, especially that it would feature disputed theories, including that ancient Greek culture was neither original nor European.[159]

Perhaps no recent battle has been higher profile than the national debate over the 1619 Project, a *New York Times* initiative featuring numerous articles, a Pulitzer Prize for project impresario and reporter Nikole Hannah-Jones, and a *Times*–Pulitzer Foundation packaging for use in schools. The Project's basic premise was that the true founding of the United States was not 1776 but 1619, when the first enslaved Africans stepped foot in America.[160] Among the most eye-catching claims was that the primary driver for American independence was fear that the British government was going to outlaw slavery, which was the key to the American economy.[161]

For the project's originators and defenders, it was a long overdue corrective to American history and a wake-up call to the American public about deep-seated racism. To its detractors, it was an error-riddled crusade to portray the country as fundamentally evil rather than grounded in principles of democracy and freedom. Said President Donald Trump at an event announcing a commission to promote "patriotic education," which became the 1776 Commission:

> The left has warped, distorted, and defiled the American story with deceptions, falsehoods, and lies. There is no better example than the *New York Times'* totally discredited 1619 Project. This project rewrites American history to teach our children that we were founded on the principle of oppression, not freedom.[162]

Trump had earlier threatened to withhold federal funding from California schools if the state introduced the project into its curriculum, and legislation was submitted in the Senate and House to take such action nationally.[163]

From the other direction, early in the administration of President Joe Biden the U.S. Department of Education published "proposed priorities" for the American History and Civics Education grant program. The notice cited the 1619 Project and "anti-racism" champion Ibram X. Kendi in calling for proposals that "take into account systemic marginalization, biases, inequities, and discriminatory policy and practice in American history."[164]

To some people it sounded like code for critical race theory, which they believed found all white people guilty of racism simply by virtue of their skin.[165] At the same time, legislatures in several, mainly Republican-controlled states were debating bills to make it illegal to teach in public schools "divisive concepts" such as "an individual, by virtue of the individual's race or sex, is inherently racist, sexist, or oppressive, whether consciously or unconsciously."[166] The entire nation had been thrust into warfare over how the schools would teach African American—and foundational United States—history.

WHY NOT MORE CONFLICT?

While conflict has been a constant companion of public schooling, all people have not been perpetually at each other's throats. Indeed, one could conceivably look at the grand scope of American history, with its relative stability despite incessant political contests, waves of immigrants, class struggles, culture wars, and so on, and conclude that public schooling succeeded in unifying diverse and ever-evolving people. Sure, people tussled, and some were bruised or worse, but as historian Diane Ravitch asserts at the end of *The Great School Wars*:

> The common school idea, for all the buffeting it has taken in the past 150 years, has survived because it is appropriate to a democratic, heterogeneous society. It presumes that children should be taught those values which are basic to a free and just society, including respect for the individual's rights, a sense of social responsibility, and above all, perhaps, a devotion to comity, that precious value of a democratic society which grants the legitimacy of opposing views and permits groups to compete without seeking to crush one another.[167]

It is a bit surprising that Ravitch wrote this after chronicling how in New York City alone Roman Catholics, African Americans, and other groups often felt *exactly* like they were being crushed. But perhaps she is right that diverse people generally came together through public schooling and learned to get along, while building broad commitment to individual rights.

Or perhaps not. Certainly not all districts containing diverse peoples have hosted scenes of civil war. But peace was often kept not because the public schools brought diverse people together, but because they *did not*. As reviewed, many barred some groups completely, and marginalized others so they had little choice but to stay out. And public schooling was, for a long time, grounded in small, homogenous communities. There basically was no diversity.

Homogeneous Districts

How small were districts for most of American history? National numbers only go back to the 1937–38 school year, but even looking at those gives a sense of how very local public schools have been. In 1937–38 there were 119,001 districts in the United States, serving a population of 128,824,829 people.[168] Each district encompassed, on average, only 1,083 people. In 2018, in contrast, there were only 13,452 districts and a population of 328,529,911, or an average of 24,422 people per district—more than a *20-fold* increase.[169]

Of course, districts were being consolidated before 1937 while the population grew, so the 1937 averages are likely much larger than what they were for many decades preceding them. New York, for instance, had nearly 12,000 districts around 1870—about 1,500 shy of the *entire country* today—and a population of 4,382,759. That is roughly just 365 people per district.[170] And for most of American history people consumed far less schooling than today. As recently as 1960 fewer than half of Americans over the age of 25 had completed high school.[171]

Districts tended to be homogeneous not just because they were small, but because, as discussed, Americans often settled in ethnically similar groups. Because daily life is easier when our neighbors share our language, courtesies, foods, and favorite leisure activities, similar people tend to congregate together. This has been especially true for immigrants, who have come to American shores and, especially for first-generation newcomers, gathered in ethnic enclaves. As sociologist Milton M. Gordon observes, "The newcomer needs the comfortable sociological and psychological milieu which the communality of his own group provides."[172]

Given the human proclivity to live among similar people, local education control has helped keep peace, but by *not* mixing. National data to prove this do not exist, but there is lower-level evidence. Historian Benjamin Justice pieced together historical records for much of nineteenth-century New York State, and found that towns and districts tended to have ethnically, religiously, and linguistically homogeneous populations. Where districts did not have such populations, Justice found that different groups would often work to establish new districts so diverse groups could separate, and get education tailored to their desires.[173]

In New York City, Justice reports that most Jews—a group likely to have had an especially difficult time finding acceptable schools in an overwhelmingly Christian country—were comfortable with public schools because they were not as controlling as what they had left in Europe, and because their children attended schools that were nearly all Jewish.[174] Engineering such homogeneity reached a constitutional end in 1994, when the U.S. Supreme Court ruled that New York's Kiryas Joel Village School District—shaped to exactly fit a town populated exclusively by orthodox Jewish Satmars—was unconstitutional government favoring of a specific religious sect.[175]

What Justice unearthed about New York is in keeping with how historian Robert Wiebe has observed peace maintained through much of American history. Religiously at-odds groups only fought, Wiebe writes, for "as long as it took their camps to disperse."[176] Much as Thomas Hooker left Massachusetts over political and religious differences, founding Connecticut, Justice reports that in 1878 Protestants in a predominantly Catholic district in Washington County, New York, started the de facto Protestant "Raceville" district.[177] Historian Jonathan Zimmerman calls local control a "safety valve" for hostilities.[178]

Local Compromise

In addition to allowing diverse groups to be separate and, hence, largely self-governing, local control has empowered the development of diverse compromises short of separation. Communities have been able to construct arrangements that have suited their unique needs, and in so doing foster innovation so that communities facing similar tensions might find already tested solutions. Districts can function like U.S. Supreme Court Justice Louis Brandeis's famous "laboratories of democracy," only at the local rather than state level.[179]

Arrangements in which Roman Catholic school buildings and staff were incorporated into districts were found in many states in the mid- to late 1800s, including districts in Georgia; the Gallitzen Borough School District in Pennsylvania; Lowell, Massachusetts; and several districts in New York. Basically, a Catholic school would provide its facilities to districts at a nominal rent—$1 annually in the well-known case of Poughkeepsie, New York—and furnish nonreligious instruction during the school day. The district would pay for maintenance, textbooks, teacher salaries, and other expenses, and control the program of instruction.[180]

Such plans accommodated rapidly growing populations for a while, but eventually fell apart. Catholics increasingly sought schools that were overtly Catholic throughout the school day, and a movement toward less strict religious requirements in public schools grew.[181] Poughkeepsie began its arrangement in 1873 and ended it in 1898.[182]

Language, like religion, was a potential source of great conflict, as seen in late-nineteenth century battles over instruction in German. But communities often found ways to accommodate those differences, too. Many New York districts serving large German-speaking communities in the latter nineteenth century offered German as an elective.[183] By the early twentieth century, after curbs on immigration had lessened assimilation fears, districts serving large numbers of children from various ethnic groups increasingly used textbooks and activities that emphasized the contributions of those groups.

As Tyack reports, in the 1920s and 1930s:

> Polish pupils in Toledo, Ohio . . . studied their parents' history and culture; students in Neptune, New Jersey, created ethnic family trees and learned the history of their ancestors; in Santa Barbara, California, pupils prepared exhibits of Chinese art, Scandinavian crafts, and Pacific cultures; and Mexican children in Phoenix, Arizona, attended a class, taught in Spanish, on Mexican history and culture.[184]

Small size and homogeneity also seemed to facilitate expanding the scope of public schooling. Goldin and Katz found that smaller, wealthier, and more homogeneous districts tended to be leaders in establishing public high schools.[185] This was almost certainly the case at least in part because agreement on establishing such schools, and what they would teach, was easier to reach in more insular districts than places with more diverse citizens.

Lowest-Common-Denominator Content

Unfortunately, a primary strategy to maintain peace is a threat to educational outcomes: removing curricular content that any group might find objectionable. If there are ideas over which people disagree, either soft-pedal or remove them. Doing that could—and often does—eliminate important content from which kids would benefit.

Such lowest-common-denominator "solutions" have been evident in the religious tensions that have plagued the schools. Recall that for orthodox Protestants, especially before the major influx of Catholics, watering down of religious belief was a major worry about Horace Mann's common schooling proposals. At least some insisted that education deprived of distinct sectarian doctrines was hollow. Such pablum, however, was necessary to prevent common schools from alienating almost all denominations unable to make *theirs* the doctrines taught.

Lamentation over lowest-common-denominator material was also seen among Catholic leaders as time went on and religious content—which many in the hierarchy had long decried as too Protestant—was removed to make schools tolerable to all, including "free thinkers" espousing no religion. Catholic leaders eventually condemned the public schools as God-free zones. As Bishop Bernard McQuaid of Rochester, New York, characterized matters in the 1870s, public schools with religious exercises may have been de facto Protestant, but those without were "godless and un-American."[186]

Pressure to exclude potentially divisive content has seemingly become more intense as the public education system has become much more centralized, and districts have included more diverse constituencies. Diane Ravitch documented the deleterious effects of such pressure in language arts and social studies. Her 2003 book *The Language Police* chronicles how groups on the left, right, and in between have fought against heaps of class content, books, and even standardized testing items that anyone might find offensive or just disquieting.[187]

On the right, activists have crusaded against content they find immoral or un-American, including efforts to remove books from school libraries or reading lists such as J. D. Salinger's *The Catcher in the Rye* and John Steinbeck's *The Grapes of Wrath*, and blocking textbooks thought to contain too little discussion of "great men" such as the Founding Fathers. On the left, sensitivity has often been the main concern, targeting books such as *The Adventures of Huckleberry Finn* that contain racial slurs, or testing items that portray minority groups in potentially negative light.[188]

Ravitch offers several examples from her time helping to craft voluntary national tests—eventually abandoned—in the 1990s. After her committee had identified what they thought were high-quality reading selections, several were rejected by the testing contractor's "bias and sensitivity" review panel. Among items rejected was the story of a blind man hiking to the peak of Mount McKinley (now Denali), the tallest mountain in North America. Not only was it wrong to suggest a blind person might face greater obstacles climbing a mountain than a sighted person, many test takers might not be from mountainous regions, putting them at a disadvantage.[189]

As powerful as Ravitch's compilation is, it is anecdotal. In 2010, Pennsylvania State University political scientists Michael Berkman and Eric Plutzer furnished more systematic evidence, publishing the results of a nationally representative survey of public high school biology teachers. They found that while some teachers taught rigorous evolution, defined as meeting National Research Council benchmarks, and some taught outright creationism, 67 percent either soft-pedaled or skipped evolution. Reported Berkman and Plutzer, "In this struggle, few teachers court controversy; quite the contrary, the most common theme emerging from teachers' responses was that they are highly attuned to the sensibilities of their students and seek to adapt their teaching goals to their environment."[190]

In 2020, Plutzer, Glenn Branch, and Ann Reid replicated the 2007 study and found declining avoidance of rigorous evolution. Still, about one-third of teachers taught creationism, gave mixed messages, or avoided the topic, and 45 percent reported spending less than two hours of instruction time on evolution. That was only down from 52 percent in 2007.[191]

Plutzer and co-authors published findings in 2016 from a survey of public middle and high school science teachers about their handling of climate change. Only about 5 percent skipped the topic, but roughly a third taught that climate change "is primarily being caused by human release of greenhouse gases" and that "many scientists believe that recent increases in temperature are likely due to natural causes."[192] "Primarily" appearing in only one statement can reconcile the two, but Plutzer and his co-authors saw offering both as "explicitly contradictory." They also saw the limits of policy: "Especially for political or cultural conservatives, simply offering teachers more traditional science education may not lead to better classroom practice."

Exclusion

The last, and most repugnant, way in which public schooling has avoided conflict has been the outright exclusion of minority groups, or legally mandated segregation within public schooling.

Blacks, as already discussed, were prohibited from receiving any education at various times in the South, and legally forced segregation was only officially struck down with *Brown v. Board of Education* in 1954. It took many years after that to overcome "massive resistance." At best, many states have only complied with the law for around 50 years, and many people still doubt how fully states and districts have embraced desegregation. Indeed, several communities seem to be de facto re-segregating; the group EdBuild reported that 73 communities left their existing districts to form new, typically wealthier and whiter ones between 2000 and 2019.[193]

It would also be wrong to think legal prohibitions against equal access to public schooling have been strictly a Dixie phenomenon. While northern states were more inclined to allow blacks access to all schools, it often vanished. Carter Woodson discussed districts in Pennsylvania, New York, Rhode Island, Connecticut, and Massachusetts where for a time blacks were admitted to white schools, only to eventually have arrangements made for their separate education. Western states such as Ohio, Indiana, and Illinois were sites of long struggles for African American access first to public schooling funds, then to integrated institutions.[194]

It was not just African Americans who were excluded from the public schools for significant stretches of American history. California for a time prohibited people of Chinese or Japanese derivation from becoming citizens and, hence, from using the public schools. In the 1930s, Mexican Americans and Indians were subject to segregated Golden State schooling.[195] And to the large extent that Native Americans were forced onto reservations, they too were kept from attending integrated schools.

CONCLUSION

A mythological image of public schooling might be as America's kitchen, with smiling chefs gathering and combining ingredients in the great melting pot. Sure, they applied some heat that may have roiled the dish a bit, but the process was much more akin to a warm, comforting bath than a scalding, hard boil. The problem is, reality was frequently very different.

Often the system did very little to bring diverse people together. Envision, perhaps, the iconic little red schoolhouse with a line of identical children marching in. Peace was preserved, but largely because no potentially disruptive melting was attempted. Where diverse people were brought together, harmony was often not in the offing. Instead, there was arguing and animosity in the schoolhouse that almost certainly exacerbated divisions, and on rare occasions precipitated violence and even death.

Public schooling *reality* and the gauzy, triumphalist, great-unifier *dream* of public schooling do not meet. History is clear that government cannot both force diverse people into schools together and foster cohesion and harmony. In light of this, it is hard to imagine how anyone could think public schools would foster social harmony. But as the next chapter tackles, several theories have been, and are, offered to back public-schooling-as-unifier.

NOTES

1. Lisa Kocian, "6th-Grade Book Stirs Rethinking," *Boston Globe*, November 12, 2006; Lisa Kocian, "Korean Officials Join Fray on Book," *Boston Globe*, February 15, 2007.

2. Stephen Arons, *Compelling Belief: The Culture of American Schooling* (Amherst, MA: The University of Massachusetts Press, 1983), xi.

3. Clive R. Belfield and Henry M. Levin, *Privatizing Educational Choice: Consequences for Parents, Schools, and Public Policy* (Boulder, CO: Paradigm, 2005), 51.

4. Christopher J. Lucas, *Our Western Educational Heritage* (New York: Macmillan, 1972), 11.

5. Lawrence A. Cremin, *American Education: The Colonial Experience, 1607–1783* (New York: Harper Torchbooks, 1970), 124.

6. Ellwood P. Cubberley, *The History of Education* (New York: Kessinger Publishing, 1920), 474.

7. Wayne J. Urban and Jennings L. Wagoner, Jr., *American Education: A History*. 3rd ed. (Boston: McGraw-Hill, 2004), 27–28.

8. Urban and Wagoner, *American Education: A History*, 42.

9. Jon Teaford, "The Transformation of Massachusetts Education: 1670–1780," in *The Social History of American Education*, eds. B. Edward McClellan and William J. Reese (Urbana: University of Illinois Press, 1988), 23–35.

10. Cubberley, *The History of Education*, 233.

11. Horace Mann, "Report for 1846," in *Life and Works of Horace Mann*, ed. Mary Mann (Boston: Horace B. Fuller, 1868), 527–528.

12. Mann, "Report for 1846," 531.

13. Carl F. Kaestle, *Pillars of the Republic: Common Schools and American Society, 1780–1860* (New York: Hill & Wang, 1983), 183–184.

14. Cubberley, *The History of Education*, 422.

15. Ibid., 423.

16. Albert Fishlow, "Levels of Nineteenth-Century American Investment in Education," *The Journal of Economic History* 26, no. 4 (December 1966), 418.

17. Bernard Bailyn, *Education in the Forming of American Society* (New York: W. W. Norton and Company, 1960), 41–45.

18. Robert F. Seybolt, *Source Studies in American Colonial Education: The Private School* (Urbana, IL: University of Illinois, 1925).

19. Urban and Wagoner, *American Education*, 25–27.

20. Seybolt, *Source Studies in American Colonial Education.*

21. Cubberley, *The History of Education*, 314.

22. Cremin, *American Education: The Colonial Experience, 1607–1783*, 547.

23. Horace Mann, "Report for 1848," 734.

24. Cremin, *American Education: The Colonial Experience, 1607–1783*, 450.

25. Robin Shields, "Publishing the Declaration of Independence," *Journeys and Crossing, Library of Congress*, transcript of video presentation, http://www.loc.gov/rr/program/journey/declaration-transcript.html, July 20, 2010.

26. See, for instance, Noah Webster, "On the Education of Youth in America," in Frederick Rudolph, ed., *Essays on Education in the Early Republic* (Cambridge, MA: The Belknap Press of Harvard University Press, 1965), 66.

27. Urban and Wagoner, *American Education*, 81.

28. U.S. Census Bureau, "1830 Fast Facts," https://www.census.gov/history/www/through_the_decades/fast_facts/1830_fast_facts.html, accessed June 16, 2021.

29. Lawrence A. Cremin, *American Education: The National Experience, 1783–1876*, (New York: Harper Colophon Books, 1980), 268.

30. Urban and Wagoner, *American Education,* 81.

31. Ron Chernow, "George Washington: The Reluctant President," *Smithsonian Magazine,*   http://www.smithsonianmag.com/history/george-washington-the-reluctant-president-49492/?no-ist, February 2011.

32. Cremin, *American Education: The Colonial Experience, 1607–1783*, 256–264.

33. Alexis de Tocqueville, *Democracy in America*, Vol. 1 (New York: Vintage Classics, 1990), 94.

34. Benjamin Franklin, *Proposals Relating to the Education of Youth in Pennsilvania*, Penn University Archives and Records Center, https://archives.upenn.edu/digitized-resources/docs-pubs/franklin-proposals, accessed July 30, 2021.

35. Samuel Knox, "An Essay on the Best System of Liberal Education, Adapted to the Genius of the Government of the United States," in *Essays on Education in the Early Republic*, ed. Frederick Rudolph (Cambridge, MA: The Belknap Press of Harvard University Press, 1965), 302.

36. Noah Webster, "On the Education of Youth in America," in *Essays on Education in the Early Republic*, ed. Frederick Rudolph, 50.

37. Benjamin Rush, "Thoughts upon the Mode of Education Proper in a Republic," in Frederick Rudolph, ed., *Essays on Education in the Early Republic* (Cambridge, MA: The Belknap Press of Harvard University Press, 1965), 12–13.

38. Charles Lesley Glenn, Jr., *The Myth of the Common School* (Amherst, MA: University of Massachusetts Press, 1987), 132.

39. Committee report quoted in Charles Lesley Glenn, Jr., *The Myth of the Common School*, 120–121.

40. Edward Newton in *The Common School Controversy; Consisting of Three Letters of the Secretary of the Board of Education, of the State of Massachusetts, in Reply to Charges Preferred against the Board, by the Editor of the Christian Witness and by Edward A. Newton, Esq., of Pittsfield, One a Member of the Board; to Which Are Added Extracts from the Daily Press, in Regard to the Controversy* (Boston: J. N. Bradley & Co., 1844), 23.

41. Matthew Hale Smith quoted in Charles Lesley Glenn, Jr., *The Myth of the Common School*, 187.

42. Lewis Joseph Sherrill, *Presbyterian Parochial Schools: 1846–1870* (New Haven, CT: Yale University Press, 1932), 22.

43. Mann, "Report for 1848," 729–730.

44. Ibid., 700.

45. Horace Mann, "First Annual Report," in *Lectures, and Annual Reports, on Education*, ed. Mary Mann (Boston: Lee and Shepard, 1872), 417–418.

46. Samuel Harrison Smith, "Remarks on Education," in *Essays on Education in the Early Republic*, ed. Frederick Rudolph (Cambridge, MA: The Belknap Press of Harvard University Press, 1965), 219.

47. Horace Bushnell, *Common Schools: A Discourse on the Modifications Demanded by the Roman Catholics* (Hartford, CT: Press of Case, Tiffany and Company, 1853), 9–10.

48. Newton, in *The Common School Controversy*, 5.

49. Horace Mann in *The Common School Controversy; Consisting of Three Letters of the Secretary of the Board of Education, of the State of Massachusetts, in Reply to Charges Preferred against the Board, by the Editor of the Christian Witness and by Edward A. Newton, Esq., of Pittsfield, One a Member of the Board; to Which Are Added Extracts from the Daily Press, in Regard to the Controversy*, 11.

50. Josiah Strong, *Our Country: Its Possible Future and Its Present Crisis* (New York: The Baker and Taylor Co., 1885), p. 67.

51. "Canons and Decrees of the Council of Trent: The Fourth Session," James Waterworth, trans. http://www.bible-researcher.com/trent1.html, accessed July 30, 2021.

52. Humanities Research Institute, John Foxe's The Acts and Monuments Online, https://www.dhi.ac.uk/foxe/index.php.

53. Cremin, *American Education: The Colonial Experience, 1607–1783*, 43–44.

54. Milton M. Gordon, *Assimilation in American Life: The Role of Race, Religion, and National Origins* (New York: Oxford University Press, 1964), 195.

55. Will Herberg, *Protestant-Catholic-Jew* (Chicago: The University of Chicago Press, 1983), 141.

56. Lloyd P. Jorgenson, *The State and the Non-Public Schools: 1825–1925* (Columbia, MO: University of Missouri Press, 1987), 25.

57. Horace Mann, "Report for 1848," in *Life and Works of Horace Mann*, ed. Mary Mann (Boston: Horace B. Fuller, 1868), 734.

58. Jorgenson, *The State and the Non-Public Schools,* 38.

59. Lyman Beecher, *A Plea for the West* (New York, Leavitt, Lord and Co., 1835), 12.

60. Beecher, *Plea for the West*, 62–63.

61. Ibid., 63–64.

62. Mass Humanities, "Charlestown Convent Lies in Ruin," *Mass Moments*, http://massmoments.org/moment.cfm?mid=234, accessed July 30, 2021.

63. Bushnell, *Common Schools*, 3–4.

64. For discussion of specific offending texts see *Complete Works of the Rev. John Hughes, D.D, Archbishop of New York, Comprising His Sermons, Lectures, Speeches, Etc.,* ed. Lawrence Kehoe, vol. 1 (New York: Lawrence Kehoe, 1866), 51–53, 69–72, 145, and 170.

65. Quoted in Diane Ravitch, *The Great School Wars: A History of the New York City Public Schools* (Baltimore: The Johns Hopkins University Press, 2000), 45.

66. *Complete Works of the Rev. John Hughes*, 143.

67. Ravitch, *Great School Wars*, 20–26.

68. Steven K. Green, *The Bible, the School, and the Constitution: The Clash That Shaped Modern Church-State Doctrine* (New York: Oxford University Press, 2012), 57.

69. Ravitch, *Great School Wars*, 63–66.

70. Ibid., 72–75.

71. Green, *The Bible, the School, and the Constitution*, 80.

72. Vincent P. Lannie and Bernard C. Diethorn, "For the Honor and the Glory of God: The Philadelphia Bible Riots of 1840," *History of Education Quarterly* 8, no. 1 (Spring 1968). Note that the date in the title was corrected to "1844" in the subsequent issue 8, no. 2 (Summer 1968).

73. Francis Kenrick, believed to be writing as "Sentinel," quoted in Lannie and Diethorn, "For the Honor and Glory of God," 51.

74. Lannie and Diethorn, "For the Honor and Glory of God," 49.

75. Ibid., 70.

76. Ibid., 75.

77. Catholic school enrollment figure from John J. Convey, *Catholic Schools Make a Difference: Twenty-Five Years of Research* (Washington, DC: National Catholic Education Association, 1992). Catholic school enrollment as a percentage of total elementary and secondary enrollment calculated using U.S. Bureau of the Census, Statistical Abstract of the United States: 1994, Table no. 240, 162.

78. Jorgenson, *The State and the Non-public Schools*, 90–93.

79. David Tyack, *Seeking Common Ground: Public Schools in Diverse Society* (Cambridge: Harvard University Press, 2003), 168.

80. Green, 36–40.

81. Ibid., 98–104.

82. Ibid., 119–121.

83. Jorgenson, 170–175.

84. *Pierce v. Society of Sisters*, 268 U.S. 510 (1925).

85. Green, *The Bible, the School, and the Constitution*, 44.

86. Ibid., 187.

87. Ballotpedia, "Blaine Amendment (U.S. Constitution)," https://ballotpedia.org/Blaine_Amendment_(U.S._Constitution)#cite_note-quotedisclaimer-3.

88. Green, *The Bible, the School, and the Constitution*, 117–135.

89. History Channel, "1925: Monkey Trial Begins," *This Day in History, July 10*, http://www.history.com/this-day-in-history/monkey-trial-begins.

90. "Days Six and Seven: Transcript of Scopes Trial, Friday July 17 and Monday July 20, 1925," The Clarence Darrow Digital Collection, University of Minnesota Law Library, http://darrow.law.umn.edu/documents/Scopes%206th%20&%207th%20days.pdf.

91. Ibid., 299.

92. *Minersville School District v. Gobitis*, 310 U.S. 586 (1940).

93. George U. Wenner, *Religious Education and the Public School: An American Problem* (New York: Bonnell, Silver and Co., 1907), 40. What "her" refers to is a bit unclear in the text, but it appears to be churches or the Church rather than America.

94. United Evangelical Action, quoted in Jonathan Zimmerman, *Whose America: Culture Wars in the Public Schools* (Cambridge: Harvard University Press, 2002), 147.

95. *McCollum v. Board of Education*, 333 U.S. 203 (1948).

96. *Zorach v. Clausen*, 343 U.S. 306 (1952).

97. Jorgenson, *The State and the Non-public Schools*, 198.

98. Released Time Education, "History of RTCE," https://www.rtce.org/history.html, accessed July 30, 2021; and James A. Swezey and Katherine G.

Schultz, "Released-Time Programs in Religion Education," Faculty Publications and Presentations, Paper #226, May 2013, http://digitalcommons.liberty.edu/educ_fac_pubs/226

99. *Abington School Dist. v. Schempp*, 374 U.S. 203 (1963).

100. *Engel v. Vitale*, 370 U.S. 421 (1962).

101. Zimmerman, *Whose America?*, 160–185.

102. Jorgenson, *The State and the Non-public Schools*, 199–203.

103. Terrel H. Bell, *The Thirteenth Man: A Reagan Cabinet Memoir* (New York: The Free Press, 1988), 130.

104. Cato Institute, Public Schooling Battle Map, http://www.cato.org/education-fight-map?Submit=Reset, accessed May 19, 2021.

105. David Skinner, "A Battle over Books," *Humanities*, September/October 2010, https://www.neh.gov/humanities/2010/septemberoctober/statement/battle-over-books; West Virginia Humanities Council, "The Kanawha County Textbook Controversy," The West Virginia Encyclopedia, https://www.wvencyclopedia.org/print/ExhibitHall/13, accessed November 27, 2017; James T. Wooten, "Bomb Indictments Latest Battle in Textbook War," *New York Times*, January 27, 1975.

106. National Education Association, "Kanawha County West Virginia: A Textbook Study in Cultural Conflict," February 1975, 9, https://files.eric.ed.gov/fulltext/ED106165.pdf.

107. Todd A. DeMitchell, Suzanne Eckes, and Richard Fossey, "Sexual Orientation and the Public School Teacher," *Public Interest Law Journal* 19 (2009), 65–105.

108. Cubberley, *The History of Education*, 508.

109. Ellwood P. Cubberley, *Changing Conceptions of Education* (Boston: Houghton Mifflin Company, 1909), 15–16.

110. It should be noted that in some places Asian and Mexican immigrants were segregated. See Tyack, *Seeking Common Ground*, 83–85, and Asia Society, "Asian Americans Then and Now," https://asiasociety.org/education/asian-americans-then-and-now, accessed July 30, 2021.

111. Numbers available in Douglas Brinkley, *History of the United States* (New York: Viking, 1998), 272–273.

112. John W. Meyer, et al., "Public Education as Nation-building in America: Enrollments and Bureaucratization in the American States, 1870–1830," *American Journal of Sociology*, 85, no. 3 (November 1979), 596.

113. Tyack, *Seeking Common Ground*, 103–104.

114. Ibid., 22.

115. Ibid., 87.

116. Ibid., 56.

117. Ravitch, *Great School Wars*, 176.

118. Bennett Law printed in Christian Koerner, *The Bennett Law and the German Protestant Parochial Schools of Wisconsin* (Milwaukee, WI: Germania Publishing Company, 1890), 3–4.

119. Declaration and Resolutions printed in Koerner.

120. Platform printed in Koerner, *The Bennett Law*.

121. Ibid., 10.

122. Tyack, *The One Best System*, 239.

123. Louis Adamec, *From Many Lands* (New York: Harper and Brothers, 1940), 93.

124. Zimmerman, *Whose America?*, 13–31.

125. Paul J. Ramsey, "The War against German-American Culture: The Removal of German-Language Instruction from the Indianapolis School, 1917–1919," *Indiana Magazine of History*, 90, no. 4 (December 2002): 297–302.

126. Lynne Cheney, "The End of History," *Wall Street Journal*, October 20, 1994.

127. Gary B. Nash and Ross E. Dunn, "History Standards and Culture Wars," *Social Education*, 59, no. 1 (1995): 5–7.

128. George B. Sanchez, "TUSD Ethnic Studies Targeted," *Arizona Daily Star*, June 12, 2008; "Raza Studies Director Defends Controversial Program," *Arizona Republic*, August 18, 2008.

129. Howard Fischer, "Measure Backs 'American Values' in State Schools," *East Valley-Scottsdale Tribune*, April 16, 2008.

130. Arizona State Legislature, A.R.S. §15–112, "Prohibited Courses and Classes," https://www.azleg.gov/ars/15/00112.htm.

131. Charla Bear, "American Indian Boarding Schools Haunt Many," National Public Radio, May 12, 2008, https://www.npr.org/templates/story/story.php?storyId=16516865.

132. Barbara Landis, "Carlisle Indian Industrial School History," http://home.epix.net/~landis/histry.html.

133. Carolyn J. Marr, "Assimilation through Education: Indian Boarding Schools in the Pacific Northwest," University of Washington, https://content.lib.washington.edu/aipnw/marr.html.

134. American Library Association, "Top Ten Frequently Challenged Books Lists of the 21st Century," Banned and Challenged Books, http://www.ala.org/bbooks/frequentlychallengedbooks/top10.

135. Carter G. Woodson, *The Education of the Negro* (Brooklyn, NY: A & B Publishing Group, 1999), 93–108.

136. Public Broadcasting System, "The Slave Experience: Education, Arts, and Culture," *Slavery and the Making of America*, http://www.pbs.org/wnet/slavery/experience/education/docs1.html.

137. University of Dayton, "Slave Codes of the State of Georgia," http://academic.udayton.edu/race/02rights/slavelaw.htm.

138. Urban and Wagoner, *American Education: A History*, 112.

139. Leonard W. Levy and Douglas L. Jones, eds., *Jim Crow in Boston: The Origin of the Separate but Equal Doctrine* (New York: De Capo Press, 1974).

140. Carter G. Woodson, *The Miseducation of the Negro* (Middletown, DE: Seven Treasures Publications, 2010), 20.

141. Ibid., 81–82.

142. W. E. B. Du Bois, *The Souls of Black Folk* (New York: Dover Publications, 1994), 109.

143. Richard Wormser, "W. E. B. Du Bois," *The Rise and Fall of Jim Crow*, http://www.pbs.org/wnet/jimcrow/stories_people_dubois.html, accessed September 16, 2019.

144. W. E. Burghardt Du Bois, "Does the Negro Need Separate Schools?" *The Journal of Negro Education* 4, no. 3 (July 1935): 328–335.

145. Alex Haley, *The Autobiography of Malcolm X* (New York, NY: Ballantine Books, 2015), 250–251.

146. National Advisory Commission on Civil Disorders, *Report of the National Advisory Commission on Civil Disorders* (New York: Bantam Books, 1968), 144.

147. James T. Patterson, *Brown v. Board of Education: A Civil Rights Milestone and Its Troubled Legacy* (New York: Oxford University Press, 2001), 168–169.

148. Vanessa Siddle Walker, *The Lost Education of Horace Tate: Uncovering the Hidden Heroes Who Fought for Justice in Schools* (New York: The New Press, 2018), 337.

149. Thomas W. Collins and George W. Noblit, "Stratification and Resegregation: The Case of Crossover High School, Memphis, Tennessee," National Institute of Education, 1976, 52.

150. Collins and Noblit, "Stratification and Resegregation," 55.

151. Ravitch, *Great School Wars*, 369.

152. Quoted in Matthew F. Delmont, *Why Busing Failed: Race, Media, and the National Resistance to School Desegregation* (Oakland: University of California Press, 2016), 1.

153. Collins and Noblit, "Stratification and Resegregation," 154.

154. Sam Dillon, "Law to Segregate Omaha Schools Divides Nebraska," *New York Times*, April 15, 2006.

155. See Justice Anthony Kennedy's controlling concurring opinion in *Parents Involved in Community Schools v. Seattle School District No. 1*, 551 U.S. 701 (2007).

156. Sarah Garland, *Divided We Fail: The Story of an African American Community That Ended the Era of School Desegregation* (Boston: Beacon Press, 2013), 194.

157. CNN, "Oakland school board amends Ebonics policy," CNN Interactive, January 16, 1997, http://www.cnn.com/US/9701/16/black.english/.

158. Noreen S. Ahmed-Ullah, "CPS Unveils Curriculum for African-American Studies," *Chicago Tribune*, December 12, 2013.

159. Chuck Ross, "See What They'll Be Teaching in the Chicago Public Schools," *Daily Caller*, April 21, 2014.

160. On its website the *New York Times* originally described 1619 as the United States' "true founding," but that was eventually removed, though when is not clear. Jordan Davidson, "The *New York Times* Deceptively Edits False Claim at the Center of 1619 Project," *Federalist*, https://thefederalist.com/2020/09/21/nyt-deceptively-edits-false-claim-at-the-center-of-1619-project/, September 21, 2020. As of September 21, 2020, however, the Pulitzer Center's page for the 1619 curriculum still said the Project challenged Americans to see 1619 "as our nation's foundational date." Pulitzer Center, The 1619 Project Curriculum, https://pulitzercenter.org/lesson-plan-grouping/1619-project-curriculum.

161. For a summary of the major disputes see Adam Serwer, "The Fight over the 1619 Project Is Not about the Facts," *Atlantic*, December 23, 2019, https://www.theatlantic.com/ideas/archive/2019/12/historians-clash-1619-project/604093/.

162. White House, "Remarks by President Trump at the White House Conference on American History," Press Release, September 17, 2020, https://www.whitehouse.gov/briefings-statements/remarks-president-trump-white-house-conference-american-history/.

163. Tristan Justice, "House Republicans Introduce Legislation to Bar Federal Funding of Schools Teaching Fake History," *Federalist*, September 17, 2020, https://thefederalist.com/2020/09/17/house-republicans-introduce-legislation-to-bar-federal-funding-of-schools-teaching-fake-history/.

164. Federal Register, Proposed Priorities: American History and Civics Education, April 19, 2021, https://www.federalregister.gov/documents/2021/04/19/2021-08068/proposed-priorities-american-history-and-civics-education.

165. See, for instance, Stanley Kurtz, "Biden Set to Push Critical Race Theory on U.S. Schools," *National Review Online*, April 19, 2021, https://www.nationalreview.com/corner/biden-set-to-push-critical-race-theory-on-u-s-schools/.

166. Many states used the same list of "divisive concepts" as was in Iowa's legislation, "An Act providing for requirements related to racism or sexism trainings at, and diversity and inclusion efforts by, governmental agencies and entities, school districts, and public postsecondary educational institutions," March 16, 2021, https://www.legis.iowa.gov/docs/publications/LGR/89/HF802.pdf.

167. Ravitch, *Great School Wars*, 402.

168. District data from U.S. Department of Education, *120 Years of American Education: A Statistical Portrait*, Table 20, January 1993, https://nces.ed.gov/pubs93/93442.pdf. Population data from U.S. Census Bureau, "Historical National Population Estimates: July 1, 1900 to July 1, 1999," https://www2.census.gov/programs-surveys/popest/tables/1900-1980/national/totals/popclockest.txt.

169. Digest of Education Statistics, "Number of public school districts and public and private elementary and secondary schools: Selected years, 1869–70 through 2018–19," https://nces.ed.gov/programs/digest/d20/tables/dt20_214.10.asp; Population data for July 1, 2018, from U.S. Census Bureau, "U.S. and World Population Clock," https://www.census.gov/popclock/.

170. District number from Benjamin Justice, *The War that Wasn't: Religious Conflict and Compromise in the Common Schools of New York State, 1865–1900* (Albany, NY: State University of New York Press, 2005), 47. Population from U.S. Census Bureau, Population of States and Counties of the United States: 1790–1990 (Washington, DC: Government Printing Office, 1996), 3.

171. Digest of Education Statistics, "Rates of high school completion and bachelor's degree attainment among persons age 25 and over, by race/ethnicity and sex: Selected years, 1910 through 2019," https://nces.ed.gov/programs/digest/d19/tables/dt19_104.10.asp.

172. Gordon, *Assimilation in American Life*, 242.

173. Justice, *The War That Wasn't*, 67–140.

174. Ibid., 173.

175. *Board of Education of Kiryas Joel Village School District v. Grumet*, 512 U.S. 687 (1994).

176. Robert H. Wiebe, *The Segmented Society: An Introduction to the Meaning of America* (New York, NY: Oxford University Press, 1979), 29.

177. Justice, *The War That Wasn't*, 77.

178. Zimmerman, *Whose America?*, 4.

179. *New State Ice Co. v. Liebmann*, 285 U.S. 262 (1932).

180. Jorgenson, *The State and the Non-public Schools*, 112–121.

181. Ibid., 121.

182. Justice, *The War That Wasn't*, 197–199.

183. Ibid., 151. For some examples of earlier local accommodations of diverse groups, see Kaestle, 164–166.

184. Tyack, *Seeking Common Ground*, 79.

185. Claudia Goldin and Lawrence F. Katz, "Human Capital and Social Capital: The Rise of Secondary Schooling in America, 1910 to 1940," NBER Working Paper No. 6439, March 1998.

186. McQuaid quoted in Justice, *The War That Wasn't*, 174. McQuaid quoted in Justice, 174.

187. Diane Ravitch, *The Language Police: How Pressure Groups Restrict What Students Learn* (New York: Alfred A. Knopf, 2003).

188. Ibid., 62–96.

189. Ibid., 10–11.

190. Michael Berkman and Eric Plutzer, *Evolution, Creationism, and the Battle to Control America's Classrooms* (New York: Cambridge University Press, 2010), 220.

191. Eric Plutzer, Glenn Branch, and Ann Reid, "Teaching Evolution in U.S. Public Schools: A Continuing Challenge," *Evolution: Education and Outreach* 13, no. 14 (2020).

192. Eric Plutzer, et al., "Climate Confusion among U.S. Teachers," *Science* 351, no. 6274 (February 12, 2016).

193. EdBuild, "Fractured: The Accelerating Breakdown of America's School Districts, 2019 Update," https://edbuild.org/content/fractured.

194. Woodson, *The Education of the Negro*, 189–206.

195. Tyack, *Seeking Common Ground*, 82–85.

Chapter 3

Why Think Public Schools Would Unify?

Wake County, North Carolina, has been touted as an exemplar of first racial, then income-based, school integration. To avoid compelled busing in the early 1980s, the district, created in the 1970s by a state-forced merger of Raleigh City and suburban Wake County, designed a system of magnet schools and race-balancing assignments aimed at having no school with minority enrollment below 15 or above 45 percent. In the 1990s, a federal court invalidated race-based assignment and the district moved to an academic- and income-based system. No school would have more than 40 percent low-income students or 25 percent reading below grade level.

By the 2000s, many Wake families had tired of the confusing, unpredictable assignment system that often sent their children far from the schools nearest their homes. In 2010, they elected a Republican-majority school board that championed neighborhood assignments. Opponents suspected an effort to return to apartheid-like conditions, and personal identity became a blistering flash point, with the board majority accused of being carpet-bagging Northerners or flat-out racists. Raleigh mayor Charles Meeker said the majority were "people who are not from the area, who do not share our values."

The district's turmoil garnered national attention, and one protest, of which there were many, resulted in the arrest of 19 people for trespassing and disorderly conduct. After so much upheaval the Republicans lost their majority in 2011. But that did not mean a return to the old income-based assignment system. The new Democratic majority moved to a system in which income, and to a large extent race, were much less important than they had been.

Several years later, school assignment continued to be a heated topic, and many who sought to return to the old system were disappointed. "As Civil Rights advocates WE were seeking to maintain our diverse school system," wrote Calla Wright, president of the Coalition of Concerned Citizens for

*African American Children, to school board members in August 2016. "As
elected officials, it is embarrassing to know that we have made very little
change in the student assignment plan."*[1]

Human beings, with our limited minds, tend to want to see life and society
as organizable, as things that a wise person, or some group of wise people,
can engineer to run smoothly and effectively. And it is certainly tempting to
give in to that. After all, who wants to feel subject to seemingly irrational,
powerful forces beyond their control?

Efforts to control society through education, as public schooling supporters
from Benjamin Rush to Amy Gutmann have explicitly advocated, are drives
to engineer messy, entropic human life. But what the evidence powerfully
indicates is that efforts to control the interactions and relationships of millions
of people, under ever-changing circumstances, do not work, and certainly
not without oppressive government force. At best, the desired results may be
achieved in *spite* of the engineering attempts. At worst, the engineering fires
off myriad unintended consequences including social conflict, inequality, and
sometimes *true* chaos.

THE BROKEN THEORY

Most early public schooling supporters did not argue in formal, theoretical
terms, but tended to assert as almost self-evident that, as Rush put it, "our
schools of learning, by producing one general and uniform system of education, will render the mass of the people more homogeneous."[2] They assumed
that a uniform system would create uniform thoughts and feelings. Indeed, as
social psychologist John B. McConahay has observed, "Americans . . . have
a great deal of faith in the beneficial effects of just getting people of different racial and ethnic groups together. Drake and Cayton have called this an
'almost mystical faith.'"[3]

Despite largely faith-based support for the unifying effect of public schooling, there have been thinkers who have endeavored to explain, in rigorous
philosophical and theoretical treatments, why public schooling is necessary.

Social Reproduction and Social Control

Probably the best known theoretical construct for what unity-driven public
schooling advocates have sought is "social capital," though most did not use
the relatively new term. Sociologist Robert Putnam is perhaps most responsible for popularizing the concept, especially through his bestselling *Bowling*

Alone, which catalogued decades of declines in shared experiences, from participation in Kiwanis clubs, to unions, to, well, bowling leagues.[4] Chapter six examines this more deeply, but an assumed effect of public schooling has been that it will build bridges among diverse people by inculcating common norms, language, and culture.

A philosophical understanding of what education systems accomplish, at least from a social perspective, is perhaps best laid out by sociologists Pierre Bourdieu and Jean-Claude Passeron, who argue that the root purpose of education systems is perpetuating the existing social order, or "social reproduction." Elementary and secondary education passes on and evaluates cultural markers such as appreciation for different types of music, or ways of speaking, and in so doing helps to mete out higher education, employment, and status.[5] John Dewey also saw education serving social reproduction, though he called it "renewal" or "continuity."[6]

Bourdieu and Passeron did not advocate such a function, seeing it as oppressive, but they nonetheless observed it. They noted that in France—admired by Mann and other American public schooling advocates for its uniform education system—the rigorous examination system, which uses both written and oral assessments, opens the doors to elite, national postsecondary institutions. Indeed, so uniform—one might say "common"—is the French system that a French education minister supposedly looked at his watch at 3 o'clock in the afternoon and declared, "At this moment pupils in year five in every French school will be studying Racine."[7]

Political scientist Amy Gutmann does not share Bourdieu and Passeron's qualms about social reproduction. In *Democratic Education*, she argues not just for a reproductive role, but for education to be *intentionally* and *explicitly* controlled by government to uniformly shape society's newest generation. She dubs her process "conscious social reproduction."[8]

Education must be primarily controlled by government, Gutmann argues, to overcome the biases children would have inculcated in them were education controlled by families. Such top-down control is legitimate, in Gutmann's eyes, as long as a "democratic" process determines what the schools teach, and the education system does not exclude anyone. In other words, a top-down, majority-rules, collective decision-making process is essential to maintaining and perpetuating the social order, though that order is supposed to be grounded in such non-collective values as religious toleration, intellectual pluralism, and individual rights.[9]

Gutmann's intention is not to have public schooling oppress, but at least in its general contours to protect freedom. This passage, in which Gutmann takes on the Lockean view that individuals and families must be allowed self-government, encapsulates much of her rationale for vesting education authority in government:

> A state makes choice possible by teaching its future citizens respect for opposing points of view and ways of life. It makes choice meaningful by equipping children with the intellectual skills necessary to evaluate ways of life different from that of their parents. History suggests that without state provision or regulation of education, children will be taught neither mutual respect among persons nor rational deliberations among ways of life.[10]

The claim that educational freedom will result in intolerance and, presumably, conflict is supremely serious, and human beings have certainly warred with one another throughout history. Gutmann is also far from alone in asserting that government education control is necessary to temper biases and sometimes violent inclinations. Emile Durkheim asserted that "the child reared exclusively in his family becomes its creature: he reproduces all its peculiarities, all its characteristics, even to the point of the tics of the family physiognomy."[11] More recently, dissenting in a ruling supporting private school choice, Justice John Paul Stevens wrote:

> I have been influenced by my understanding of the impact of religious strife on the decisions of our forbears [sic] to migrate to this continent, and on the decisions of neighbors in the Balkans, Northern Ireland, and the Middle East to mistrust one another. Whenever we remove a brick from the wall that was designed to separate religion and government, we increase the risk of religious strife and weaken the foundation of our democracy.[12]

The gaping hole in these assertions has been the failure to rigorously demonstrate—or to really even try—that government control has succeeded in curbing prejudice and fostering peaceful coexistence, and that it has done so more successfully than educational freedom would have. Gutmann cites no specific evidence to support her crucial accusation that, essentially, we need government-controlled education lest families teach intolerance. She simply proclaims it.

Of course, the previous chapter showed that government schooling in the United States is scarred by repeated intolerance for people outside the norm, and warfare over who gets what. Such ugliness is not restricted to the United States. Much of the conflict in the Balkans has been driven by desires to escape forced "unity," not to kill each other over ancient prejudices. Decades of dictators failed to eliminate deep, personal identities, with Yugoslavia splitting into ethnic pieces with the fall of communism. The violence largely stemmed from efforts to keep peoples who wanted autonomy—Croats, Bosnians, Kosovars—in the national fold.

Looking specifically at education, in the nineteenth century the Netherlands attempted to maintain a common school system but found it impossible. Catholics, Protestants of various sects, and secularists fought bitterly—a contest called the *Schoolstrijd*, or "school struggle"[13]—for control. Indeed, the drive for an independent Belgium, achieved in 1830, was in part fueled by Catholic anger over the Protestant-skewed Dutch school system.[14]

The Dutch government at one point attempted to bring peace by eliminating content that offended Catholics, but in so doing stoked the ire of orthodox Protestants while failing to give Catholics what they wanted: more Catholic content, not less religion overall. Yes, it was the same explosive recipe that ignited the Philadelphia Bible Riots, except with secularists also a major faction. The secularists were dominated by members of the upper class, so there was an element of class warfare as well.

Through most of the nineteenth century Dutch Catholics and orthodox Protestants fought for schooling equality to little avail, but an 1878 law that increased the staffing and physical requirements for all elementary schools, while providing a national subsidy only to public institutions, put public sentiment over the edge. It united many Protestants and Catholics, who in 1889 combined their political might to pass a law enabling all schools, public and confessional, to receive equal subsidies.

To this day, Dutch families may receive public funding at the school of their choice. As historian Charles Glenn put it, "In the Netherlands the effort to implement the common school in the interest of creating national unity . . . was for decades the primary cause of national disunity. By contrast, the 'Pacification' . . . freed political and social energies to address the challenges of the postwar world."[15]

Revolutionary France had an even more intense education effort to forge national unity. In an effort to destroy the influence of the Catholic Church and create loyalty to the state, attendance at private schools was outlawed for a time, and when allowed had to be religion-free. As revolutionary leader Georges Danton stated, "Children belong to the Republic more than they do to their parents. . . . It is in national schools that children must suck republican milk. The Republic is one and indivisible; public instruction must be related to this center of unity."[16]

This, too, failed. Countless French people continued to go to their churches and priests for education even when doing so was illegal, and revolutionary governments eventually had to incorporate independent Catholic schools into the French system. Today, as in the Netherlands, French private schools receive public support, though almost all non-public education is Catholic.[17]

Some countries have, of course, maintained largely uniform education systems, but those nations have often been either religiously and ethnically homogeneous, or autocratic. The latter was the case with Prussia, which built a government schooling system greatly admired by Horace Mann and others. Mann was not insensitive to the oppressive nature of the Prussian government, but thought that public schools could be used as much for good as ill. He argued, "If Prussia can pervert the benign influences of education to the support of arbitrary power, we surely can employ them for the support and perpetuation of republican institutions."[18]

It did not, apparently, occur to Mann that government education control might be more compatible with government control of everything than with freedom. And even in Prussia, as Mann noted, the state had to accommodate religious differences, allowing people to choose Protestant or Catholic schools. Mann wrote that, while he was unaware of much popular complaint about compulsory attendance, there was noteworthy unhappiness when children were "compelled to receive instruction in a religious creed from which their parents dissent."[19]

One of Prussia's progeny was Nazi-era Germany, and the education system it employed to indoctrinate youth and instill hatred of Jews, Gypsies, the French, and anyone else deemed enemies of the Fatherland. Today, in intentionally stark contrast, Germany has a highly decentralized education system, with the country's 16 states having almost complete autonomy over their schooling systems. Meanwhile, countries such as Japan and China—which have also at times used their public schooling systems to instill aggressive nationalism—have ethnically and religiously uniform populations, certainly compared to the United States.

In China in particular, ethnic or cultural independence is often brutally repressed. And while the United States has, for much of its history, been a magnet for immigrants, East Asian nations have often been committed to keeping foreigners out. This is reflected in modern demographics.

In 2020, the United States was home to several racial groups that constituted at least 1 percent of the population, 6 religious groupings of that size, and had a net immigration rate of 3 migrants per 1,000 population. Japan, in contrast, had a 98.1 percent Japanese population, only 4 major religious groups, and zero net immigration. South Korea was totally homogeneous ethnically, had only 4 major religious groupings, and had a net immigration rate of 2.3 migrants per 1,000 population. China was dominated by one ethnic group—91.6 percent are Han Chinese—and had only 5 major religious groups. It had a *negative* net migration rate.[20]

Contact without Control

Perhaps the most famous American education theorist is John Dewey, whose ideas remain highly influential among educators. Dewey offered a decidedly gentler approach to using public schooling to engineer unity than did paternalistic predecessors such as Benjamin Rush and Horace Mann, or contemporary Ellwood Cubberley, all of whom presented public schooling as a machine into which mismatched children would be fed and hammered, contorted, and pressed into "American" form.

The latter sort of thinking manifested itself in public schooling dominated by what historian David Tyack has dubbed "administrative progressives." It was rule by experts, who created highly regimented systems and, using "scientific" assessments such as IQ tests, sorted children. As William T. Harris, a leading administrative progressive, explained, "The first requisite of the school is *Order*: each pupil must be taught first and foremost to conform his behavior to a general standard."[21]

Regimentation was not only intended to make instruction easier to deliver. No, the industrial life the experts decided most students were destined for required "conformity to the time of the train, to the starting of work in the manufactory." Harris wanted, essentially, an assembly line: "The pupil must have his lessons ready at the appointed time, must rise at the tap of the bell, move to the line, return; in short, go through the evolutions with equal precision."

Dewey believed this factory model was pedagogically mistaken and dehumanizing. He also believed it an ineffective way to build bridges among diverse racial, religious, and ethnic groups. Forced feeding did not make sense if the goal was to make children truly imbibe—truly *feel*—kinship with their fellow human beings, not to mention understand the way their world worked. What Dewey envisioned was not dictate-and-discipline schooling, but education by student-directed, cooperative activity. As he wrote at the end of *Democracy and Education*:

> [T]he school must itself be a community life in all which that implies. Social perceptions and interests can be developed only in a genuinely social medium—one where there is give and take in the building of a common experience. Informational statements about things can be acquired in relative isolation by any one who previously has had enough intercourse with others to have learned language. But realization of the *meaning* of the linguistic signs is quite another matter. That involves a context of work and play in association with others. The plea which has been made for education through continued constructive activities in this book rests upon the fact they afford an opportunity for a social atmosphere. In place of a school set apart from life as a place for learning lessons, we have a miniature social group in which study and growth are incidents of present shared experience. Playgrounds, shops, workrooms, laboratories not only direct the natural active tendencies of youth, but they involve intercourse, communication, and cooperation;—all extending the perception of connections.[22]

Dewey was grasping what later theorists would perceive as necessary to build social cohesion: personal interactions among members of different groups in pursuit of mutual self-interest. In Dewey's case, children of differing backgrounds would work together on projects of interest to them, guided—not dominated—by authority figures. Helping each other to reach the conclusion they all desired would overcome divisions such as race, religion, and class.

The first problem for Dewey, and anyone who would create social cohesion through schools, was the huge difficulty of bringing diverse people into close enough proximity to create contact. Recall for much of American history schools were the domain of more than 100,000 districts, which tended to serve homogeneous communities. Beyond education, it appears to be *very* natural for people to congregate with people like themselves, often in *very* specific ways. As commentator David Brooks chronicled about this proclivity sociologists call *homophily*:

> Looking through the market research, one can sometimes be amazed by how efficiently people cluster—and by how predictable we all are. If you wanted to sell imported wine, obviously you would have to find places where rich people live. But did you know that the sixteen counties with the greatest proportion of imported-wine drinkers are all in the same three metropolitan areas (New York, San Francisco, and Washington, D.C.)? If you tried to open a motor-home dealership in Montgomery County, Pennsylvania, you'd probably go broke, because people in this ring of the Philadelphia suburbs think RVs are kind of uncool. But if you traveled just a short way north, to Monroe County, Pennsylvania, you would find yourself in the fifth motor-home-friendliest county in America.[23]

Of course, this extraordinary micro-level sorting is dwarfed by the macro level already discussed, including by religion, ethnicity, and race. But both illustrate that sorting toward homogeneity is a natural inclination.

This inclination has meant that students have often not been sharing chalk and Lincoln Logs with diverse classmates, and communities have been able to avoid contentious topics and volatile group interactions even if state authorities have ordered they do otherwise. It is also why Dewey's famous Laboratory School never achieved his dream, dealing primarily with the well-to-do children of University of Chicago professors and other white, affluent families.[24] Even if diverse schools can shrink social distance, the problem that must first be solved has proven a most Gordian of knots: How do you get diverse children together in the first place?

PHYSICAL FORCE

The presumption of many well-intentioned people for how to bring diverse groups together has simply been to force it. But if public schooling is democratically controlled, and the majority of people do not want mixing, the system will not likely produce the force necessary. Those who have thought that a divided populace would democratically form—or allow to be formed—a religiously, ethnically, racially, or philosophically integrated system have placed hope above reason.

Of course, some thinkers, like Ellwood Cubberley, did not trust the people to control public schooling. They ultimately believed that common schooling had to be *imposed* on the very people who were supposed to democratically rule the schools. Top-down imposition is what tended to occur in urban districts during the decades surrounding the turn of the twentieth century, with massive consolidation to eliminate small, ethnically distinctive districts, and transition from democratic control to largely "scientific," bureaucratic governance. But forcing physical integration was an especially difficult thing to do in still large and widely dispersed rural and even suburban communities.

The greatest test of the ability to engineer racial *integration* in schools was the Herculean effort to end government-engineered *separation* in southern—and eventually northern and western—states. It was launched by the unanimous 1954 U.S. Supreme Court *Brown v. Board of Education* decision striking down legally forced segregated schooling. Famously, the ruling stated that "separate education facilities are inherently unequal."[25]

The government drive to end segregation did not start off Herculean. The court did not rule on remedies for segregation until 1955, in what came to be known as "Brown II," which called for desegregation with "all deliberate speed." Deliberate sloth is often what occurred, including "massive resistance" in Virginia that included laws calling for the closure of any school that sought to integrate, and awarding vouchers for families seeking to avoid integration. Arkansas governor Orval Faubus infamously employed National Guard troops to bar black students from Little Rock High School. Many states and towns saw other intentional delays.

There was also, however, a natural sorting problem, illustrated on a micro level by David Brooks's discussion of RVs and wine. On the macro level, by immigrant settlements. People tend to want to live with others like themselves, so white people tend to live with other white people, and black people with other black people. And since schools often serve specific geographical areas, separation is often the result not of law, but human nature.

To overcome this, federal courts eventually ordered what seemed like the only possible solution: physically move children out of their same-group neighborhoods and into schools serving other-group communities. Over time this was reduced to one word—*busing*—that became like fingernails on a chalkboard to many who hear it. But even people who, at least in the abstract, favor integrated schools often oppose moving children out of their local school.

A 2011 summary of surveys found that support for black and white students attending school together had grown remarkably since the 1950s, rising from 49 percent support to 95 percent between 1956 and 2007. At the same time, a very large majority of Americans did not want such integration to come at the expense of attending one's nearest school.[26] Depending on the poll, 60 to 85 percent of respondents typically agreed with something along the lines of "it is better to attend the school in one's community, even if it means students will be of the same race, than to have them bused elsewhere."

The annual Phi Delta Kappa International survey asked similar questions in 2017, and found the same local-beats-diverse dynamic. A majority said racial and ethnic mixing in schools was either "extremely" or "very" important, but when asked how they would feel if their child had to travel farther to go to a more diverse school, only 25 percent said it would be worth it.[27] A 2017 survey of Americans ages 18–34 found that 64 percent of this relatively young, and presumably more idealistic, group agreed that "students should go to local community schools even if it means most students are of the same race."[28]

A July 2019 Gallup survey perhaps offered a little bit of encouragement for busing, finding 43 percent of respondents favoring a requirement that "school districts . . . bus a certain percentage of students to a neighboring school district to make schools more racially diverse."[29] However, 55 percent—a solid majority—were opposed. And the survey did not refer to the respondents' children or communities, or offer the better-to-stay-near-home option.

In addition to nearest-school bias, research suggests that Americans do not want integration at the expense of educational quality, with parents selecting schools they think will produce the best academic outcomes.[30] There also appears to be a white aversion to schools with increasing African American enrollments even after controlling for school quality indicators such as relative standing on standardized tests, and the degree of security one passes through to enter the building.[31] And social desirability bias—people telling pollsters what sounds morally "right"—means these results may overstate how much people desire diverse schools.

Opposition to coerced integration may remain because of painful national memories of busing. Many violent episodes accompanied busing plans, both in schools among students, and outside among adults. For example, 46 buses and other vehicles were blown up in Denver, Colorado, in February 1970, in response to a busing order upheld by the U.S. Supreme Court in *Keyes v.*

Denver School District No. 1, the primary case opening non-Southern states to desegregation orders.[32] Buses were sabotaged in Pontiac, Michigan, where six members of the Ku Klux Klan bombed 10 in August 1971. There was also desegregation-related violence in Lubbock, Texas; Jonesboro, Georgia; and Jacksonville, Florida; and a bus bombing by black youths in Ayden, North Carolina.[33]

Perhaps nothing seared the ugly side of forced integration into the American consciousness more than Boston's busing battle. The famous 1976 photograph of a white teenager appearing to lunge with an Old Glory–bearing flagpole at a black man in a three-piece suit—attorney Ted Landsmark—in front of iconic Faneuil Hall froze savage conflict in the American mind.[34] But Boston was also the site of marches and boycotts, and class and racial conflict, for years as it and the state sought to deal with segregation both before Judge Arthur Garrity's June 1974 busing order and after.

It was not a conflict strictly or even primarily about getting on a bus, but about ethnic, racial, and class-based communities—especially African American and Irish—and parents trying to do what they thought best for their children. Given the intimate ethnic bonds in conflict, it would be little wonder if Mayor Kevin White actually said what he has been purported to have uttered as he peered over Quincy Market: "Sometimes when I look through this window, I see Belfast out there."[35] Perhaps because busing engenders so much anger in adults, sociologist James Moody has found evidence that it actually exacerbates racial divisions among students.[36]

Importantly, not all jurisdictions subject to busing saw such upheaval. Some embraced it, and many just acquiesced. But for many white people, there was another alternative: leave. Just as people in the previous century had used local control to congregate with people like themselves, many white Americans used their ability to change residences to escape forced integration.

The ability to move to access unintegrated schools was protected by the 1974 *Milliken v. Bradley* decision, in which the U.S. Supreme Court held that districts could not be issued desegregation orders absent compelling evidence that their boundaries had been drawn with segregationist intent.[37] The upshot was that predominantly white, suburban districts could not be incorporated into busing orders with the urban, and predominantly African American, cores they often surrounded. Flight was essentially guaranteed to provide shelter from unwanted integration.

The ability to leave is one reason that between 1970 and 1980 the average nonwhite student in a district under a desegregation order saw the percentage of white children in their school rise only from 37 percent to 43 percent. By

1995 that would dip to 34 percent.[38] Economist Sarah Reber has found that about one-third of integration gains were eventually lost due to white flight.[39]

Notably, while flight in direct response to desegregation orders has been well documented, it appears it was an ongoing phenomenon regardless of school integration orders. Economist Steven Rivkin has estimated that only 9 percentage points of the change in white enrollment in 40 large, central-city school districts between 1968 and 1988 were attributable to the implementation of mandatory desegregation. The rest was the result of ongoing demographic change, often people moving regardless of school assignments.[40] Several researchers have found that many whites simply ignored forced desegregation, with 50 percent or more of white children ordered to go to previously black schools not showing up at their newly assigned institutions.[41]

This is consistent with what research reveals about how whites and African Americans feel about mixed-race neighborhoods. While different measures find different mixes, the evidence is fairly clear that African Americans tend to want to live in neighborhoods in which they are a large percentage of the population—significantly larger than their roughly 13 percent share of the overall U.S. population. Whites, meanwhile, want to live in communities with much smaller concentrations of African Americans.

Sociologist Camille Zubrinsky Charles has reported on experiments in which respondents identified their preferred neighborhood racial mixes on cards showing groups of houses. Based on 2000 data, whites want, on average, neighborhoods that are 57 percent white and only 17 percent black. They also want only 13 percent Hispanic and 13 percent Asian neighbors, which suggests that whites' desires to live primarily with people like themselves extends beyond just African Americans. Blacks, meanwhile, want to live in neighborhoods that are 30 percent white and 42 percent black, as well as only 14 percent Hispanic and 13 percent Asian. [42]

Interestingly, for whites, blacks, and Hispanics, Asians elicited the highest percentage of respondents saying they did not want them as neighbors. This may indicate that avoiding integration is at least partially driven by fear of the unfamiliar, rather than a simple story of black/white animosity. Asians are the newest and smallest, and therefore perhaps least familiar, of the country's major ethnic groups.

This kind of *stated* preference suggests a desire among blacks and whites to live in neighborhoods predominantly of their own race. The *reality* of where people live puts stratification in even starker relief. Data from 2001 show African Americans living in census tracts that were, on average, 63 percent non-Hispanic black and only 28 percent white, and whites living in tracts on average 84 percent non-Hispanic white and only 7 percent black.[43] Segregation declined somewhat between 2000 and 2010, but the average urban African American still lived in a neighborhood that would have to see more than 50 percent of the black population move to achieve a racial mix on par with their entire metropolitan area.[44]

This breakdown might not reflect mixes were people completely free to live where they choose. Restrictive covenants, redlining, and discriminatory federal mortgage and development insurance policies have kept blacks out of white neighborhoods, and real estate agents may still treat otherwise similar African Americans and whites differently.[45] Policies, of course, reflect a desire of some white people to remain separate from blacks, but may impede voluntary race-mixing that would have otherwise occurred.

That said, stated preferences might overestimate integration due to desirability bias. Also, differing composition preferences might produce less integration than both groups want, as an influx of one can create a tipping point yielding a mass exodus of the other.[46] According to research by David Card, Alexandre Mas, and Jesse Rothstein, around 13 percent African American residents is the point at which whites tend to move, and racial homogeneity eventually results.[47] The good news is 13 percent is just about proportional to blacks' overall percentage of the national population. The bad news is it is well below the percentage of African Americans that blacks say they want to live with.

Importantly, busing, which has sometimes been used to keep blacks *out* of white schools,[48] has not always been particularly popular with African Americans. Many black parents have objected to their children being forced into long daily bus rides. And as discussed in the previous chapter, many African Americans have wanted control over their children's schools in order to teach African American history and culture, to hire black teachers, and to be run by African American communities.

As mother Inez Andry told the San Francisco school board in 1968, "We don't want to go to no other neighborhood. But we want education, the kind we need in our neighborhood . . . Black books, more black principals, some more black people on the school board. . . . "[49] A 1971 Gallup poll found a large majority of white parents opposed busing "children from one district to another," but so did a plurality of African Americans: 47 to 45 percent.[50] And busing did not just affect black and white communities. Many San Francisco Chinese families fought a proposal to bus children out of Chinese-dominated public schools that taught their culture.[51]

CONTACT THEORY

That we can unite diverse people by just pushing them together seems to make sense to many people, and it has animated public schooling advocates for centuries. Why does it fail? Because it is hopelessly unrealistic, likely driven much more by good intentions than clear thought and observation.

People will not quietly abandon or compromise away their religious, racial, and ethnic bonds and comforts, or basic values, just because someone tells them that they should for the good of the community, state, or country. As the twentieth century experience of the Balkans suggests, even togetherness at gunpoint will disintegrate when the big gun is holstered. People want to control their own lives, and typically to live with others with whom they identify.

If people will not jettison their religion or racial identity, how can an education system ever do what we want: foster social harmony while providing rigorous learning? Enter Gordon Allport, a Harvard psychologist who wrote *The Nature of Prejudice*, a seminal work positing that intergroup contact—but *not just* contact—is essential to overcome group divides. Allport basically argued that all human beings have to stereotype unknown others, at least at first, because our minds are finite and we need to use limited cues and clues to assess things and people with which we are unfamiliar.

> "We spend most of our waking life calling upon pre-formed categories," Allport wrote. "When the sky darkens and the barometer falls we prejudge that rain will fall. . . . When an angry looking dog charges down the street, we categorize him as a 'mad dog' and avoid him." This, Allport stated, was unavoidable. "Open-mindedness is considered to be a virtue. But, strictly speaking, it cannot occur. A new experience *must* be redacted into old categories."[52]

If this is largely the case, if we have to stereotype unknowns, then getting members of different groups to know each other is crucial to unifying people of all races, religions, and classes. Make them *knowns* instead of *unknowns*. In addition, by meeting individuals belonging to diverse groups and, essentially, seeing them as fellow human beings, we can dispel stereotypes such as all Asians are academic superstars, or black people athletic, or white people cold.

The first problem, as we have seen, is establishing that contact. Other things being equal, people typically do not choose it, and when government has attempted to force it the effect has been like squeezing together two positively charged magnets: the moment policy makers let go, the magnets shoot apart. And, of course, trying to force togetherness has produced a great deal of animosity and divisive conflict.

It is extremely difficult, if not impossible, to have sustained, forced togetherness. That was understood by Allport, who published *The Nature of Prejudice* in 1954, meaning the writing occurred before *Brown v. Board*, and well before forced desegregation busing. Allport wrote:

What is needed is *freedom for both assimilation and for pluralism to occur according to the needs and desires of the minority group itself* [italics added]. Neither policy can be forced. The evolution of societies is a slow process. It can come about with minimum friction *only if we take a relaxed and permissive attitude toward the process* [italics added].[53]

What would be the most effective—or maybe just least explosive—way to promote and sustain intergroup contact? Allport offers four conditions, two mandatory, two helpful but not essential, for successful contact. The four have been italicized for emphasis in this quote from *The Nature of Prejudice*:

Prejudice . . . may be reduced by *equal status contact* between majority and minority groups in the *pursuit of common goals*. The effect is greatly enhanced if this contact is *sanctioned by institutional supports* (i.e., by law, custom or local atmosphere), and provided it is of a sort that leads to the *perception of common interests and common humanity* between members of the two groups.[54]

It is insufficient, posits Allport, to simply put people of different groups in the same place, such as a school. No, the people must be considered of "equal status"—not one group inferior and the other superior—and should be working toward something mutually advantageous: "common goals." It is also helpful for the contact to be, essentially, approved by custom or some legal authority, and to highlight that members of different groups are all human beings with similar hopes and goals.

Basically, in addition to requiring members of different groups to work toward something from which all will benefit, contact must emphasize commonalities. Social psychologist Jonathan Haidt discusses this in *The Righteous Mind: Why Good People Are Divided by Politics and Religion*: "A great deal of research in social psychology shows that people are warmer and more trusting toward people who look like them, dress like them, or even just share their first name or birthday." Key to unity is "drowning . . . differences in a sea of similarities, shared goals, and mutual interdependencies."[55] Some call this creating "crosscutting social identities."[56]

Noting again that he was writing before *Brown v. Board* and busing, Allport did not think schools would be very efficacious places for overcoming prejudice; the influence of prejudice in families can be too strong to overcome, and schools must respond to parents.[57] Allport did, though, have some hope along the lines of Dewey. He thought that if schools were integrated, non-authoritarian, and involved children in intercultural activities that relayed factual and cultural information about different groups, as well as taught non-prejudiced ways of thinking, they could potentially help to break down barriers.[58]

The flip side of contact conducive to bridge-building is contact that rein-forces or exacerbates divides, perhaps by reinforcing negative stereotypes, or by creating a sense of group competition instead of cooperation. Social psychologist Patricia Devine notes that people not internally inclined against prejudice are often embittered by officially sanctioned efforts to quash preju-dice, causing them to become more hostile to outgroups.[59] The "Crossover" high school study captured in one quote the sentiment of several white honors students who saw their social status in the integrated school decline: "I've become a racist since attending Crossover."[60]

How has Allport's contact theory held up, both in education and out? In 2006, social psychologists Thomas Pettigrew and Linda Tropp published a huge meta-analysis of intergroup contact studies. A meta-analysis combines the statistical findings of many separate studies to estimate overall effects of a variable or variables, in this case the effect of intergroup contact on prejudice. The studies included assessed contact in various settings and among numer-ous groups, including people of different races, religions, and ages.[61]

Pettigrew and Tropp did not just assess the effect of contact, but contact with and without Allport's provisos, with and without choice for those mak-ing contact, and other important variables. What they found crunching 515 studies with 696 total samples was that intergroup contact tends to lessen social distance, and the effect is greater when Allport's four provisos are present. The overall effects were small but significant, with a mean of -0.215, the minus sign indicating that greater contact was associated with less preju-dice.[62] Studies of optimal contact—all of Allport's conditions met—had a mean effect size of -0.287.[63]

Some evidence suggested that having institutional support was especially powerful. However, Pettigrew and Tropp stated that with caution due to many of the studies being highly structured, and other evidence showing the need for equal status and mutual self-interest, in conjunction with institutional support, to get improved effects. In light of these qualifications, the firm-est conclusion was that all four provisos together were important, not just one or two.

As is usually the case with social science research, Pettigrew and Tropp's findings should be taken with a few grains of salt. While the researchers worked hard to overcome difficulties inherent to meta-analyses, such as the "file drawer" problem in which studies that find no effects are less likely to be published, it is difficult to completely control things that might bias find-ings. Can you be sure you captured representative unpublished work? Or can the results of experiments using small numbers of psychology students at a single university inform expectations for, say, a busing program encompass-ing thousands of grade schoolers?

Pettigrew and Tropp's analysis suggests choice might not help with inter-group relations. With 114 of the 696 samples categorized as situations in which subjects had no choice but to experience inter-group contact, Pettigrew and Tropp reported that studies allowing *no* choice had bigger effect sizes than those with choice. Assuming that is accurate, forced contact, such as through busing, might work better to build bridges.

Pettigrew and Tropp's effort does not show that to be broadly accurate. When their samples are reduced to those categorized as having no choice; in published studies; that deal with race, ethnicity, and religion; and that were not laboratory experiments, only 19 samples remain.[64] Of those, only 15 were in the United States, and of those 15 only 8 had sample sizes above 100 people. Only one had a sample size above 1,000, a study of World War II combat units with compelling common goals—work together or die—but hellish bonding conditions no one would want to replicate for children.[65] Several studies also predate major integration efforts, and those in education include colleges, Israeli schools, and a project mimicking study abroad.

What do the studies that are focused on American education show? Looking only at studies that were published; about race/ethnicity or religion; set in the United States; in schools; and dealing with children or adolescents, the number of findings is reduced to 34, and all but 5 involved at least "some" choice. Overall, with or without choice, the findings indicate contact is associated with reduced prejudice.

Finally, it is not clear that all the studies categorized as having no choice really had no choice. One examined racial integration at a summer camp, but parents chose to send their children to the camp and likely would have known, or at least would have known it was possible, that the camp would be integrated.[66] Parents were also told a research project would be conducted, and the camp was organized by the Council for Interracial Projects, Inc., though whether parents knew that was unclear. The campers were also carefully selected to be split by race 50/50, so choice or not, the results were not analogous to coerced school integration.

Another study, the analysis of the program intended to replicate study abroad, would have by definition included people already inclined to choose contact outside of their group.[67] Deutsch and Collins's study of housing integration, classified as without choice, relied on affordable housing shortages in New York City and Newark, New Jersey, to conclude that integration was compelled in New York affordable housing units.[68] But it is hard to believe that, if sufficiently motivated, very prejudiced people could not have found other arrangements than integrated housing, such as living with a family member or just on the street.

That said, integrated housing is more in line with Allport's provisos than is forced school integration. Every tenant would be of equal, low-income status, and have common interests in such things as making sure the building they all share stays clean and functional. Forced school integration, in contrast, often involved loss of control for one group, and learning is ultimately an individual endeavor.

Another meta-analysis, conducted by social psychologists Gunnar Lemmer and Ulrich Wagner, focused on interethnic contact interventions informed by contact theory that were implemented in the "real world"—no psychology labs. Studies of policies such as school desegregation and housing projects were also excluded because such contact has typically not been structured or restricted to ethnicity. Lemmer and Wagner, like Pettigrew and Tropp, found contact tended to decrease social distance between in and out groups, but most of the contact appeared to be chosen (the authors did not specifically discuss choice) and much was not focused on American K–12 students.[69]

Chapter 6 will look more widely and deeply at the research on the integration effects of numerous school-assignment policies, and whether Allport's provisos requiring voluntarism matter. For now, suffice it to say that the largest study-of-studies of contact theory does not demonstrate what some opposed to school choice might suggest: that choice is anathema to integration. The meta-analysis does not have the kind of research necessary—large scale, real world, and with clear choice or compulsion—to draw definitive conclusions, but it does suggest that contact theory is on to something.

CONCLUSION

No rigorously thought-through and tested theory undergirds assertions that government-controlled schooling, pushing diverse people physically together, unifies society. There seems to mainly be an *assumption* that public schooling will do this. Meanwhile, the historical evidence speaks powerfully against the assumption.

A more nuanced and deeper theory stands against the simple notion that any contact—even forced—will narrow gulfs. Contact theory holds that contact must include such components as equal status among groups and pursuit of common goals to have much chance of success. The problem with that for public schooling advocates is that it points powerfully to school choice— equal status requires voluntarism, and competing for resources or control of schools is the opposite of pursuing common goals.

Perhaps public schooling's impotence at fostering social cohesion, or worse, its tendency to exacerbate divides by forcing zero-sum conflicts, is why the focus of policy over the last few decades has been test scores and not social goals. Standardized test results have been the ultimate measures of success under federal laws dating back to the 1988 reauthorization of the

Elementary and Secondary Education Act, which for the first time called for states to identify schools that were not succeeding and show that students receiving federal aid were making academic progress. That movement, however, peaked around 2011, when the federal government incentivized states to use the Common Core national curriculum standards and national tests.

That micromanagement lit a fire under an already percolating revolution against education obsessively focused on test scores and "accountability." A return to "democratically controlled," local education was emerging as a battle cry. And such control, many theorists believe, may itself be a unifying force.

It is to democratic control that the next chapter turns. It will examine what exactly "democracy" means when people invoke it and ponder whether their formulations are consistent with truly fundamental American values.

NOTES

1. Richard D. Kahlenberg, *All Together Now: Creating Middle-Class Schools through Public School Choice* (Washington, DC: Brookings Institution Press, 2001), 251–254; Allen G. Breed, "North Carolina: Fear of 'Resegregation' Sparks Unrest," BET News.com, July 16, 2010; Chris Reinolds Kozelle, "19 Arrested as Protesters Claim School Plan Would Resegregate System," CNN.com, July 23, 2010; T. Keung Hui, "Draft Wake County Assignment Plan Does Little on School Diversity," *News Observer*, September 6, 2016.

2. Benjamin Rush, "Thoughts upon the Mode of Education Proper in a Republic," in *Essays on Education in the Early Republic*, ed. Frederick Rudolph (Cambridge, MA: The Belknap Press of Harvard University Press, 1965), 9.

3. John B. McConahay, "The Effects of School Desegregation upon Students' Racial Attitudes and Behavior: A Critical Review of the Literature and a Prolegomenon to Future Research," *Law and Contemporary Problems* 42, no. 3 (Summer 1978): 102.

4. Robert D. Putnam, *Bowling Alone: The Collapse and Revival of American Community* (New York: Simon & Schuster, 2000).

5. Pierre Bourdieu and Jean-Claude Passeron, *Reproduction in Education, Society, and Culture*, 2nd ed. (Thousand Oaks, CA: SAGE Publications, 2000).

6. John Dewey, *Democracy and Education* (New York: Barnes & Noble Books, 2005), 2.

7. Anne Corbett, "Secular, Free and Compulsory," in Anne Corbett and Bob Moon, eds., *Education in France: Continuity and Change in the Mitterand Years, 1981–1995* (London: Routledge, 1996), 5.

8. Amy Gutmann, *Democratic Education* (Princeton, NJ: Princeton Paperbacks, 1999), 289.

9. Gutmann, *Democratic Education*, 289.

10. Ibid., 30–31.

11. Emile Durkheim, *Moral Education*, trans. Peter L. Phillips Simpson (Mineola, NY: Dover Publications, 2002), 144–145.

12. *Zelman, Superintendent of Public Instruction of Ohio,* et al. *v. Simmons-Harris* et al., 536 U.S. 639 (2002).

13. Charles Glenn, *The Myth of the Common School* (Amherst, MA: University of Massachusetts Press, 1988), 52.

14. Glenn, *Myth of the Common School.*

15. Ibid., 249.

16. Danton cited in Glenn, *Myth of the Common School,* 22.

17. The European Commission reports that as of the 2007–08 school year, "Private education (pre-school + primary school) in France is nearly 97% catholic." Directorate-General for Education and Culture, European Commission, *The Education System in France: 2007/08,* 41.

18. Horace Mann, "Report for 1843," in Mary Mann, ed., *Life and Works of Horace Mann* (Boston: Horace B. Fuller, 1868), 242.

19. Mann, "Report for 1843," 367.

20. Country data from Central Intelligence Agency, "The World Factbook," https://www.cia.gov/library/publications/resources/the-world-factbook/, accessed July 7, 2020.

21. Harris quoted in David B. Tyack, *The One Best System: A History of American Urban Education* (Cambridge, MA: Harvard University Press, 1974), 43.

22. Dewey, *Democracy and Education*, 390.

23. David Brooks, "People Like Us," *The Atlantic Monthly*, September 2003.

24. Diane Ravitch, *Left Back: A Century of Battles over School Reform* (New York: Touchstone, 2000), 174.

25. *Brown v. Board of Education of Topeka*, 347 U.S. 483 (1954).

26. Erica Frankenberg and Rebecca Jacobson, "The Polls—Trends: School Integration Polls," *Public Opinion Quarterly* 75, no. 4 (Winter 2011): 789–801.

27. Phi Delta Kappa, "The 49th Annual PDK Poll of the Public's Attitudes Toward the Public Schools," September 2017, K6, https://pdkpoll.org/wp-content/uploads/2020/05/pdkpoll49_2017.pdf.

28. GenForward, "GenForward July 2017 Toplines," August 2017, http://genforwardsurvey.com/assets/uploads/2017/09/GenForward-July-Toplines-_-Education.pdf.

29. Justin McCarthy, "Most Americans Say Segregation in Schools a Serious Problem," Gallup, September 17, 2019, https://news.gallup.com/poll/266756/americans-say-segregation-schools-serious-problem.aspx.

30. Allison Roda and Amy Stuart Wells, "School Choice Policies and Racial Segregation: Where White Parents' Good Intentions, Anxiety, and Privilege Collide," *American Journal of Education* 119, no. 2, February 2013: 261–293; Atila Abdulkadiroglu, et al., "Do Parents Value School Effectiveness," NBER Working Paper No. 23912, October 2017.

31. Chase M. Billingham and Matthew O. Hunt, "School Racial Composition and Parental Choice: New Evidence on the Preferences of White Parents in the United States," *Sociology of Education* 89, no. 2: 99–117.

32. Claire Martin, "DPS Bus Chief Kept Wheels Turning," *Denver Post*, July 28, 2005.

33. "6 Klansmen Arraigned in Bus Bombings; New Violence Erupts," *Chicago Tribune*, September 11, 1971.

34. For an in-depth discussion of that famous photo see Louis P. Masur, *The Soiling of Old Glory: The Story of a Photograph That Shocked America* (New York: Bloomsbury Press, 2008).

35. J. Anthony Lucas, *Common Ground: A Turbulent Decade in the Lives of Three American Families* (New York: Vintage Press, 1986), 610.

36. James Moody, "Race, School Integration, and Friendship Segregation in America," *American Journal of Sociology* 107, no. 3 (November 2001): 706.

37. *Milliken v. Bradley*, 418 U.S. 717 (1974).

38. Sarah J. Reber, "Court-Ordered Desegregation: Successes and Failures Integrating American Schools Since *Brown versus Board of Education*," *Journal of Human Resources* 40, no. 3 (Summer 2005): 565.

39. Reber, "Court-Ordered Desegregation," 560.

40. Steven G. Rivkin, "Residential Segregation and School Integration," *Sociology of Education* 76, no. 4 (October 1994): 279–292.

41. Christine H. Rossell, "The Desegregation Efficiency of Magnet Schools," *Urban Affairs Review* 38, no. 5 (May 2003): 2.

42. Camille Zubrinsky Charles, "The Dynamics of Racial Residential Segregation," *Annual Review of Sociology* 29 (2003): 167–207.

43. Scott J. South, Kyle Crowder, and Jeremy Pais, "Metropolitan Structure and Neighborhood Attainment: Exploring Intermetropolitan Variation in Residential Segregation" 48, no. 4 (November 2011): 1263–1292.

44. Edward Glaeser and Jacob Vigdor, "The End of the Segregated Century: Racial Separation in America's Neighborhoods: 1890–2010," Manhattan Institute *Civic Report* no. 66, January 2012.

45. See, for instance, Richard Rothstein, *The Color of Law: A Forgotten History of How Our Government Segregated America* (New York: W. W. Norton & Company, 2017).

46. For a detailed walk through this process, see Thomas C. Schelling, "Dynamic Models of Segregation," *Journal of Mathematical Sociology* 1 (1971): 143–186.

47. David Card, Alexandre Mas, and Jesse Rothstein, "Are Mixed Neighborhoods Always Unstable? Two-Sided and One-Sided Tipping," NBER Working Paper 14470.

48. Matthew F. Delmont, *Why Busing Failed: Race, Media, and the National Resistance to School Desegregation* (Oakland, CA: University of California Press, 2016), 2.

49. Quoted in Delmont, *Why Busing Failed*, 168.

50. Mary Costello, "School Busing and Politics," *Editorial Research Reports 1972*, vol. 1 (Washington, DC: CQ Press, 1972), http://library.cqpress.com/cqresearcher/document.php?id=cqresrre1972030100.

51. Editorial, *Honolulu Star-Bulletin*, September 2, 1971, reproduced in *The School Busing Controversy: 1970–75* (New York: Facts on File, 1975), 50.

52. Gordon W. Allport, *The Nature of Prejudice* (Boston: The Beacon Press, 1954), 20.

53. Allport, *The Nature of Prejudice*, 240.

54. Ibid., 281.

55. Jonathan Haidt, *The Righteous Mind: Why Good People Are Divided by Politics and Religion* (New York: Vintage Books, 2013), 277.

56. Janet Ward Schofield, "Improving Intergroup Relations among Students," in *Handbook of Research on Multicultural Education*, eds. James A. Banks and Cherry A. McGee Banks (New York: Macmillan Library Reference, 1995), 640.

57. Allport, *The Nature of Prejudice*, 296.

58. Ibid., 510–513.

59. Patricia G. Devine, "Breaking the Prejudice Habit: Allport's 'Inner Conflict' Revisited" in *On the Nature of Prejudice: Fifty Years after Allport*, eds. John F. Dovidio, Peter Glick, and Laurie A. Rudman (Malden, MA: Blackwell Publishing, 2005), 340.

60. Thomas W. Collins and George W. Noblit, "Stratification and Resegregation: The Case of Crossover High School, Memphis, Tennessee," National Institute of Education, 1976, 152.

61. Thomas F. Pettigrew and Linda R. Tropp, "The Meta-Analytic Test of Intergroup Contact Theory," *Journal of Personality and Social Psychology* 90, no. 5, 2006, 751–783.

62. Ibid., 757.

63. Ibid., 760.

64. For a quick discussion of the dangers of reaching conclusions based on research conducted especially in American college labs, see Eric M. Johnson, "The WEIRD Evolution of Human Psychology," *Scientific American*, December 7, 2011, https://blogs.scientificamerican.com/primate-diaries/the-weird-evolution-of-human-psychology/.

65. Samuel A. Stouffer et al., *American Soldier: Combat and Its Aftermath, Vol. II* (Princeton, NJ: Princeton University Press, 1949).

66. Gerald L. Clore et al., "Interracial Attitudes and Behavior at a Summer Camp," *Journal of Personality and Psychology* 6, no. 2 (February 1978): 107–116.

67. Cynthia Stohl, "The A.M.I.G.O. Project: A Multicultural Intergroup Opportunity," *International Journal of Intercultural Relations* 9, no. 2 (1985): 151–175.

68. Morton Deutsch and Mary Evans Collins, *Interracial Housing: A Psychological Evaluation of a Social Experiment* (Minneapolis, MN: University of Minnesota Press, 1951).

69. Gunnar Lemmer and Ulrich Wagner, "Can We Really Reduce Ethnic Prejudice outside the Lab? A Meta-analysis of Direct and Indirect Contact Interventions," *European Journal of Social Psychology* 45, no. 2 (March 2015): 152–168.

Chapter 4

The "Democracy" Problem

Texas, the second largest state by population, has a board of education that approves curricula for every district, as well as textbooks for which districts receive state funds if they adopt them. In other words, the state board— with members elected by the people of Texas—decides what will be taught throughout the state. That has made it a political and social lightning rod for decades, as every group in the diverse state has been forced to weigh in on what Lone Star children will learn.

In perhaps the most meta of disputes, in 2010 a major bone of contention in proposed state social studies standards was whether the United States is a "democracy," as it is often described, or a "constitutional republic," in which a constitution lays out specific powers granted to government by the people, and representatives vote on behalf of their constituents. What was meta was that in "democratically controlled" schooling, a fierce fight raged over whether to teach children that the country is democratically controlled.

Lots of Texans—and political theorists—disagree about terms such as "democracy" and "constitutional republic." And that hot-button issue was accompanied by many others, including the influence of Moses on American government, and the solvency of Social Security, matters the Republican majority sought to address in the curriculum and erase a perceived liberal bias. There was, though, at least one thing all sides seemed to fear: the state board would push one "correct" answer on every public school, and it would not be their *answer.*

Ultimately the changes, including the new description of American government, were passed on a 9 to 5 vote. Reported the Washington Post, *"'I have let down the students in our state,' said board member Mary Helen Berlanga (D). 'What we have done today is something that a classroom teacher would not even have accepted,' she said, sweeping a pile of history books from her desk onto the floor."*

Of course, the other side was pleased, and the outcome had *to be just: "democracy" had spoken.*[1]

Education apparently has a lot to do with democracy. To run through just a handful of American book titles tying the two together, there is John Dewey's *Democracy and Education*, Amy Gutmann's *Democratic Public Education*, David Mathews' *Reclaiming Education by Reclaiming Our Democracy*, E.D. Hirsch, Jr.'s *The Making of Americans: Democracy and Our Schools*, Johan Neem's *Democracy's Schools: The Rise of Public Education in America*, and Derek Black's *Schoolhouse Burning: Public Education and the Assault on American Democracy*.

Diving deeper than title, we see that these and other books specifically connect public schooling, not just education, to democracy. Political scientist Benjamin Barber has asserted that public schools are the "institutions where we learn what it means to be a public and start down the road toward common national and civic identity. They are the forges of our citizenship and the bedrock of our democracy."[2]

School founder and public schooling activist Deborah Meier writes in her book *In Schools We Trust: Creating Communities of Learning in an Era of Testing and Standardization*, "All the habits of mind and work that go into democratic institutional life must be practiced in our schools until they truly become habits."[3]

And Jeffrey Henig, in *Rethinking School Choice: Limits of the Market Metaphor*, opines that "because public schools are the vehicle for education most feasibly and appropriately subject to democratic control, government policy toward public schools is the major opportunity that democratic societies have for upgrading the quality of insight and sensitivity on which future majority decisions will rely."[4]

Many people perceive intimate, essential connections between public schooling and democracy. But they often appear to mean different things when they refer to "democracy," and see different relationships between it and the schools. This is a big problem, because nailing down the definition of democracy—not simply invoking it in vague, sentimental ways—is crucial to understanding the real-world implications of education system designs, as is specifying how, exactly, one expects democracy and education to interact.

TRIP DOWN DEMOCRACY LANE

Before breaking down what modern theorists mean when they talk about "democracy," and tackling education's relationship to it, it is worth spending a few moments reviewing how political theorists and philosophers have viewed democracy through the ages. What that reveals, largely, is that the imprecision we see in pronouncements today is, in fact, time honored. Democracy can feature lots of attributes, some by definition, others by implication.

Ancient Greece, of course, is regarded as the birthplace of democracy, so it seems reasonable to start with Socrates, Plato, and Aristotle to ferret out a basic definition of "democracy." One or two common denominators can be found among them, but that seems to be it. Democracy is associated with some degree of popular—as opposed to tyrannical or oligarchic—control of government, and as a result some degree of power leveled among the people. But that may be the extent of agreement.

In *The Republic*, Plato, via Socrates's dialogue with Glaucon, does little to define "democracy," perhaps because Plato and Socrates's goal is to identify an ideal government, and they do not think democracy is it. What one gets from Socrates is that in a democracy the people have power, attained after the poor of a once-oligarchic society have overthrown the wealthy and taken power for themselves. The people may organize into some sort of vote-driven assembly to make collective decisions, but ultimately Socrates describes democracy as anarchy; all men do as they please—they have "liberty"—and what laws and penalties exist are flouted.

In democracies, Socrates says, "There's no compulsion either to exercise authority if you are capable of it, or to submit to authority if you don't want to." He adds, "You must have noticed that in a democracy men sentenced to death or exile stay on, none the less, and go about among their fellows, with no more notice taken of their comings and goings than if they were invisible spirits."[5] There is no "majority rule," as moderns tend to associate with democracy, because there is no "rule" at all. Other, that is, than an individual over himself.

Complete self-rule may sound ideal, at least to libertarian ears, but it should not, warns Socrates. Many people, driven by their greed and leveling ethos, will grow covetous of the rich and increasingly exert political force to redistribute their wealth. The rich will attempt to defend themselves, but in so doing will be accused of attempting to re-create the recently overthrown oligarchy. The people will feel compelled to root out such intrigue, creating a ripe environment for a small group, and eventually one leader, to arise, promising to destroy the would-be oligarchs. In so doing, the grounds for tyranny will be seeded.[6]

Plato's student Aristotle gave democracy a more detailed explanation and examination than Socrates, incorporating discussion of who, in fact, has power, and in what ways it is exercised. Aristotle agreed with Plato and Socrates in viewing democracy as a way for the poor to rule for their own advantage, and opposed to a "polity" in which "the multitude govern for the *common* [italics added] advantage."[7] Indeed, democracy is not about majority rule per se—though Aristotle says that that is the common perception—but it *ends up* as majority rule because the poor are typically far more numerous than the rich. And *any* rule is prone toward injustice.

From this baseline, Aristotle discusses various forms of democracy, moving to a conception beyond rule by the poor. He discusses a system in which neither the rich nor the poor predominate. More importantly, he tackles rule of law versus rule of the majority. The latter is when "the multitude is in control . . . when decrees, but not the law, are in control."[8] And how should majority rule, and the rights and desires of rich and poor, be balanced? Perhaps, Aristotle argues, via a system in which both the rich and poor vote, and majority rules when majorities of *both* groups agree, or when majorities can be assembled combining the votes of the two.

Aristotle's is a more nuanced assessment of democracy than Plato and Socrates's, though all agree that democracy has, at its root, victory of the poor over the rich in accumulating political power, with majority rule being a coincidence of the class divide, not a fundamental feature. Meanwhile, Aristotle seems more sensitive to the reality that a majority can *directly* exert tyranny, as opposed to democracy *descending* into anarchy and then producing tyranny. Part of his solution is to have basically two co-equal legislative houses, a clear departure from mere majority rule.

Moving centuries beyond the Greeks come Thomas Hobbes, John Locke, and Montesquieu, who were heavy influencers of America's Founders. All gave a sense of what democracy—or, at least, some kind of rule by "the people"—could be. And one in particular defined the end that democracy, as later envisioned by the Founders, was supposed to serve: securing individual liberty.

Hobbes, as some might remember from their basic U.S. history or civics classes, was primarily interested in promoting and defending monarchy (some might recall the sketch of the king, composed of hundreds of people, looming over the hills and village on their *Leviathan* cover). And what was democracy to Hobbes? A legitimate sovereign power just like a monarchy, and like a monarchy, "a real Unitie" of all people:

> in one and the same Person, made by Covenant of every man with every man, in such manner, as if every man should say to every man, *I Authorize and give up my Right of Governing my selfe, to this man, or this Assembly of men, on this condition, that thou give up thy Right to him, and Authorise all his Actions in like manner* (Italics in original).[9]

Hobbes says a "democracy" is an "assembly of all that will come together." Though composed of many people, and, according to Hobbes, conflated with individual liberty by Aristotle, democracy must have one assembly. Its power must be supreme, lest men return to a state of "Warre"—all at liberty to take from one another according to their strength and cunning—which Hobbes says existed absent a supreme government. Men have no liberty on which the assembly cannot encroach. Essentially, the only difference between a monarchy and democracy is whether one's sovereignty is surrendered to a single person or assembly.[10]

It was Locke, a favorite of the Founders,[11] who explained that the purpose of rule by the people is to preserve individual liberty and property. Humanity, Locke argues, was born into a "state of perfect freedom" and "equality." When human beings would have first appeared on Earth, all men would have started off equals in terms of power, and would have been free to do as they chose within the "law of nature."[12]

Alas, some people would steal from others, or force them to do their bidding, which would violate the state of freedom. Locke asserts that men have a right to resist such force and punish offenders, but lest men be judges in their own cases, government should be instituted to arbitrate conflicts. Locke says that where there is no common authority, and no law, to which to appeal when force is used or threatened, humanity is in a "state of war," a conclusion not coincidentally like the "war of all against all" that Hobbes saw as the state of nature. To avoid this, human beings enter society.[13]

To enter society, individuals must relinquish some of their freedom; any laws proscribing actions, including using force against others, reduce liberty, at least in the short run. But as long as the function of government is to prohibit the use of force or fraud—the latter being, essentially, force through deception—the orbit of freedom for all is ultimately maximized. Writes Locke: "The end of law is not to abolish or restrain, but *to preserve and enlarge Freedom*. For *Liberty* is to be free from restraint and violence from others which cannot be, where there is no Law."[14]

Democracy, by Locke's lights, is the form of government that results when free people voluntarily enter into a society of laws. And majority rule is the only reasonable way to have that society function as one unit, "when any number of Men have so *consented to make one Community* of Government, they are thereby presently incorporated, and make *one Body Politick*, wherein the *Majority* have a Right to act and conclude the rest."[15]

Crucially, Locke argues that *no government has the right* to take property from people without their consent, because the primary justification for entering into society is to *secure* property, including *one's property in oneself.* He also states that the best form of government for protecting *individual liberty*—which is why government is created—is democracy with frequent elections:

> Hence it is a mistake to think, that the Supream or *Legislative Power* of any Commonwealth, can do what it will, and dispose of the Estates of the Subject *arbitrarily*, or take any part of them at pleasure. This is not much to be fear'd in Governments where the *Legislative* consists, wholly or in part, in Assemblies

which are variable, whose Members upon the Dissolution of the Assembly, are
Subjects under the common Laws of their Country, equally with the rest. But in
Governments, where the *Legislative* is in one lasting Assembly always in being,
or in one Man, as in Absolute Monarchies, there is danger still, that they will
think themselves to have a distinct interest, from the rest of the Community;
and so will be apt to increase their own Riches and Power, by taking, what they
think fit, from the People.[16]

For Locke, democracy is—or at least should be—majority rule, but in frequently turning-over assemblies that cannot take property from any person
without his or her consent. To this he would add a subordinate power to exe-
cute laws, especially when assemblies are not occurring, and a "federative"
power to deal with people outside of the society, such as other nations. These
would be in the hands of a single person. Essentially, the role of the president.

Charles-Louis de Secondat, Baron de La Brède et de Montesquieu—better known simply as Montesquieu—wrote in *The Spirit of the Laws* that a
democracy appears to be the type of government in which the people have
the most freedom to do as they please, though he draws a distinction between
this freedom and liberty. "Liberty," he writes, "can consist only in having the
power to do what one should want to do and in no way being constrained to
do what one should not want to do. . . . Liberty is the right to do everything
the law permits."[17]

This somewhat contradictory definition of liberty aside, Montesquieu's
primary contribution to what democracy is—or more important, how it can
be constructed to ensure rule of law and not arbitrary rule of men—is in
elaborating on the separation of powers. Montesquieu advises dividing power
among legislative, executive, and judicial branches and dividing the legislative branch into two houses, one of the nobility and one "the people," as
Aristotle proposed. A central benefit is different branches and bodies check-
ing each other, preventing rash or despotic actions and preserving individual
liberty to the greatest extent possible.

Socrates, Plato, Aristotle, Montesquieu, and many others feared that
democracy would degenerate into tyranny. When the more numerous groups
realize their ability to take from the less numerous—typically the poor taking from the rich—they become strongly inclined, due to basic human greed,
to do so. This poisonous combination of envy and numerical advantage is
then exploited by demagogues, who will rail about conspiracies by the rich
or some other minority group with something to be plundered, and whip up
popular sentiment against them. The result is often tyranny of the majority,
and then tyranny of a, well, *tyrant*.

This powerful inclination toward tyranny is what the American Founders
sought with great energy to overcome. It is in the *Federalist Papers* that we

see this major threat of democracy most methodically and comprehensively addressed. The authors explain especially why the new national government under the proposed constitution would not be a democracy as understood by Socrates, Aristotle, and Hobbes—an all-powerful assembly—but a system of power divisions as Locke had begun to lay out, and Montesquieu cemented. Preservation of individual liberty was the goal.

As James Madison stated in *Federalist* no. 10:

> From this view of the subject it may be concluded that a pure democracy, by which I mean a society consisting of a small number of citizens, who assemble and administer the government in person, can admit of no cure for the mischiefs of faction. A common passion or interest will, in almost every case, be felt by a majority of the whole; a communication and concert result from the form of government itself; and there is nothing to check the inducements to sacrifice the weaker party or an obnoxious individual. Hence it is that such democracies have ever been spectacles of turbulence and contention; have ever been found incompatible with personal security or the rights of property; and have in general been as short in their lives as they have been violent in their deaths.[18]

The basic mechanisms to prevent tyranny in the Constitution are myriad, starting with republicanism—the people select representatives rather than voting in assemblies directly—as the basic governmental form, which Madison hoped would result in relatively wise, dispassionate rule. Next, the republic covers a geographically and numerically extensive area, diffusing factions and making their coordination more difficult. The powers of the national government are also separate from those of the state governments, and strictly defined. Finally, the national government is divided into legislative, executive, and judicial branches, each with checks on the other, and the legislative branch is broken into the House of Representatives, representing the people, and the Senate, representing states.

Soon after ratification, amendments were added to the Constitution to further protect individual rights. The Bill of Rights specifically says that incursions on worship, speech, and others freedoms are not permitted to the national government, and eventually the Fourteenth Amendment applied the prohibitions to state and local governments. The framers clearly intended something far from democracy, defined as a single assembly with unlimited power as long as a majority supports it. They wanted limited government, largely to protect individuals against tyranny of the majority, or a powerful minority, to which democracy is inclined.

What about at the state level, where most governance occurred at the time of the Constitution's ratification? In *Federalist* no. 47 Madison looked at the connections among the branches of government in most states and found that they tended to adhere to Montesquieu's separation, though often with stronger connections between the legislative and other branches than the complete break that some objectors to the federal Constitution called for.[19] Many also enumerated individual rights and protections from government power, in keeping with British traditions reaching back to the Magna Carta in 1215.

Interestingly, as Hamilton noted in *Federalist* no. 84, the *absence* of enumerated rights was thought by some to *maximize* liberty in the federal context, where only specific powers were granted to the government, necessarily leaving all others to the people:

> They would contain various exceptions to power which are not granted; and on this very account, would afford a colorable pretext to claim more than were granted. For why declare that things shall not be done which there is no power to do? Why, for instance, should it be said that the liberty of the press shall not be restrained, when no power is given by which restrictions may be imposed?[20]

By 1787 it was fairly clear among philosophers that "democracy" referred to a sovereign assembly of the people in which majorities ruled. It was also clear that no states, nor the new national government, were to be democracies, but constitutional republics with explicit protections for individuals against government intrusion.

From Majority Rule to Government Control, Because Democracy Fails

Through the nineteenth century, "democracy" tended to be defined as vague control by "the people," through some sort of voting and majority rule, with those permitted to vote starting very narrow, largely white males with property. Over time those restrictions ebbed. First property qualifications disappeared, then some racial curbs, then restriction of the franchise to men, all inching closer to rule by the people broadly.

Against that flow, historian Eric Foner observes, by the Progressive Era's height around the early twentieth century, the term "democracy" was often being invoked to restrict who had power. Political and social elites were invoking it not, it appears, to give "the people" more direct control over government, but to give government more control over the people. The term was becoming a euphemism for control by government experts, making it even more obtuse than the old debates. Writes Foner:

> "He didn't believe in democracy; he believed simply in government." H.L. Mencken's quip about Theodore Roosevelt came uncomfortably close to the mark for many Progressive advocates of an empowered national state. The

government could best exercise intelligent control over society through a "democracy" run by impartial experts and in many respects unaccountable to citizenry. The technocratic impulse toward order, efficiency, and centralized management—all, ostensibly, in the service of social justice—was an important theme of Progressive reform.[21]

This move toward technocratic, elite government may have been no more clearly illustrated than it was in education with, as already discussed, small, locally controlled districts often intentionally destroyed and consolidated into larger districts to remove them from what many progressives saw as corrupt, ethnically homogeneous, ill-informed democratic governance. "The people" could not directly control their own districts because, many progressives concluded, they simply did not know what was good for them. "Democracy" became the rhetorical sugar to make the medicine of expert control go down more easily.

Today, the same technocratic, power-consolidating ethos has pushed authority to even more distant strata of government. Much of the backing for it has stemmed from the conclusion that democratic control of education does not work. It is an evolution that largely bypassed states and went directly to the federal government, reaching its pinnacle in the No Child Left Behind Act (NCLB), enacted with bipartisan support in early 2002.

Inspired by systems of uniform standards and tests, and high-stakes consequences for schools, in a few states, the George W. Bush administration worked to extend the model nationwide through reauthorization of the Elementary and Secondary Education Act (ESEA). Since the ESEA was enacted with many other Great Society programs in 1965, it has been the primary vehicle by which Washington has delivered K–12 monies to states. It was largely that act that precipitated major growth in state education bureaucracies, with states expected to do most of the work of administering and overseeing large federal grant programs.

Over time, as it became clear that federal dollars were not translating into better academic outcomes, the thinking behind federal funding shifted from subsidizing low-income districts to pushing academic improvement. As noted in the previous chapter, that change started with the 1988 ESEA reauthorization, but NCLB took ESEA to its most controlling version, requiring that states, in exchange for funds, adopt uniform state standards, tests, and a cascade of interventions for schools that failed to make "adequate yearly progress" toward all students being "proficient" in mathematics and reading by 2014. It also laid out "highly qualified teacher" rules and other micromanaging guidance.

The only thing that exceeded the centralizing power of NCLB was federal influence via funding to ameliorate the Great Recession's negative effects on state spending. A relatively small part of 2009's nearly $800 billion American Recovery and Reinvestment Act was $4.35 billion over which the secretary of education had largely unilateral control, which he turned into a prize pot for a competition among states. Eventually dubbed "Race to the Top," the contest required states to submit plans that would be rewarded points by reviewers, and top scorers would get some dough.

Among the requirements for states to get maximum points was adopting standards and aligned tests common to a majority of states, and to create "longitudinal data systems" to track students from pre-kindergarten through college or entering the workforce.[22] Only one set of national standards existed at the time applications were due (and even those were still under development): the Common Core. Also, part of the RTTT money was directed to state consortia to create Core-aligned tests. The Obama administration doubled down on many of these policies by offering states waivers from many of NCLB's most onerous provisions if they complied.[23]

A major justification for this federal control was the belief that local democracy, in the form of school boards, often failed. School boards, many argued, had become tools of special interests, especially teacher unions, that did not want to be held accountable for district failures, while few voters participated in board elections. As Lisa Graham Keegan, former superintendent of Arizona schools, and Chester Finn, president of the conservative Thomas B. Fordham Institute, wrote in 2004:

> The teacher unions now dominate many a school board election, or at least have the capacity to do so. . . . When the board is quiet and rocks no education boats, the union rests. But . . . when the board undertakes the kinds of reforms that the union doesn't favor, the union will mobilize to elect friendly candidates.[24]

Keegan, Finn, and many others also concluded that districts and states, left to their own devices, would either overlook or actively keep down minority and low-income students. As George W. Bush famously and repeatedly declared, NCLB was needed to overcome "the soft bigotry of low expectations."

Only at the end of 2015 did the federal government loosen its increasingly tight reins, passing the Every Student Succeeds Act (ESSA), another reauthorization of the ESEA. ESSA eliminated "adequate yearly progress" requirements and the prescriptive interventions that went with it, and prohibited the Department of Education from trying to influence states to adopt national standards, in particular the Common Core. States were still, though, required to have uniform standards and tests, and to intervene with the lowest performing schools; democratically controlled school districts still could not be trusted to work.

DEMOCRACY AND EDUCATION

How has "democracy" been framed in major treatments of education? What has been its proposed relationship to education? What are the dangers of the various treatments?

The visions of democracy that can frequently be discerned in discussions of education can be reduced to six major ones, though no doubt other divisions are possible, and there can be significant overlap in the views of people who subscribe to different ones. The most common conceptions of the nexus between education and democracy seem to be the following:

1. **Informed Citizens:** When government is controlled by the people, it is important that citizens be sufficiently educated to understand political matters and make informed decisions about them.
2. **Virtuous Citizens:** When government is controlled by the people, it is important that citizens be sufficiently virtuous that they are not a danger to others and to a healthy society.
3. **Social Control:** The job of education is to engineer society and the people in it, and the process is fair as long as a participatory mechanism—democracy—is followed.
4. **System of Togetherness:** Education controlled by a democratic process brings diverse people together and forces them to hash out their differences, preparing them for peaceful coexistence in all facets of social life.
5. **Schools of Togetherness:** Public schooling brings diverse students together and teaches them common humanity and how to get along.
6. **Levelers:** Democracy is about equality, and everyone has an equal chance to succeed when they have equal preparation for life.

At first glance those may or may not make sense. But they need to be unpacked.

Informed Citizens

That in a nation in which the people are sovereign the people must be sufficiently well educated to think critically about political matters, and therefore some "free" government schooling is necessary, is probably most closely associated with Thomas Jefferson. As discussed in chapter 1, Jefferson famously proposed a system for Virginia in which all children would attend publicly provided schools for three years, and then the "natural aristocracy" would be brought to the fore as the best students were "raked from the rubbish." Over several levels and rakings, an intellectual elite would eventually study *gratis* at the state university.

While the "natural aristocracy" concept was consistent with a common conviction that elites were few and far between, and should be groomed without regard to class to assume positions of political leadership, the proposal that all people be given a basic education free of charge was somewhat novel. While certainly noting that reading and arithmetic could help people in their practical, daily lives, the primary justification for the proposal was empowering people to be vigilant, empowered citizens:

> But of all the views of this law none is more important, none more legitimate, than that of rendering the people safe, as they are the ultimate, guardians of their own liberty. For this purpose the reading in the first stage, where *they* will receive their whole education, is proposed, as has been said, to be chiefly historical. History by apprising them of the past will enable them to judge of the future; it will avail them of the experience of other times and other nations; it will qualify them as judges of the actions and designs of men; it will enable them to know ambition under every disguise it may assume; and knowing it, to defeat its views. . . . Every government degenerates when trusted to the rulers of the people alone. The people themselves therefore are its only safe depositories. And to render even them safe their minds must be improved to a certain degree.[25]

Jefferson's focus was clear: universal public schooling was to equip the people to discern when those whom they might elect, or who might seek power in other ways, were a threat to their liberty. This would include being able to detect, perhaps, the tyrant that many thinkers believed would arise from democracy. Directly connected to the need to perceive such dangers is that power in the hands of the people was a check on ruling elites. Jefferson's was, to a large extent, a defensive stance: the people must be educated so they would know when their freedom was in jeopardy.

While Jefferson is often invoked by defenders of universal public schooling, his justification for it—educate citizens to detect threats to their liberty—tends to get less attention than simply his advocating government provision. He is often featured in a simplistic message that the Founders thought that public schooling was important, and therefore it *must* be. That seems especially compelling when you include no less an enemy of government power than Jefferson.

Virtuous Citizens

More broadly propounded than Jefferson's goal of a citizenry equipped to thwart threats to liberty was the intent to shape children into virtuous citizens;

presumably a very desirable aim if the people were to have all of the political power. By simple logic, if the people are in control of government and are virtuous, the outcomes of governance will also be steeped in virtue. But this leaves at least one crucial question: What constitutes virtue?

While many early public schooling advocates and writers featured the need to infuse virtue in the people—among them Benjamin Rush, Noah Webster, and Samuel Harrison Smith—the most important was common school "father" Horace Mann. And virtue was, indeed, his primary aim. But what, to Mann, constituted virtue?

Mann's conceptualization reduced to holding basic Protestant beliefs and putting the needs of others above one's own. Inculcating such feelings within students would, presumably, make them inclined to use their freedom in sober, selfless ways. As Mann wrote in his twelfth, and final, annual report:

> It may be an easy thing to make a republic; but it is a very laborious thing to make republicans; and woe to the republic that rests upon no greater foundation than ignorance, selfishness, and passion! Such a republic may grow in numbers and in wealth. As an avaricious man adds acres to his lands, so its rapacious government may increase its own darkness by annexing provinces and states to its ignorant domain. Its armies may be invincible, and its fleets may strike terror into nations on the opposite side of the globe at the same hour. Vast in its extent, and enriched by the prodigality of Nature, it may possess every capacity and opportunity of being great and of doing good. But, if such a republic be devoid of intelligence, it will only the more closely resemble an obscene giant who has waxed strong in his youth, and grown wanton in his strength; whose brain has been developed only in the region of the appetites and passions, and not in the organs of reason and conscience; and who, therefore, is boastful of his bulk alone, and glories in the weight of his heel, and in the destruction of his arm. Such a republic, with all its noble capacities for beneficence, will rush with the speed of a whirlwind to an ignominious end; and all good men of after-times would be fain to weep over its downfall, did not their scorn and contempt at its folly and its wickedness repress all sorrow for its fate.[26]

Perhaps surprising given the ills that Mann sees a unified republic might inflict, virtue for many early writers, including Mann, included a willing-ness—an internal compulsion, even—to sacrifice one's personal desires and ambitions when called to serve one's state or country. As Rush contended:

> Our country includes family, friends, and property, and should be preferred to them all. Let our pupil be taught that he does not belong to himself, but that he is public property. Let him be taught to love his family, but let him be taught at the same time that he must forsake and even forget them when the welfare of his country requires it.[27]

Rush's view has perhaps intentional parallels to Jesus's admonition to would-be disciples, "If anyone comes to me and does not hate father and mother, wife and children, brothers and sisters—yes, even their own life— such a person cannot be my disciple."[28] Rush probably did not want to put the state on par with God, but he certainly elevated attachment to the state, at the expense even of family.

John Adams was of a somewhat similar bent to Mann and Rush, calling on public schooling to create virtuous citizens, which would translate into love of, and service to, their country, as well as lending itself to the belief that the people themselves are sovereign. Writing to his British friend John Jebb in 1785, Adams asserted:

> When Children and Youth hear their Parents and Neighbours and all about them applauding the Love of Country or Labour of Liberty and all the Virtues Habits and Faculties which constitute a good Citizen, that is a Patriot and an Hero— those Children indeavour to acquire those qualities and a sensible and Virtuous People will never fail to form Multitudes of Patriots and Heroes.[29]

Beyond the borders of the United States, Emile Durkheim, often thought to be the father of sociology, saw education as the key to replacing morality based in religion with morality based in one's attachment to, and care for, others. In particular, not unlike many in the Founding Era who hoped to unite the people of the new United States in fraternal feelings, Durkheim believed that inculcating attachment to one's country was paramount. "[M]orality begins where and when social life begins, but there are nonetheless different degrees of morality," Durkheim writes. "Now there is one that enjoys a real primacy over all the others—the political society, the nation."[30]

Social Control

The goal of reproducing society has already been discussed at length, and it is one form of social control. Another has been to *change* society by implanting in children different values, beliefs, and understandings than those of their parents, communities, or even most of society. This has been the aim of many policymakers and theorists, including some progressives who seemed to desire both social reproduction *and* change through the schools. Change by destroying the cultures and values of many ethnic groups, and reproduction by judging students' aptitudes and abilities, and deeming most destined for the economic status quo: factory work.

Some progressives were aiming for especially radical reformation of society through public schooling. George Counts, an American educator, academic, and one-time head of the American Federation of Teachers, told the members of the Progressive Education Association, in speeches assembled in *Dare the School Build a New Social Order?,* that it was the job of educators to indoctrinate children in revolutionary social ideas:

> Progressive Education . . . must . . . face squarely and courageously every social issue, come to grips with life in all its stark reality, establish an organic relationship with the community, develop a realistic and comprehensive theory of welfare, fashion a compelling and challenging vision of human destiny, and become less frightened than it is today of the bogies *imposition* and *indoctrination*.[31]

For Counts, the key connection between democracy and education was not democratic control of the schools, but that the schools be harnessed to shape students so they would demand Counts's preferred vision of democracy: leveling of political power and wealth largely by pulling down the wealthy, with little regard for the components and processes of government:

> Democracy of course should not be identified with political forms and functions—with the federal constitution, the popular election of officials, or the practice of universal suffrage. . . . The most genuine expression of democracy in the United States has little to do with political institutions: it is a sentiment with respect to the moral equality of men: it is an aspiration towards a society in which this sentiment will find complete fulfillment.[32]

He went on:

> We must . . . insist on two things: first, that technology be released from the fetters and the domination of every type of special privilege; and second, that the resulting system of production and distribution be made to serve directly the masses of the people. Within these limits, as I see it, our democratic tradition must of necessity evolve and gradually assume an essentially collectivist pattern. The only conceivable alternative is the abandonment of the last vestige of democracy and the frank adoption of some modern form of feudalism.[33]

The Educational Frontier, a 1933 book by seven progressive authors, including John Dewey and William Heard Kilpatrick, is similarly focused on public schooling to remake American society, stating that "individualism" is a mindset that has dominated American thought but is dangerous and outmoded in the Industrial Era. The authors see many "evils" in society and determine them to be "rooted . . . in the very structure of our *laissez faire* profits system economy."[34] They assert that the education system should be used to challenge existing structures and spur experimentation away from individualism.

Their revolutionary approach "is the only one compatible with the democratic way of life. . . . Every extension of intelligence as the method of action enlarges the area of common understanding."[35] The people would have to be prodded by educators to think against the old ways, and when they did they would themselves prod education for more change. And the direction of that change, as also advocated by Counts, would be toward the toppling-the-rich democracy that Socrates warned about.

While Counts and the *Educational Frontier* authors may have been among the more up-front proponents of using the schools to engineer a new society, they were hardly alone. It was, for instance, an inescapable consequence of inculcating virtue. And Benjamin Rush, while not saying he wanted to remake society, was straightforward in stating that a primary function of public schooling was, essentially, to make all children the same so that they would not pose a threat of instability when granted freedom and democratic power. The intent was to basically mold the individual while a child so their freedom as an adult would be "safe."

A different twist on the social reproduction nexus with democracy is Amy Gutmann's thesis that social control is a necessary aim of education. In her view, recall, it is fine to impose educational decisions as long as a "deliberative" and "democratic" process was used to make the decisions, and they do not result in discrimination against, or repression of, specific groups. A public schooling system does not so much serve a democratic nation as employing a vaguely democratic process justifies *whatever education decisions are made*.

Note that the carveouts that seem to protect liberty—the nondiscrimination and nonrepression provisos—are truncated. Gutmann defines "nonrepression" as preventing "the state, and any group within it, from using education to restrict rational deliberation of competing conceptions of the good life and society."[36] Of course, Gutmann gets to define "rational," for instance saying that the Old Order Amish would be tough to defend under nonrepression because their lifestyle requires "resistance to rational deliberation."[37] And "nondiscrimination"? It just means no one may be excluded from education, doing nothing to protect against tyranny of the majority, or a powerful minority, in deciding what is taught, and how.

System of Togetherness

Today, the "system of togetherness" conception of the necessity of public schooling to democracy may be the most widely held among high-profile public schooling advocates. It asserts that public schooling, done right, essentially *is* democracy, because it is the only arena in which adults can have a full, concrete say in their community's future. It perhaps best captures the idea that public schooling is a public good, something that contributes far beyond the benefits individuals derive. Beyond skills and knowledge people can sell to employers, public schooling creates good citizens, common bonds, and enables all people to help shape the collective future.

Adherents to this conception tend to stress that truly democratic education requires primarily local decision-making, and must be as close as possible to the New England town meeting, in which each citizen can speak and vote on every issue. The idealized little red schoolhouse may capture this most viscerally, evoking images of rural folks gathering for spelling bees, picnics, and other social affairs.[38] Or maybe Norman Rockwell's *Freedom of Speech*, depicting a leathery man in a blue flannel shirt and dingy, drab jacket standing to speak on some matter of importance to a small Vermont town.

The focus on localism and democracy is closely akin to—and probably derived from—the broad, 1960s progressive backlash against centralized, technocratic control of "democratic" government that was itself the product of progressive reforms. Of course, in the latter case elites who distrusted sometimes corrupt and parochial local control consolidated authority and put "experts" in charge.[39] The localism reaction to that was very much a "New Left" versus "Old Left" movement, though many conservatives, moderates, and liberals alike have strong attachments to local control of education.

Several education thinkers probably belong under this New Left heading. Included would be historian David Tyack, progressive educator Deborah Meier, president of the Charles F. Kettering Foundation David Mathews, and historian and public schooling activist Diane Ravitch.[40] A prominent reason many adherents cherish locally controlled public schooling is that its governance effectively forces everyone in a community together, and in so doing is itself a school of sorts, one in which adults of myriad views and backgrounds learn to debate, reason, and compromise with one another.

"In socially diverse places the common ground in school policies was often procedural, a willingness to follow democratic rules in arriving at decisions," Tyack writes. "At its best, school governance was itself educational, as citizens debated with one another about how the community should educate the next generation."[41] Ravitch is more ebullient:

> The neighborhood school is the place where parents meet to share concerns about their children and the place where they learn the practice of democracy. They create a sense of community among strangers. As we lose public schools, we lose the one local institution where people congregate and mobilize to solve local problems, where individuals learn to speak up and debate and engage in democratic give-and-take with their neighbors. For more than a century they have been an essential element of our democratic institutions. We abandon them at our peril.[42]

Schools of Togetherness

It may seem odd to have both a "system of togetherness" and "schools of togetherness," but there is a difference. While the former emphasizes the benefits of bringing adults together in democratic deliberation, the latter is focused on bringing diverse children together so that they can discover each other's common humanity and live peacefully and effectively together in a democratic country. The former values the effect of democratic deliberation on adults, the latter the preparation of children for democratic adulthood. What they have in common is preparing people to overcome their differences and live harmoniously in associated life.

John Dewey stands at the front of this group, as he most famously emphasized student-centered and directed learning among children of diverse backgrounds, with a goal of dissolving barriers of class, race, and religion. Of course, he was not alone. Traces of this can be found in Mann, Webster, and others who argued that a benefit of public schooling would be drawing together, or at least blurring distinctions among, children of different classes, ethnicities, or regions. But these thinkers typically ignored student-directed learning, and thus, as mentioned in the last chapter, the mutual self-interest and pursuit of common goals crucial for "bridging."

The ideal of "schools of togetherness" lives on, at least in the abstract. Probably few people who believe that schools are best when their student bodies are diverse feel that way explicitly because they think such compositions are ideal for a harmonious life in a country where the people are sovereign. Regardless, as discussed earlier, huge majorities say they want such diverse schools. Presumably, this is because even if they do not explicitly connect integrated students and democracy, they intuitively sense that it would be beneficial if a nation of diverse people had their children in classes with diverse others.

This is quite possibly what animates "public schooling ideology"—a devotion to public schooling no matter how it performs—identified by Terry Moe in his polling discussed in chapter one. Of course, as already tackled, this sense has not come close to translating into truly diverse schools, much less classrooms. As people have both stated and demonstrated with their feet, they may think integration is important, but not at the expense of attending the school closest to one's oft-segregated home.

A very direct function of the public schools should probably go under this heading, one that often gets lost in philosophical and political grappling over what public schooling is supposed to do: teaching civics. Public schools should inform children about the concrete components of their shared government: how bills become laws, federalism, jury duty, voting, and all the other mechanism and tools of "democracy." The necessity of public schools, in this regard, is to ensure that all children are taught these ties of citizenship rather than keeping education private and leaving "to chance" whether children receive such instruction.

Levelers

While it did not enjoy the prominence of creating virtuous or easily managed citizens in the formative years of public schooling, the belief that universal public schooling would level society by giving everyone the tools to perform to the peak of their natural ability was also a selling point. It may be the conception most consistent with what seems to be a popular use of "democratic": making everyone equal. Jefferson and Mann discussed it, as did others. Even administrative progressives likely believed it, only with the proviso that they were far more capable of determining a child's natural ability than the child or his parents.

This leveling is distinct from what Socrates warned about, and was embraced by Counts and other members of the social control school. This is about enabling the poor to rise, not pulling down the wealthy. In this framing, the public schools are sometimes described as a ladder that enables even children born into the lowest of circumstances to climb as high as their abilities allow. The schools equip children with the knowledge and skills they need regardless of their families' ability to pay. As Mary McCorkle, a South Dakota teachers' union official once said, "Our public schools are the great equalizer, the provider of opportunity for all our students."[43]

That public schooling is an equalizer may be the most commonly held conception today, though again many people likely do not think explicitly in those terms. Policy for decades has been driven by essentially one goal—raising test scores—and the primacy of "achievement" has been clear since at least the 1983 publication of *A Nation at Risk*, a federal report that intoned, "If an unfriendly foreign power had attempted to impose on America the mediocre educational performance that exists today, we might well have viewed it as an act of war."[44] This reached its apogee with the No Child Left Behind Act.

The leveling construction of democracy is not so much about a form of government as a state of society; everyone roughly equal. NCLB called for progress not just for students overall, but raising the performance of lagging groups—African Americans, low-income students, English language learners—to the level of leaders. This is what oft-heard "closing the achievement gap" is about. Not that the focus on gaps, which were for a long time studiously and legally ignored, is brand new. The inherent inequality of "separate but equal" was central to *Brown v. Board* in 1954, and "achievement gap" came into use around the mid-1960s.[45]

CONCLUSION

It is constantly asserted that public schooling is essential to democracy. But far too often that assertion is put forth without defining what the speaker means by "democracy." Perhaps as a result there seem to be numerous, often poorly differentiated, conceptions of the relationship between public schooling and our supposedly democratic system of government. The end result can range from elite, bureaucratic control of schooling in which "experts" decide what all children will be and should learn, to local control in which every citizen is able to vote on every decision, exercising true democratic power and, perhaps, teaching people to live harmoniously.

These are, of course, often incompatible goals. You cannot have both true, democratic local control and centralized, expert decision-making. Similarly, you cannot have students conducting self-directed work and school boards requiring teachers to deliver lessons on, say, the importance of voting. And as the next chapter plumbs deeply, you cannot logically say that the purpose of democracy is to protect liberty *and* that the education system best suited for democracy is one in which a majority, or powerful minority, dictates what *every* child will learn.

NOTES

1. Michael Birnbaum, "Texas Board Approves Social Studies Standards That Perceived Liberal Bias," *Washington Post*, May 22, 2010; Need to Know Editor, "Texas School Board Approves Controversial Textbook Changes," PBS, May 23, 2010.

2. Benjamin R. Barber, "Public Schooling: Education for Democracy," in *The Public Purpose of Education and Schooling*, eds. John I. Goodlad and Timothy J. McMannon (San Francisco: Jossey-Bass, 1997), 22.

3. Deborah Meier, *In Schools We Trust: Creating Communities of Learning in an Era of Testing and Standardization* (Boston: Beacon Press, 2002), 177.

4. Jeffrey R. Henig, *Rethinking School Choice: Limits of the Market Metaphor* (Princeton, NJ: Princeton University Press, 1994), 10.

5. Plato, *The Republic*, trans. Desmond Lee (London: Penguin Books, 1987), 376.

6. Plato, *The Republic*, 386.

7. *The Politics of Aristotle*, trans. Peter L. Phillips Simpson (Chapel Hill, NC: The University of North Carolina Press, 1997), 142.

8. *The Politics of Aristotle*, 180.

9. Thomas Hobbes, *Leviathan*, ed. Crawford B. Macpherson (London: Penguin Books, 1968), 227.

10. Hobbes, *Leviathan*, 266.

11. Lorraine Smith Pangle and Thomas L. Pangle, *The Learning of Liberty: The Educational Ideas of the American Founders* (Lawrence, KS: University of Kansas Press, 1993), 55.

12. John Locke, *Two Treatises of Government*, ed. Peter Laslett (Cambridge, UK: Cambridge University Press, 1994), 269.

13. Locke, *Two Treatises,* 278–282.

14. Ibid., 306.

15. Ibid., 331.

16. Ibid., 361.

17. Montesquieu, *The Spirit of the Laws*, eds. Anne Cohler, Basia Miller, and Harold Stone, (Cambridge, UK: Cambridge University Press, 1992), 155.

18. James Madison, *Federalist* no. 10, in *The Federalist Papers*, ed. Clinton Rossiter (New York: Mentor Books, 1961), 81.

19. Madison, *Federalist no. 47,* 303–308.

20. Alexander Hamilton, *Federalist no. 84, The Federalist Papers*, 513–514.

21. Eric Foner, *The Story of American Freedom* (New York: W. W. Norton & Company, 1998), 154–155.

22. U.S. Department of Education, "Race to the Top Program Executive Summary," November 2009, https://www2.ed.gov/programs/racetothetop/executive-summary.pdf; and Department of Education, 34 CFR Subtitle B, Chapter II, Race to the Top Fund; Final Rule, *Code of Federal Regulations*, November 18, 2009, https://www.gpo.gov/fdsys/pkg/FR-2009-11-18/pdf/E9-27426.pdf.

23. U.S. Department of Education, "ESEA Flexibility," June 7, 2012, https://www2.ed.gov/policy/elsec/guid/esea-flexibility/index.html.

24. Lisa Graham Keegan and Chester E. Finn, Jr., "Lost at Sea: Time to Jettison One of the Chief Obstacles to Reform: The Local School Board," *Education Next* 4, no. 3 (Summer 2004), 16.

25. Thomas Jefferson, "Notes on the State of Virginia," in *Jefferson: Writings*, comp. Merrill D. Peterson (New York: Literary Classics of the U.S., 1984), 274.

26. Horace Mann, "Report for 1848," in *Life and Works of Horace Mann*, ed. Mary Mann (Boston: Horace B. Fuller, 1868), 689.

27. Benjamin Rush, "Thoughts upon the Mode of Education Proper in a Republic," in *Essays on Education in the Early Republic*, ed. Frederick Rudolph (Cambridge, MA: The Belknap Press of Harvard University Press, 1965), 13–14.

28. Luke 14:26 (New International Version).

29. John Adams, "John Adams to John Jebb, September 10, 1785," Founders Online, https://founders.archives.gov/documents/Adams/06-17-02-0232.

30. Emile Durkheim, *Moral Education* (Mineola, NY: Dover Publications, 2002), 79.

31. George S. Counts, *Dare the School Build a New Social Order?* (Carbondale, IL: Southern Illinois University Press, 1978), 7.

32. Counts, *Dare the School*, 37–38.

33. Ibid., 42–43.

34. William H. Kilpatrick et al., *The Educational Frontier* (New York: The Century Company, 1933), 145.

35. Kilpatrick, et al., *The Educational Frontier*, 317.

36. Amy Gutmann, *Democratic Education* (Princeton, NJ: Princeton Paperbacks, 1999), 44.

37. Gutmann, *Democratic Education*.

38. For a great discussion of the heavily freighted little red schoolhouse, see Jonathan Zimmerman, *Small Wonder: The Little Red Schoolhouse in History and Memory* (New Haven, CT: Yale University Press, 2009).

39. Foner, *Story of American Freedom*, 289–290.

40. See David Tyack, *Seeking Common Ground: Public Schools in a Diverse Society* (Cambridge, MA: Harvard University Press, 2003); Meier, *In Schools We Trust: Creating Communities of Learning in an Era of Testing and Standardization*; David Mathews, *Reclaiming Public Education by Reclaiming Our Democracy* (Dayton, OH: Kettering Foundation Press, 2006); Diane Ravitch, *The Death and Life of the Great American School System: How Testing and Choice Are Undermining Education*.

41. Tyack, *Seeking Common Ground*, 184.

42. Ravitch, *Death and Life of the Great American School System*, 220–221.

43. James Nord, "Backers Lay Groundwork for South Dakota's School Choice Law," *Rapid City Journal*, June 10, 2016, http://rapidcityjournal.com/news/latest/backers-lay-groundwork-for-south-dakota-s-school-choice-law/article_4e96a0aa-a972-5ddf-ba68-eff46839cd8d.html.

44. National Commission on Excellence in Education, *A Nation at Risk: The Imperative for Educational Reform*, April 1983, https://www2.ed.gov/pubs/NatAtRisk/risk.html.

45. Michael Salmonowicz, "A Short History of the Term 'Achievement Gap' (or Is It 'Gaps'?), *True/Slant*, October 3, 2009, http://trueslant.com/michaelsalmonowicz/2009/10/03/history-of-the-achievement-gap/.

Chapter 5

American Values

In 2004—nearly eight decades after the acrimonious spectacle of the Scopes Trial—Dover, Pennsylvania, was aflame over the teaching of the origins of life. The proximate cause was a school board dictum that all ninth-grade biology students be told that Darwinian evolution is a theory, not a fact, and that they be directed to the intelligent design-promoting book Of Pandas and People *to learn more. In December 2005, federal judge John E. Jones III ruled that the district's policy unconstitutionally advanced religion. The social fabric of the town, however, had already been set ablaze. As ABC News reported about a year earlier:*

> *The argument in Dover is of a special kind, where to let the other side win a little is to lose your own cause entirely.*
>
> *"Unfortunately, I think somebody simply has to win," [Dover resident Brian] Ream said. "My side right now is for science education."*
>
> *[Resident Ray] Mummert said, "I can't make you believe what I believe," and that he recognizes the rights of all faiths in America. But he does not want to be told—condescendingly, he feels—that there are places where his faith does not belong.*
>
> *"Part of what is so frustrating to me is this dichotomy in the life of all humans, where we want to keep God over here in this little building," he said. "'OK, so you come here and we'll tell you all about God.' Now, you come out to the public education, and we're not going to say anything about God."*[1]

For many thinkers and advocates, public schooling is wrapped up in democracy. Creating a citizenry fit for democracy—either in virtue, uniformity, or ability to deliberate and compromise for collective action—is paramount. But is this consistent and compatible with what may be *the* fundamental American value: liberty?

There is no question that social harmony, and democratic decision-making when government *must* act, are important—there's a reason we have a Democratic Party, celebrate the creation of peaceful government by popular consent, and fixate on elections. But is public schooling consistent with the truly bedrock American value of human freedom? Or does it undermine liberty in the name of the governmental system—"democracy"—that is supposed to *protect* liberty?

This chapter grapples with the great paradox of public schooling—schooling controlled by government to serve a free society—and answers the basic question: Is such an education system consistent with the most basic of American values?

The answer is "no."

WHAT IS THE FOUNDATIONAL AMERICAN VALUE?

Democracy. Patriotism. Free markets. While all of these are important and often cherished features of American life, none is the country's ultimate, indispensable, bedrock value. To varying degrees, they are all valuable only to the extent to which they preserve, and are consistent with, the true foundational value: *individual liberty*.

Roughly defined from a political standpoint, "liberty" is the ability of human beings to conduct their lives according to their own wills, not government control. The root caveat to this is but one: all other people must be able to do the same. In other words, people must be able to live free from force by others, and unable to initiate force themselves. A correlate of this is the prohibition on fraud. Lying to a person to get them to act has the same effect as force: it uses deception to make someone do something they would not freely choose.

Importantly, it is not at odds with liberty to use persuasion, or incentives in the form of shunning people whose views one finds abhorrent, or showering affection on people whose behavior you like, to try to convince them to do what you want. Liberty does not mean non-judgmentalism, or relativism about right and wrong. Properly understood, it simply means freedom from force imposed by others; to be able to choose for oneself how one will live as long as one respects the same basic right of others.

This is the only philosophy of government consistent with the most basic reality of human life: we are all individuals. There are no collective minds, even if there are decisions made for and by groups. Even as members of sometimes very intimate communities—families, neighborhoods, churches, and so on—only individuals have minds, and all decisions are, ultimately, made by individual members who must choose to either give or withhold their consent to group decisions, and to persist in or exit those groups. The individual is the only irreducible and truly autonomous component of human existence.

That protecting liberty is the ultimate, bedrock purpose of American government is clear. As the Declaration of Independence states, government is instituted "to secure" the rights to "life, liberty, and the pursuit of happiness." The preamble of the Constitution proclaims that the function of the government the Constitution establishes is to "secure the Blessings of Liberty" to all Americans. And what does the Pledge of Allegiance tout? "Liberty and justice for all."

Much of the thought around American independence sounded themes of individual liberty. In calling for independence from England, Thomas Paine's "Common Sense"—proportionate to the country's population at the time, the top-selling publication in American history—declared that "this new world hath been the asylum for the persecuted lovers of civil and religious liberty from *every part* of Europe."[2] For John Locke, the primary role of government was to secure the people's individual liberty and property. As noted in the previous chapter, Locke wrote in his *Second Treatise of Government*:

> *the end of Law* is not to abolish or restrain, but *to preserve and enlarge Freedom*: For in all the states of created beings capable of Laws, *where there is no Law, there is no Freedom*. For *Liberty* is to be free from restraint and violence from others which cannot be, where there is no Law.[3]

George Washington, in a message to state governments upon his retirement from the Continental Army, wrote about "four things . . . essential to the well being" of the country: an "indissoluble" union of states; "Public Justice," "a proper Peace Establishment"; and a "pacific and friendly disposition" among all people in the country. And "Liberty is the Basis" for all those "pillars."[4]

Liberty was at the center of formational American political philosophy. Its importance can still be seen several decades after enactment of the Constitution. Alexis de Tocqueville, in his famous reflections on the United States in the 1830s, observed not just that Americans were far more independent of government than Europeans, but that religion, aided by the separation of church and state, compelled people to act justly with one another without the force of government: "The Americans combine the notions of Christianity and of liberty so intimately in their minds that it is impossible to make them conceive the one without the other."[5]

In 1848, the "Declaration of Sentiments" produced at the Seneca Falls women's rights convention deliberately mimicked the Declaration of Independence, including invoking the rights of "life, liberty, and the pursuit of happiness."[6] While the declaration contained much on social and cultural inequality, especially in churches, it decried, first and foremost, women's having been denied "the elective franchise," and when it came to husbands and wives, "the law giving him power to deprive her of her liberty."

Those who inveighed against slavery also invoked liberty as the essential characteristic of the nation. William Lloyd Garrison, after invoking the Founders in the 1833 "Declaration of Sentiments of the American Anti-Slavery Convention," opined, "The right to enjoy liberty is inalienable. . . . Every man has a right to his own body—to the products of his own labor—to the protection of law—and to the common advantages of society."[7] Asked Frederick Douglass in an 1852 oration on the 4th of July, "Would you have me argue that man is entitled to liberty? That he is the rightful owner of his own body? You have already declared it."[8]

Finally, what is the most renowned symbol of the United States, save, perhaps, its flag? The Statue of *Liberty*. And to whom does the description at its base call out?

Your tired, your poor,
Your huddled masses yearning to breathe free.

And what is breathing "free" if not having liberty?

Crucially, liberty is not the same thing as atomization or self-reliance. Liberty allows for countless ways of living in community with other people, whether through bowling leagues or joining a, well, commune. Indeed, liberty is a prerequisite for real community—a network of interpersonal relationships based in mutual consent—which is also consistent with Gordon Allport's provisos for successful intergroup contact. Emotional ties among people cannot be forced. They must come from each person.

DEMOCRACY AND LIBERTY

To read many treatments of history, you could well believe that democracy, not liberty, is the foundational American value, as many public schooling champions have suggested. And representative government—often broadly and imprecisely called "democracy"—is important. It was central to Locke, who held that legitimate government could only rightly come from a legislative body chosen by the people. The Constitution established an elected national government, which each state had also done. And the great rallying cry leading to the revolution was "no taxation without representation." Democracy and liberty seem to go hand in hand.

Or do they? As historian Eric Foner has pointed out, while the Founders very much wanted "the people," as opposed to a monarch, to be sovereign, the seeming dual centrality of individual freedom and government by the people would ultimately be in great tension. What happens when "the people" want to impose something on free individuals against their will? Or take things from them?

Despite the obvious potential for clashes, in the national discourse, both in revolutionary and modern days, the terms "freedom" and "liberty" have often been used interchangeably with "democracy," presenting potentially oppositional concepts as if they were one. As Foner writes of the revolutionary era:

> Many leaders of the Revolution seem to the modern eye simultaneously republican (in their concern for the public good and citizens' obligations to the polity) and liberal (in their preoccupation with individual rights). Both political ideologies could inspire a commitment to constitutional government, freedom of speech and religion, and restraints on arbitrary power. Both emphasized the security of property as a foundation of freedom.[9]

One major reason that the Founders could simultaneously support liberty and republicanism is that they thought the two were intimately connected, as articulated by Locke. People of their own free will give up some of the liberty enjoyed in the state of nature to enter society with other people, and in so doing to secure their natural liberty against the depredations of others. Essentially, people enter society to ensure that one person's liberty ends where another's nose begins, to borrow shorthand for the libertarian view of government.

That necessitates the creation of government. But government is only legitimate if it is *freely entered into* and *controlled by the governed*. The goal of government is to "secure liberty," and the basic form of government most consistent with individual liberty is one in which individuals have equal say.

Simple democracy, however, is not sufficient to uphold individual liberty, leaving political minorities subject to the power of majorities. To deal with this, many early American states had bills of rights to protect specific freedoms. Most, following Montesquieu, also had at least some separation of power among legislative houses, executives, and judiciaries.

The national government was, of course, designed to restrain its own scope and power. The Constitution creates multiple checks and balances among branches, only gives the government specific powers, and eventually included the Bill of Rights. As mentioned in the previous chapter, one of the major ratification debates was whether the document would include a list of specific, individual rights that would be protected from government encroachment. The primary argument *against* such a listing was itself grounded in protecting liberty: an enumeration of rights could imply that all rights *not* explicitly mentioned could be curbed.

In recognition of this threat, the Bill of Rights contains two amendments that explicitly state what the enumerated-power logic of the Constitution already contains. The Ninth Amendment says that "the enumeration . . . of certain rights shall not be construed to deny or disparage others retained by the people." The Tenth Amendment states that any power not given to Washington resides with the states or people.

Basically, if the Constitution does not explicitly give the national government a power, it does not have it. It resides with the people, unless they give it to their states. And through the Fourteenth Amendment, ratified in 1868, protections of specific rights are incorporated against state and local government incursions.

American "democracy"—representative government with extensive checks and balances among powers—was intended to preserve and protect liberty, which was the lodestar of American political formation. This directly invalidates many of the "democratic" justifications for public schooling, which subjugate individual liberty to collective decision-making. What does this mean for the validity of various models of education and democracy discussed in the last chapter?

Informed Citizens

When it comes to respecting liberty, this is among the less problematic conceptions of the role of public schooling in a democracy, because it is aimed at enabling the people to make wise and defensive political decisions more than to "fit" them for safe and easy governance. With an emphasis especially on history, however, it hits a snag we see constantly bedeviling people: who gets to decide what—and whose—history is taught, and interpret what it means? One need look no further than the Revolutionary period—the era when Thomas Jefferson, the exemplar of the "informed citizens" school, made his name—to see how interpretations of history vary.

One heavily debated question has been whether the Founders truly desired liberty, or were just rich men trying to avoid taxes and keep their slaves. And did keeping slaves make them intolerable hypocrites?[10] Historian Jonathan Zimmerman has shown that treatment of the Revolution in the public schools changed, with historians in the 1920s downplaying negative views of Great Britain in early American history and, seemingly, positive aspects of the Revolution. Meanwhile, various ethnic groups with beefs against the British took issue with the change, while arguing to have their contributions to the Revolution magnified.

It is said, "History is written by the winners," and there certainly seems to be truth to that. As mentioned in chapter two, the teaching of history in Tucson, Arizona, was long a conflagration. Among many things, powerful opponents of the ethnic studies curriculum bemoaned that it taught that Mexican territory ceded to the United States after the Mexican–American War, including large tracts of present-day California, Nevada, Utah, Arizona, New Mexico, Texas, and Colorado, was illegally obtained and rightfully belongs to Mexico.[11]

This is debatable, but hardly beyond the pale. Henry David Thoreau spent a night in jail for refusing to pay a Massachusetts tax in support of the Mexican–American War, which he thought an illegitimate attack on another country in an effort to expand slavery. That evening of imprisonment inspired Thoreau's famous essay "Civil Disobedience," and historians to this day debate whether the war was justified by Mexican aggression or driven by American imperialism.

The state of Arizona, however, seemingly ruled that taking that side was unacceptable, passing a law in 2010 prohibiting lessons in public schools that would "promote the overthrow of the United States government . . . promote resentment toward a race or class of people . . . (or) advocate ethnic solidarity instead of treatment of pupils as individuals."[12] Depending on the rigor of the enforcement, the law could forbid any teaching suggesting that any group had ever been mistreated, or had mistreated others. It could, in fact, sideline minority views and free inquiry, and impose orthodoxy by force, rather than preparing students to detect threats of tyranny.

State responses to the controversial 1619 Project and ideas subsumed under "critical race theory" pose the same danger. In 2021, many states considered legislation forbidding such teachings as "the United States" is "fundamentally or systemically racist."[13] The stated intent was typically to block inaccurate teaching about the country, and certainly there is reason to believe the United States is not systematically racist. Our ideal, again, is liberty, and many races have become fully integrated, legally equal Americans.

That said, there is evidence of systemic racism, including centuries of slavery and legally mandated segregation, discriminatory housing policy, and police misconduct against African Americans. Understandably, some people saw the proposals as attempts to block the teaching of uncomfortable history. "Educators in states where such bills become law would be blocked from teaching about the racist roots of Western society, generally, and the United States, specifically, and how racism continues to plague us," wrote African American educator Rann Miller.[14]

History is complicated and contentious. Public schools employing it to train children how to ferret out dangerous politicians or politics would have a hard time identifying the historical saints and scoundrels, doing so without upsetting related modern-day groups, and sounding alarms before it was too late to block the bad guys. The "informed citizens" justification for public schooling, while at first blush appearing to pose little threat to liberty, brings into play a potentially dreadful weapon: government control over the retelling of all of human existence.

Virtuous Citizens

The contentiousness of history may be surprising—isn't it just "one damned thing after another"?—but rancor over what constitutes a virtuous citizen should not shock at all. From debates thousands of years old among philosophical schools, to religious disputes today, "virtue" is a constant battleground. And we know it has disrupted public schools from the ringing of the very first bell.

As discussed, Mann and other public schooling advocates saw "virtue" as a combination of selflessness and Protestant values, the latter vaguely characterized by no allegiance to a politically connected, established church, and individual interpretation of scripture. As soon as public schooling advocates started to concretize this, however, old allies sometimes came to loggerheads. Recall that Benjamin Rush and Noah Webster were at odds over the place of the Bible in schools; Rush thought it essential, Webster thought it trivializing. Rush argued that virtue includes a paramount sense of duty to the state, Mann warned that a citizenry wanting in virtue would create a monstrous state to crush others.

Returning to the Mexican–American War, a monster is exactly what some people believed the country had become. Indeed, the jingoistic concept of Manifest Destiny would pit the ideas of Rush against those of Mann. Manifest Destiny essentially held that the right thing for the United States—and hence virtuous citizens—was to export American dominion, by force if necessary. In contrast, recall that Mann feared the republic becoming an "obscene giant . . . whose brain has been developed only in the region of the appetites and passions." This is very similar to how, in "Civil Disobedience," Thoreau described the nation:

> A common and natural result of an undue respect for law is, that you may see a file of soldiers, colonel, captain, corporal, privates, powder-monkeys, and all, marching in admirable order over hill and dale to the wars, against their wills, ay, against their common sense and consciences, which makes it very steep marching indeed, and produces a palpitation of the heart. They have no doubt that it is a damnable business in which they are concerned; they are all peaceably inclined. Now, what are they? Men at all? or small movable forts and magazines, at the service of some unscrupulous man in power? . . . The mass of men serve the state thus, not as men mainly, but as machines, with their bodies.[15]

Beyond associating virtue with selfless service to the state is the idea that virtue is inherently connected to Protestant values. This would hardly be a universal view for many Americans, even just from a theological perspective. Roman Catholics, of course, consider it virtuous to obey the teachings of the Church. Jews, adherence to the Mosaic law. Muslims, to the teachings of Muhammad. And for many people, virtue need not have a religious basis at all.

Conflicts over what is the "right" thing to do are common occurrences in modern public schooling. Recall that the Cato Institute's Public Schooling Battle Map includes a category of conflicts called "moral values" that contains battles over "right" policies or actions that are not explicitly grounded in religion, freedom of speech, or other clear categories. In other words, it is a bit of a catch-all. But it also captures battles for which the "virtuous" action is not obvious or agreed upon.[16]

Government schools inculcating virtue can only work without violating liberty if individuals—the people democracy is supposed to protect—all agree on what constitutes virtue, including concrete attitudes, attachments, and acts. But they do not, meaning that when government forces one concept of virtue on everyone, it directly violates freedom of conscience, thought, and belief.

Social Control

There is no way to square social control with liberty. Whether it is to transform society through public schooling àla George Counts, or "social reproduction" through "deliberative democracy," using a government schooling system to engineer society is inherently in conflict with liberty. If the goal is to transform society through the schools, the change will have to be imposed against the will of some, and quite possibly many millions of people. It may also trample on fundamental beliefs and values, including religious convictions that are supposed to be immune from government actions under the First Amendment.

On the flip side, if the status quo is maintained, that too will represent inequality under the law—those who want or need change will remain subjugated. Think Mexican Americans in places like Tucson who wish to learn about their families' histories. Or Christians in states that require "comprehensive" sex ed who want their kids to get abstinence-only instruction because they believe it is the only morally acceptable approach.

The social control framework basically demands top-down control, often via mechanisms that are at best only marginally democratic. Elites during the Progressive Era consolidated school districts and imposed uniformity and "scientific management," though through a putatively democratic process.

Meanwhile, deliberative democracy only holds that everyone affected by a policy should get to *say* something about it, and does not even spell out how loudly or often. As long as one gets to utter one's thoughts, one must accept whatever the majority imposes.

This leads to tyranny of the majority or politically powerful minorities. What it does not do is protect individual liberty. Indeed, it would make acceptable what the U.S. Supreme Court ruled against in *Pierce v. Society of Sisters*: the child becoming "the mere creature of the state," as long as a majority voted to do so, and those against it got to emit a peep.

Legal scholar Stephen Arons wrote two books on the consequences of top-down control education. He itemized the conflict and inherent inequality of such a system, capturing the inescapable danger of trying to create uniformly thinking adults: "Under these conditions the government becomes a kind of perpetual-motion machine, legitimizing its long-term policies through the world view and public opinion it creates."[17] Constant battles over basic values and identities—from black hairstyles violating dress codes, to battles over LGBTQ books—provide incessant testimony to the social control model's incompatibility with freedom and harmony.

There is only one way in which the social control conception of public schooling could be consonant with individual liberty: teaching that the only inviolable American value is to not impose on others by force or fraud. As John Stuart Mill wrote, "the only purpose for which power can be rightly exercised over any member of a civilized community, against his will, is to prevent harm to others."[18] But, as we have seen repeatedly, promoting that understanding is not what the major social controllers have sought to inculcate.

Most who have advocated for social control through schooling have either tried to maintain society as it is, or change it in ways they saw fit, whether it has been administrative progressives employing IQ tests to furnish the next cohort of factory drones, or Christians demanding school prayer to instill their values in the upcoming generation. The desires of students, parents, or anyone without political clout, meanwhile, have been shunted aside. And it has been cold comfort that they might have had a chance to squeak out their objections before the boot landed on them.

System of Togetherness

No conception of democracy and education places democracy higher above liberty than this one. It holds that the most important attribute of public schooling is that it forces diverse people together so they must hash out what their collective children will learn, how they will learn it, and from whom.

Aside from the reality that for most of our history public schools likely did not serve particularly heterogeneous populations, the system of togetherness framework is by its very nature doomed to the tyranny of the majority. Many citizens may be willing to compromise some of their beliefs and values to achieve desired educational ends, but that is just a soft form of tyranny. They are being forced to sacrifice things they think are important to get some semblance of the education they want.

Of course, some matters are non-negotiable, leading to heated, divisive conflicts that sometimes end up in court, or force parents to pay first for public schools, and a second time for private or homeschooling. For many of the families of the country's roughly 7.4 million private and homeschooled children, the latter is almost certainly the case.[19]

This school of thought tends to view local democratic control of education as preferable to state or national, where the voice of the average citizen is reduced to almost nothing. Adherents also tend to dislike bureaucratic, expert control, and they aim for "child-centered" instruction that treats children somewhat as individuals. Kettering Foundation president David Mathews, for instance, laments that people have lost the sense that the public schools belong to them, as such impositions as uniform standards and testing dictates have arrived from state and federal governments.[20]

One of the three things progressive educator Deborah Meier identifies as essential to creating good schools is "choice" (the others are school self-governance and small size).[21] For Mathews, the key to renewal is local people and institutions, including businesses and teachers, deciding that they own schooling and, more broadly, education of their community. But neither Meier nor Mathews can let go of government control, despite how little choice and truly local control it has ultimately allowed.

"Why save public education?" Meier asks. Because "[it] is in schools that we learn the art of living together as citizens, and it is in public schools that we are obliged to defend the idea of a public, not only a private, interest."[22] Mathews paints a rosier picture of people getting together formally and informally to reach consensus, but the end result—inequality under the law—would still pertain unless everyone completely agreed on the consensus decision.

At least some defenders of the system of togetherness framework recognize democratically controlled schools' threat to people's rights. They celebrate it: "It's within such schools that we need to learn to resist what we see as improper encroachments on our rights, and to organize and expand what we believe are our entitlements," writes Meier.[23] A feature of public schooling, in this view, is putting rights in jeopardy and forcing people to fight for them. It is also training people to claim entitlements, things they believe others must provide them. Public schooling is intentionally a zero-sum game to train for a lifetime of zero-sum games.

Yet government is not the only way that people come together. An absence of government control in no way means an absence of public-ness. Civil society—all those human interactions and groupings above the level of the individual and family, but below government—is public, but with the crucial addition of being *voluntary*. And in being voluntary, civil society is a real, bonding community, not the Potemkin togetherness of forced collective decision-making and sacrifice just to move things along. Though public schooling defenders rarely sound like it, "public" is not synonymous with "government." *All* of our interactions build society.

Of course, nearing Hobbes's "state of Warre" is almost certainly not what proponents of the system of togetherness want. By all indications they think their system will foster harmony. But either conflict, oppression, or lowest-common-denominator curricular content—nothing that offends anyone—is what they will get. Indeed, these things are too often what we have been getting for nearly two centuries.

Schools of Togetherness

Somewhat akin to the system of togetherness, the idea behind schools of togetherness is to bring diverse children into contact and, in so doing, expand their outlooks and abilities to get along, especially by allowing their largely self-driven but communal experiences to build bridges among them. The goal is to enable the children to live harmoniously when they become adults. It is a noble desire seemingly without any of the coercive, potentially dictatorial dangers of many of the previously discussed schools of thought. How could this gentle approach jeopardize individual liberty?

Perhaps executed in the basic way that John Dewey envisioned—students deciding for themselves what they will study and with whom—it may pose little threat. But utterly neutral, voluntary teaching is likely impossible in reality. Even more difficult is assembling truly diverse student bodies to begin with.

Consider how little free rein students can actually have. With one teacher, there could only realistically be so many projects occurring at one time. That would mean teachers would, at some point, likely have to say "no" to some proposals, or at the very least give more or less attention to different projects, possibly introducing bias for and against different ideas or lines of inquiry. In addition, disputes would almost certainly arise among group members working on specific projects. Could teachers mediate them without appearing to take one side or the other?

How about teaching children from different linguistic backgrounds? Teach all children in English and you handicap the non-native speakers. Try to teach them in separate languages and commonality is sacrificed, not to mention opening a fraught debate over English immersion and bilingual instruction.[24] There is also, of course, a limit to the number of languages a teacher can speak.

What of the evidence that children of different backgrounds may, as a result of culture, behave differently in class or the face of authority, or even learn differently?[25] How do you teach them all in the same way, especially if they are working on joint projects with other children? And how do you handle children's possible pursuit of religious projects or inquiries without succumbing to the pitfall of a teacher appearing to be for or against specific religious ideas?

Those potential obstacles noted, the highest hurdle for schools of togetherness is that many people will choose *not* to be together. While it would be difficult for teachers and schools to appear neutral in their treatment of different racial, linguistic, or other groups, schools of togetherness gets right the basic idea for creating bridges, going deeper than simply assuming that putting diverse children within a school's walls will overcome divisions. With its emphasis on student-driven projects, schools of togetherness incorporates Allport's provisos that contact be of equal status, be in pursuit of common goals, and inculcate feelings of common humanity.

But getting diverse children together in the first place, especially from families not already inclined toward integration—those who presumably most *need* the schools of togetherness—would be very difficult, as history has demonstrated. At the very least, achieving such contact on any broad level would require significant coercion either in housing or school assignment—you cannot live *here*, you must go to school *there*—both of which would likely engender huge resistance and threaten basic freedoms of association and self-determination. You know, *liberty*.

Levelers

This may be the conception of public schooling least clearly at odds with individual liberty. Indeed, it seems geared toward enhancing liberty by ensuring that no one's education, or lack thereof, is an accident of birth, and that everyone will get the intellectual tools they need to succeed to the best of their God-given ability. Especially having ditched Jefferson's idea that the public schooling system should "rake from the rubbish" the supposedly best minds, giving everyone access to free public schooling seems likely to promote individual empowerment.

The problem is that by most indications public schooling has not equal-
ized educational opportunity. Your school is assigned primarily based on
your home address, and where you buy or rent a home is heavily dictated
by your family's income. To the extent that income correlates with academic achievement, that means the well-off disproportionately end up in the
higher-performing schools, and the poor in the lower-performing ones. That
is, in fact, what happens, with major concentrations of wealth and poverty in
different districts, and outcomes—at least standardized test scores—reflecting that.[26]

As has been fairly clear since at least the famous "Coleman Report" of
1966, numerous variables impact children before and outside of school—
nutrition, family structure, words heard starting in infancy, and so on—and
have significantly larger effects on student outcomes than anything schools
do.[27] Of course, short of truly draconian government action, you cannot prohibit wealthier parents from taking their kids to museums, providing them
with tutoring, feeding them nutritious meals, or many other activities that
give them advantages over low-income children. Public schooling cannot be
some sort of magic equalizer.

The utopianism of leveling aside, this conception of schooling could
largely avoid the most concerning conflicts and inequality—decisions about
what and whose values, historical ideas and information, and scientific
theories to teach—if the schools taught just the three Rs: reading, 'riting,
and 'rithmatic. Sticking to those building blocks would provide all children
with the basic intellectual skills needed to live, and to attend to their own
instruction in the far more contentious fields of history, literature, biology,
philosophy, and so on.

But what about the facts-only versions of U.S. history, biology, or
Shakespeare? Teaching those things seems tame at first, but determining
what things actually are facts, and deciding which of those to teach, are often
hugely controversial. And schools, with limited time, must favor teaching
some facts over others, and as a result must favor some views of history, science, and much else over others.

As discussed, we have had ongoing debates about the Founders' real
motives in writing the Constitution, and over the reasons behind the
Mexican–American War. Or consider this: The Turkish government killed
roughly 1.5 million Armenians during World War I. Many Armenians assert
that it is a fact that this was genocide. Many Turkish Americans disagree.

In 2005 this precipitated a lawsuit against the Massachusetts Department
of Education over its curriculum covering the matter. A teacher sued to have
state-approved history guidelines changed to present information defending
Turkey, and asked, "Why is the state declaring there is no controversy when
there is?" Opponents argued that there is no *real* debate. "The historical fact

is that genocide happened; over a million Armenians were slaughtered," said State Senator Steven A. Tolman (D-Brighton).[28]

Even basic reading and writing can drag ethnic and racial identities into conflict. There are bilingualism controversies, and there was conflict over teaching African American vernacular English—so-called Ebonics. And what books should children use as they practice their reading? Controversies over such a seemingly mundane matter as that are featured in Ravitch's *The Language Police*, but may have been most visible in the late 1980s when Core Knowledge Foundation founder—and public schooling advocate— E. D. Hirsch Jr. published *Cultural Literacy: What Every American Needs to Know.*[29]

Hirsch posited that there are thousands of time-honored names, idioms, pieces of literature, and the like that children must know to be functional in American society, and he provided an exhaustive list at the end of the book. He also argued that learning to read is not simply a matter of recognizing letter sounds and decoding words, but understanding concepts so that words can be put into context and students can *comprehend* what they are reading. In other words, reading requires schools to teach specific, often dead-white-male content.

Hirsch rolled this into an argument—largely repeated in a subsequent book, *The Making of Americans: Democracy and Our Schools*—that locally controlled public schools are *necessary* to convey the thousands of building blocks that constitute cultural literacy, which are themselves crucial to cohesion in a pluralist nation.[30] Perhaps most important, Hirsch argued that it is primarily low-income and non-white students who suffer from a deficit of this knowledge.

Cultural Literacy ignited explosive debate and pushback, perhaps most vehemently from progressives and some minority group members who saw it not as advocating cultural literacy, but Eurocentric cultural hegemony. As education professor Gloria Ladson-Billings asked about *Cultural Literacy* in 1991, as well as Allan Bloom's *The Closing of the American Mind*,[31] which also focused on the decline of traditional content in education, "What, then, is the real reason for this Western civilization curriculum panic?" Her answer:

> Perhaps a look at the demographic trends in the nation's public schools provides an answer. . . . [W]ithout a concerted effort to make Western culture the dominant (or, in most cases, the only) representation of culture afforded these immigrant, non-English speaking, urban, "at-risk," and often alienated students, these students will not be the new standard-bearers of Western culture.[32]

Cultural literacy may sound like cultural imperialism, but it was rooted, at least for Hirsch, in teaching underprivileged kids a basic skill they often were not getting: reading. Hirsch also, though, recognized how political this was, in 1983 writing that "literacy is not just a formal skill; it is also a political decision."[33] In critiquing Hirsch, Ernest House, Carol Emmer, and Nancy Lawrence also saw how much personal and political weight was attached to reading: "Both natural language and especially cultural content are in fact highly political, as evidenced by the explosive political nature of bilingual education, official English referenda, and controversies over standardized test performance."[34]

Even the teaching of math, seemingly so logical, is susceptible to cultural and identity conflicts. Though quiet compared to history and literature battles, there have been persistent critiques of the European focus of math curricula, and cultural bias on tests such as the SAT.[35] "[C]urricula emphasizing terms like Pythagorean Theorem and pi perpetuate a perception that mathematics was largely developed by Greeks and other Europeans," wrote University of Illinois professor Rochelle Gutiérrez in a 2017 anthology for math teachers.[36] In 2019, Seattle Public Schools considered a new math framework presenting how math has been used to oppress and liberate people, and its roots in "empires of color."[37]

There are also class divides over pedagogy, with wealthier parents often preferring a more child-centered, Dewey-esque approach, and lower-income families tending toward traditional instruction.[38] In *Common Ground*, a deep dive into the lives of three families in the Boston busing crisis, J. Anthony Lukas chronicles how integration brought low-income students into the Bancroft School, a progressive public school created by gentrifying South Boston residents. One goal was racial integration, but bringing in diverse families pitted pedagogical traditionalists against its progressives. "Dedicated to the proposition that children of all races and classes should be educated together, it was torn by racial and class struggles rooted in divergent concepts of what an urban education ought to be," Lukas writes.[39]

Levelers want public schools to create a ladder that enables people in democratic society, free of bounds of wealth, to reach their full potential. At its heart, it may be the only conception of public schooling consistent with individual liberty. But in practice we cannot agree where the rungs should go, what shape they should be, or where the top of the ladder should end up. Even this simple conception of education for democracy turns out to be marked by pitfalls.

CONCLUSION

The bedrock of American political life is individual liberty, and all those other things we hold up as crucial—democracy, equality, the rule of law—are, ultimately, of value only to the extent that they protect it. Unfortunately, there is no conception of public schooling that does not encroach on liberty, outside of the rare—if existent at all—case of a district in which all thoughts about religion, ethnic or religious identity, class identity, language, and moral values are unanimously held. In other words, there is likely nowhere that everyone has untrammeled liberty.

But what of social cohesion? While it must not supersede liberty, it is nonetheless of great importance. Certainly we want a society in which the people, with their sundry backgrounds and beliefs, are at peace with each other, and hopefully all feel themselves part of a greater whole. The next chapter looks at the structure of education, and how to improve its performance in fostering harmony. It also reviews the empirical evidence on education systems and their effects on social cohesion, and discusses the limits of empirical research.

NOTES

1. John Donvan and Elissa Rubin, "Pa. Neighbors Feud over Darwin, 'Design,'" ABC News, January 18, 2005, http://abcnews.go.com/Nightline/Science/story?id=415444&page=1.

2. Thomas Paine, *Common Sense*, February 14, 1776, https://www.gutenberg.org/files/147/147-h/147-h.htm.

3. John Locke, *Two Treatises of Government*, ed. Peter Laslett (Cambridge, UK: Cambridge University Press, 1994), 306.

4. George Washington, "Circular to State Governments," in *Washington: Writings*, comp. John Rhodehamel (New York: Literary Classics of the U.S., 1997), 518–519.

5. Alexis de Tocqueville, *Democracy in America, vol. 1* (New York: Vintage Classics, 1990), 306.

6. The Elizabeth Cady Stanton and Susan B. Anthony Papers Project, "Declaration of Sentiments and Resolutions, Woman's Rights Convention, Held at Seneca Falls, 19–20 July 1848," http://ecssba.rutgers.edu/docs/seneca.html.

7. William Lloyd Garrison, "Declaration of the National Anti-Slavery Convention," December 14, 1833, http://fair-use.org/the-liberator/1833/12/14/declaration-of-the-national-anti-slavery-convention.

8. Frederick Douglass, "The Hypocrisy of American Slavery," July 4, 1852, http://www.historyplace.com/speeches/douglass.htm.

9. Eric Foner, *The Story of American Freedom* (New York: W.W. Norton & Co., 1998), 8.

10. See, for instance, these dueling op-eds: Sean Wilentz, "Constitutionally, Slavery Is No National Institution," *New York Times*, September 16, 2015; and David Waldstreicher, "How the Constitution Was Indeed Pro-Slavery," *Atlantic*, September 19, 2015.

11. National School Boards Association, "Tucson Teachers File Suit Challenging Arizona Law Banning Ethnic-Studies Courses on the Grounds the

Law Is 'Anti-Hispanic,'" *Legal Clips*, October 21, 2010, http://legalclips.nsba.org/2010/10/21/group-of-tucson-teachers-file-suit-challenging-arizona-law-banning-ethnic-studies-courses-on-the-grounds-the-law-is-anti-hispanic/.

12. HB 2281: Prohibited Courses; Discipline, Schools, 49th Legislature, 2nd Regular Session (2010) https://www.azleg.gov/legtext/49leg/2r/summary/h.hb2281_05-03-10_astransmittedtogovernor.doc.htm#:~:text=HB%202281%20prohibits%20a%20school,race%20or%20class%20of%20people.

13. Sarah Schwartz, "Who's Really Driving Critical Race Theory Legislation? An Investigation," *Education Week*, July 19, 2021, https://www.edweek.org/policy-politics/whos-really-driving-critical-race-theory-legislation-an-investigation/2021/07.

14. Rann Miller, "First Person: States Want to Prevent Schools from Telling the Truth about Racism in America. Here's What Educators Can Do about It," *Chalkbeat*, May 18, 2021, https://www.chalkbeat.org/2021/5/18/22441106/critical-race-theory-teaching-about-racism.

15. Henry David Thoreau, "Civil Disobedience," 1849, http://xroads.virginia.edu/~hyper2/thoreau/civil.html.

16. Cato Institute, Public Schooling Battle Map, https://www.cato.org/education-fight-map

17. Stephen Arons, *Compelling Belief: The Culture of American Schooling* (Amherst, MA: University of Massachusetts Press, 1983), 203. He delved further into the conflict and inherent inequality of public schooling in *Short Route to Chaos: Conscience, Community, and the Re-constitution of American Schooling* (Amherst, MA: University of Massachusetts Press, 1997).

18. John Stuart Mill, *On Liberty* (London: Penguin Books, 1985), 68.

19. Calculated using data from U.S. Department of Education, National Center for Education Statistics, *Digest of Education Statistics: 2019*, Table 205.10, https://nces.ed.gov/programs/digest/d19/tables/dt19_205.10.asp?current=yes; and U.S. Department of Education, National Center for Education Statistics, *Digest of Education Statistics: 2018*, Table 206.10, https://nces.ed.gov/programs/digest/d18/tables/dt18_206.10.asp?current=yes.

20. David Mathews, *Reclaiming Public Education by Reclaiming Our Democracy* (Dayton, OH: Kettering Foundation Press, 2006).

21. Deborah Meier, *In Schools We Trust: Creating Communities of Learning in an Era of Testing and Standardization* (Boston: Beacon Press, 2002), 159.

22. Meier, *In Schools We Trust*, 176.

23. Ibid., 177.

24. This was a very contentious debate in the 1990s, especially in California and other states with sizeable immigrant populations. For insight into that see Craig Donegan, "Debate Over Bilingualism: Should English Be the Nation's Official Language?" *CQ Researcher* 6, no. 3 (January 19, 1996). http://library.cqpress.com/cqresearcher/document.php?id=cqresrre1996011900. The debate died down in the 2000s, but has still sprung up in districts in California, New York City, and Virginia. See Cato Institute, Public Schooling Battle Map, http://www.cato.org/education-fight-map.

25. For research on this, see, for instance, A. Wade Boykin, Kenneth M. Tyler, and Oronde Miller, "Expressions in the Dynamics of Classroom Life," *Urban Education* 40 (2005): 521–549; Edward W. Morris, "From 'Middle Class' to 'Trailer Trash': Teachers' Perception of White Students in a Predominantly Minority School," *Sociology of Education* 78 (2005): 99–121; Kimberlé Williams Crenshaw, "Black Girls Matter: Pushed Out, Overpoliced and Underprotected," Center for Intersectionality and Social Policy Studies and African American Policy Forum, September 2015.

26. See, for instance, the searchable database at Motoko Rich, Amanda Cox, and Matthew Bloch, "Money, Race and Success: How Your School District Compares," *New York Times*, April 29, 2016, http://www.nytimes.com/interactive/2016/04/29/upshot/money-race-and-success-how-your-school-district-compares.html.

27. James S. Coleman et al., "Equality of Educational Opportunity," U.S. Department of Health, Education, and Welfare, 1966.

28. Shelley Murphy, "Suit Challenges How Armenian Genocide Is Taught," *Boston Globe*, October 28, 2005.

29. E. D. Hirsch, Jr., *Cultural Literacy: What Every American Needs to Know* (New York: Vintage Books, 1988).

30. E. D. Hirsch, Jr., *The Making of Americans: Democracy and Our Schools* (New Haven, CT: Yale University Press, 2009).

31. Allan Bloom, *The Closing of the American Mind: How Higher Education Has Failed Democracy and Impoverished the Souls of Today's Students* (New York: Simon & Schuster, 1987).

32. Gloria Ladson-Billings, "Beyond Multicultural Illiteracy," *The Journal of Negro Education* 60 (1991): 147–157.

33. E. D. Hirsch, Jr., "Cultural Literacy," *The American Scholar* 52, no. 2 (Spring 1983): pp. 159–169.

34. Ernest R. House, Carol Emmer, and Nancy Lawrence, "Cultural Literacy Reconsidered," in *Literacy for a Diverse Society: Perspectives, Practices, and Policies*, ed. Elfrieda H. Hiebert (New York: Teachers College Press, 1991), 65–66.

35. See, for instance, Arthur B. Powell and Marilyn Frankenstein, *Ethnomathematics: Challenging Eurocentrism in Mathematics Education* (Albany, NY: State University of New York Press, 1997); and Elise Takahama, "Is Math Racist? New Course Outlines Prompt Conversations about Identity, Race in Seattle Classrooms," *Chicago Tribune*, October 10, 2019.

36. Robert Gearty, "White Privilege Bolstered by Teaching Math, University Professor Says," FoxNews.com, October 24, 2017, https://www.foxnews.com/us/white-privilege-bolstered-by-teaching-math-university-professor-says.

37. Seattle Public Schools, "K–12 Math Ethnic Studies Framework (20.08.2019)," https://www.k12.wa.us/sites/default/files/public/socialstudies/pubdocs/Math%20SDS%20ES%20Framework.pdf.

38. For a good discussion of this, see Michael J. Petrilli, *The Diverse Schools Dilemma: A Parent's Guide to Socioeconomically Mixed Public Schools* (Washington, DC: Thomas B. Fordham Institute, 2012).

39. J. Anthony Lucas, *Common Ground: A Turbulent Decade in the Lives of Three American Families* (New York: Vintage Books, 1986), 338.

40. HB 2281: Prohibited Courses; Discipline, Schools, 49th Legislature, 2nd Regular Session (2010) https://www.azleg.gov/legtext/49leg/2r/summary/h.hb2281_05-03-10_astransmittedtogovernor.doc.htm#:~:text=HB%202281%20prohibits%20a%20school,race%20or%20class%20of%20people.

Chapter 6

Is Freedom the Key to Unity and Equality?

France, like many European countries, has experienced major difficulties absorbing immigrants, especially Muslims. It has suffered riots in predominantly Muslim areas and been the target of numerous terrorist attacks. The French focus intensely on assimilation, including limiting public expressions of religious values such as wearing burqas or veils that obscure a woman's face.

The French public schools—long famously centralized—are instrumental in such assimilation efforts. But it may well be Roman Catholic schools that are doing the superior job of bringing Muslim students into French society. Nadia Oualane, 14, a student of Algerian descent who wears her hair hidden under a black head scarf, explained to the New York Times, *"There is respect for our religion here." She added, gesturing at nearby buildings, "In the public school, I would not be allowed to wear a veil."*

Jean Chamoux, headmaster of the St. Mauront Catholic School in Marseille, said, "If I banned the head scarf, half the girls wouldn't go to school at all." He added, "I prefer to have them here, talk to them and tell them that they have a choice. Many actually take it off after a while. My goal is that by the time they graduate they have made a conscious choice, one way or the other." "It's ironic," said Imam Soheib Bencheikh, "but today the Catholic Church is more tolerant of—and knowledgeable about—Islam than the French state."[1]

Individual liberty must always be the foundational value of American life, as the individual is the only irreducible component of society. But this does not mean that social harmony and unity are not important goals. They are— witness the national pain we have suffered from racial, religious, and political polarization—and those who have advocated public schooling as the best mechanism to achieve harmony have, almost certainly, been well intentioned.

151

But though we might like it to be otherwise, historical and, as we shall see, to a lesser extent quantitative evidence, reveals that unity cannot be engineered by government, nor will it come as quickly as most would like.

This chapter looks first at the evidence of intergroup contact by looking at research about bringing people permanently together. Then it digs into the effect of such contact in education, with physical proximity achieved through various mechanisms. Most of the evidence will be historical, though both sections will discuss empirical findings.

Why more historical than empirical? Because (1) there is limited empirical research on how contact affects cohesion, and (2) most of what exists is unable to tell us whether a contact mechanism, especially in education—assignment by address, busing, vouchers—drives levels of cohesion or just coincides with them. To be very confident that a contact "treatment" causes a particular outcome, we would ideally have randomized controlled trials—essentially what are used for new drugs—that isolate the effect of the treatment because random chance, not someone's own choices, determines whether they are put in a treatment or control group.

Some other approaches can approximate random assignment by statistically controlling for variables that might lead to specious conclusions, but it is always difficult to control for unobservable factors such as motivation. And even randomized trial results apply only to the specific groups examined. For instance, those who enter a school voucher lottery, which randomly selects winners and losers who can then be compared, might be quite different from those who do not enter, meaning the whole group may be unrepresentative of the general population. All of this to say that empirical research can tell us something, but it is in limited supply and offers few definitive answers.

WHAT WE KNOW ABOUT BRIDGING CAPITAL AND CONTACT

In the parlance of social capital, we hope schools will create "bridging" capital: positive connections among people from socially distant groups, be they racial, religious, or class. There are different ways of measuring social capital, perhaps most notably Robert Putnam's tallying of participation in bowling leagues, Rotary Clubs, and other voluntary associations.[2] That said, the rolls of every garden club and Hash House Harrier group could be overflowing, and were they filled with ethnically, religiously, or economically homogeneous members, there might be much "bonding" capital—*within-group* connection—but little bridging.

Of course, membership is not the tie that binds. That is the positive feeling among individuals that membership fosters or indicates.

Both our everyday experience and limited empirical work show that increasing bridging capital is tough. We naturally gravitate to things that we know and are comfortable with, and often use quick cues—looks, sounds, smells—to find them. As Katherine Phillips of the Columbia Business School observed in an article touting the power of diversity, "The first thing to acknowledge about diversity is that it can be difficult. . . . Research has shown that . . . [it] can cause discomfort, rougher interactions, a lack of trust, greater perceived interpersonal conflict, lower communication, less cohesion, more concern about disrespect, and other problems."[3]

The inherent difficulty of dealing with diversity is why building bonding capital—connections among people of the same group—is infinitely easier than constructing bridges. Such capital can be good, creating efficient, supportive relationships. But as Alejandro Portes and Patricia Landolt have pointed out, bonding capital can also be dangerous. It can create balkanization, "conspiracies against the public," and "restrictions on individual freedom and business initiative" by groups that take control of specific industries or communities.[4]

Previous chapters have examined struggles to promote bridging capital in American education, but that is just one manifestation. High social-capital countries, for instance, tend to be homogeneous. Nordic countries are typically near the top of national social capital rankings, and their racial and cultural homogeneity, at least historically, is well known.[5] In those countries the barriers to trust, such as linguistic, religious, and cultural differences, are relatively low. They have a lot of bonding capital—the easy stuff—and little need for bridging.

Research by Robert Putnam, however, suggests not just that diversity has a negative connection with *bridging* capital, but that it also seems to deplete *bonding* capital. "Diversity seems to trigger not in-group/out-group division, but anomie or social isolation," he found in research published in 2007.[6] It seems that people in highly diverse places encounter difficulty finding *any* groups with which to connect.

Despite many obstacles, the United States has experienced tremendous success in bringing diverse groups together. It has rarely been easy or swift, but today Catholics, Protestants, Jews, and atheists are all well integrated into society, as are those of German, Irish, Italian, Japanese, and other ethnic extractions. And as bad as our racial relations may be, the United States elected its first African American president in 2008.

Such success may be why, in a letter objecting to an op-ed that used his 2007 diversity study to advocate immigration curbs, Putnam wrote, "In the medium to long run . . . successful immigrant societies like the U.S. create new forms of social solidarity and damp the negative effects of diversity by constructing new, more encompassing identities."[7] Indeed, an openness to diversity may be one of the country's greatest strengths. As the Kauffman Foundation has reported, 40 percent of Fortune 500 companies in 2010 had been started by either an immigrant or the child of one.[8]

How do diverse people eventually mesh? Here is how they generally *do not*: by force. Government efforts to assimilate people, which have largely been the responsibility of public schools, have been contentious, insulting, and ultimately impotent or even counterproductive, building resentments instead of bridges. As Francis Fukuyama has put it, "[s]ocial capital is like a ratchet that is more easily turned in one direction than another; it can be dissipated by the actions of governments much more readily than those governments can build it up again."[9] Government can easily force zero-sum contests, but is ill equipped to build fraternal feelings.

The answer to how diverse people have melded is not force, but what you would expect were you to contemplate human nature: self-interest. While immigrants have tended to settle in areas dominated by their ethnic and linguistic group, as discussed already life is easier if one speaks the common language, follows broadly accepted norms such as being pleasant and accommodating to neighbors, and understands the national culture by knowing, say, who the New York Yankees are—maybe even becoming a fan of a big-time sports team—or eating hot dogs on the 4th of July.

Of course, sharing norms and knowledge could apply only to bonding capital—just know those things about your immediate group—but you would have to hermetically seal off your community to keep from feeling pressure to learn the ways of broader society. Even the Amish, who still drive horse-drawn buggies and eschew electricity, have not fully done that, catching rides in automobiles and doing business with "English" clientele.[10] And would immigrants undertake arduous journeys in steerage of a steamship, or with "coyotes" crammed into gutted vans to be smuggled over the southern border, to totally re-create their old lives?

Comfort and ease of living are just the beginning of the self-interested incentives that have spurred people to expand their social horizons. Pejoratively, one might say the motivation has been downright *greedy*: when you conduct business with people outside of your group, you can greatly improve your lot. Think of the Ethiopian chef who opens a restaurant to Ethiopian and non-Ethiopian communities. Or the Catholic accountant who takes on Protestant clients. Or the Indian engineer who works for South African immigrant Elon Musk. And such business is win-win: members of different groups do not *compete*, but *cooperate* for mutual gain.

We could go back at least as far as John Stuart Mill for a discussion of the bridging effects of commerce. In *Principles of Political Economy,* Mill writes that "it is hardly possible to overrate the value . . . of placing human beings in contact with persons dissimilar to themselves, and with modes of thought and action unlike those with which they are familiar. Commerce is now what war once was, the principal source of this contact."[11]

Sociologist Ferdinand Tönnies, in *Community and Society*, discusses *gemeinschaft* and *gesellschaft*. *Gemeinschaft* is essentially feelings of connection and obligation we have when we live in close-knit groups such as families, or confined spaces such as villages. It is *gesellschaft*, basically, commerce—that extends connections beyond those bonds.

At first, *gesellschaft* does not create deep connections, as people primarily seek material gain and form no affective bonds. But commerce fuels peaceful, positive contact that sets up the conditions for stronger bridging. Indeed, writing in the late nineteenth and early twentieth centuries, Tönnies argued that the society created by commerce was in some sense "represented by the entire globe,"[12] and connections were marked by "politeness . . . exchange of words and courtesies in which everyone seems to be present for the good of everyone else and everyone seems to consider everyone else as his equal."[13]

Peter Salins, examining immigration and contact in America, concludes that *gesellschaft* eventually evolves into *gemeinschaft*. "Once immigrants and natives work together and come to appreciate each other's value, it becomes much easier to form other kinds of interest-based relationships," he writes. "Eventually, economic relationships lead to social ones, culminating in friendship and even intermarriage."[14]

In *Making Democracy Work: Civic Traditions in Modern Italy*, Putnam discusses the vital role of merchants and artisans in building social capital, with guilds building bonds among artisans of numerous types, and merchants making medieval northern Italian republics centers of trade beyond their borders. "Intimately associated with the expansion of civic republicanism was a rapid growth in commerce," Putnam writes. "As civil order was established, bold and ambitious merchants expanded their trading networks, first in the regions around the city-state and then gradually to the farthest reaches of the known world."[15]

That trade seemed to lead to more peaceful society was captured by Montesquieu. He propounded the idea of *doux commerce*—"sweet commerce"—as a self-interest-driven, edge-softening influence.[16] "Commerce cures destructive prejudices," he wrote, "and it is an almost general rule that everywhere there are gentle mores, there is commerce and that everywhere there is commerce, there are gentle mores."[17]

Adam Smith captured the same idea, writing, "Whenever commerce is introduced into any country, probity and punctuality always accompany it. . . . When a person makes perhaps 20 contracts in a day, he cannot gain so much by endeavouring to impose on his neighbours, as the very appearance of a cheat would make him lose."[18] Extending this beyond just good manners, Max Weber wrote, "No matter how calculating and hard-headed the ruling considerations in such a social relationship—as that of the merchant to his customers—may be, it is quite possible for it to involve emotional values which transcend its utilitarian significance."[19]

Remember, most distinctive groups in the United States *chose* to come to America (importantly, other than most African Americans, all Native Americans, and some Mexican Americans whose families were on lands annexed from Mexico). Of course, many new arrivals settled in ethnic ghettos, but even a seemingly isolated immigrant, as political scientist Walker Connor has written, "was constantly aware of being part of a larger cultural entity that pervaded and shaped the ghetto in countless ways, and he realized that cultural assimilation was necessary if the more obvious limits to his ambitions were to be pushed back."[20]

Michael Barone, comparing older and newer "out" groups in America— Irish and African Americans, Italians and Latinos, and Jews and Asians— observed that those coming from more commercial backgrounds integrated more quickly and effectively than those that did not. This was likely because a business background made them more accustomed to dealing productively with people from outside their group.[21]

Irish and African Americans, coming from backgrounds of legalized powerlessness, including being forbidden from holding property (or, much worse for blacks, being treated as property themselves) had little commercial tradition and took a relatively long time to assimilate. Italians and Latinos, often coming from politically corrupt and dysfunctional homelands and tending to trust only family, integrated somewhat faster but were still slow to embrace outsiders. Finally, Jews and Asians tended to come from more commercial backgrounds, and assimilated with ease compared to the other four groups.

Of course, bridging even for the fastest integrating groups has not been easy or immediate. Asians suffered a great deal of discrimination, especially in the West, and for several decades immigration from China was prohibited. Anti-Semitism has many times resurfaced. Yet all of these groups eventually assimilated, respecting basic American values even if they sometimes chose to live parts of their lives distinctly. And they did it because they wanted to.

Contrast this with government assimilation efforts. Edward Hartmann, in a detailed recounting of eventually government-driven "Americanization" initiatives during the years immediately prior to, during, and after World War I, found that many of the initiatives insulted and aggravated immigrant populations, and likely yielded little net benefit. Immigrants would integrate, but they would do so naturally, and on their own terms:

> [T]he number of immigrants who became Americanized along the formal lines advocated by the Americanization groups must have been small, indeed, when compared to the great bulk of their fellows who never saw the inside of

an American schoolroom or settlement house. The great majority of the latter became Americanized in time through the same gradual process of assimilating American customs, attitudes, speech, and ideals from their native American neighbors and their American-born children.[22]

Vasiliki Fouka examined the backlash effect statistically, finding that German-Americans in states that prohibited the teaching of the German language in schools after World War I were less likely to volunteer to fight in World War II, and more likely to identify as ethnically German, than were German Americans in states that had no such bans.[23]

Commercial interactions snap right into Gordon Allport's proviso that successful intergroup contact requires pursuit of common goals. In the case of commerce, whether it is people entering business partnerships, or buying and selling from one another, all involved hope to make themselves better off by working together, rather than one having to win and the other lose. Mutual benefit is also at work when public housing tenants cooperate in a push for building upgrades, or soldiers or sailors pull together to defeat an enemy.

Sociologist Robert Wuthnow notes that in the 1950s and 1960s, men participated in groups like Elks and Rotary for business-related networking and to demonstrate that they, and by extension their businesses, were committed, trustworthy members of their communities.[24] Economist Partha Dasgupta has observed that commercial ties beget more commercial ties, as "production and exchange via networks in one commodity can be of vital importance to the functioning of the market in another."[25] Historian Simon Szreter notes that unionization in nineteenth-century England was primarily bonding of similar, relatively high-status workers, but expanded to include lower-status workmen. Unions furnished, essentially, class-based bridging capital for those whose business was their labor.[26]

Perhaps the most powerful but least direct way that commerce builds bridging capital is by giving the country common experiences through countless products and services sold and bought for profit. Americans nationwide can talk to each other about the Super Bowl—or the literally show-stopping advertisements between possessions—or *Seinfeld* episodes, or the poultry politics of Chick-fil-A. Or Americans can chat about the finer points of Darth Vader being Luke's dad while sitting in a Hampton Inn sipping venti Starbucks coffee.

This building of common culture and experience through commerce hardly ends on the country's Atlantic or Pacific shores. In the 1990s, people all over the world dressed like—and wanted to *be like*—Mike. That is, of course, Michael Jordan. As of 2012, Coca-Cola was sold in all but two countries: North Korea and Cuba.[27] As of 2013, McDonald's restaurants could be found in 116 countries.[28] Meanwhile, Americans gladly pay for culturally bridging things from other counties, whether it is the ascendance of K-Pop[29]—highly choreographed singing and dancing bands from South Korea—or the Angry Birds franchise based on the top-selling smartphone games from the Finnish company Rovio.[30] And this just scratches the surface of how commerce-driven globalization has created bridging capital throughout the nation and the world.

WHAT THE RESEARCH SAYS ABOUT BRIDGING CAPITAL AND CONTACT

History and daily experience build a strong case for self-interest furnishing the energy and conditions for bridge building. What does research say? Unfortunately, searches using terms including "social capital," "formation," "commerce," and "bridging capital" on databases such as JSTOR, Google Scholar, and ProQuest produce far more research examining the effect of social capital on business than vice versa. A mid-August 2021 ProQuest search for "commerce" and "social capital" returned nearly 86,000 items, but for "commerce" and "bridging capital" only 946. This is consistent with the thrust of major social capital works such as *Bowling Alone*, which tend to be more concerned with what social capital can do than what can be done for it.[31]

That said, there are some interesting studies on commerce building social capital. For instance, economists Edward Glaeser, David Laibson, and Bruce Sacerdote have conducted research on whether self-interest explains individuals' differing proclivity to join groups such as Elks clubs. They found strong evidence that variables such as being in a job that involves significant social interactions, such as physicians or clergy, is correlated with joining the types of organized, voluntary associations Putnam sees as crucial.[32] That at least suggests that commercial interest has a role in individual, social capital–building decisions.

Is there evidence that commerce has helped to increase social capital beyond an individual basis? Research by Simon Ville suggests that stock and station agents in Australia from roughly 1840 to 1940 helped to build social capital both for their firms and rural farmers and herders. Agents moved to, and integrated in, small, often isolated communities, and helped farmers and herders access shipping, banking, and other national and international services to get their goods to wider markets.[33] As time went on, firm consolidation allowed clients in different, previously isolated communities to build some bridging capital with other rural communities.

Agents, for their part, would often initially sell their services at a loss to build goodwill in the communities in which they set up shop, and they would be very active in communal life. That bonding was beneficial to the agent and his firm. Ville argues that such goodwill was often reflected in firms being purchased for prices higher than the valuation of their net tangible assets. Such seeming overpayment, Ville suggests, was to purchase a firm's "reputational" value; essentially, their value based on people's hard-earned trust.

WHAT HISTORY TELLS US ABOUT
SCHOOLING AND BRIDGING CAPITAL

The first lesson of education history—at least American—is that the belief that public schooling has unified diverse people is founded more on intentions than evidence. The goal was to have Americans of sundry backgrounds attend uniform government schools and, in so doing, break down the barriers separating them. What actually occurred, as examined in chapter two was often far different. Separation was the norm because people tended to live with others like themselves, but where populations were not heterogeneous conflict or separation often ensued. And several groups were de jure or de facto barred from public schooling.

There are, in contrast, at least a few examples of private schools bringing diverse people together in early American history. Colonial Pennsylvania was home to highly decentralized education among sects. It was also, as Lawrence Cremin has written, home to schools that served "diverse clientele" (at least among Christians of European descent) without "exciting sectarian controversy."[34] Indeed, the first book on conducting schooling published in the New World was by German-speaking Pennsylvanian Christopher Dock, whose *Schulordnung* furnished plans and advice for peaceful, and religiously inclusive, schooling.[35]

Several post-bellum private institutions set up bridging conditions. In 1890s Florida, the Orange Park Normal and Industrial School, founded by the American Missionary Association, and other religious schools, taught racially integrated classes despite state warfare against them.[36] Seven years before *Brown v. Board*, Saint Louis Archbishop Joseph Ritter ordered all diocesan schools desegregated and threatened excommunication for anyone who sued to block the order.[37] A 1949 report on independent schools—typically elite, expensive institutions—found 22 had declared they would have nondiscriminatory admissions policies.[38] In 1953, Bishop Vincent Waters ordered desegregation of all Diocese of Raleigh, North Carolina, schools.[39]

It would be Pollyannaish to think that fully privatized education would have created perfect harmony during most of American history had it just been allowed to flower. Human beings are heavily inclined to favor people like themselves and to stereotype those who are different. Free choice does not magically overcome this. But the existence of such institutions as the

Orange Park Normal and Industrial School shows that positive intergroup contact through private schooling was at least possible, and sometimes occurred while it was still illegal in public schools. If nothing else, it gave people with a minority view—let us integrate—a chance to act.

Outside of the United States, Europe has received many immigrants from predominantly Muslim countries, and struggled with assimilation and social cohesion. France is perhaps most infamous for its strict assimilation demands, right down to its ban on the modest swimwear known as the "Burkini." This is not necessarily driven by anti-Muslim sentiment as much as a thirst for secularism. *Laïcité* has been an overarching goal for many French since at least the Revolution, and is connected to cultural protectionism that has produced French-language music quotas on radio broadcasts and a leading role preserving European Union rules limiting the importation of American music, television shows, and movies.[40]

While immigrants may want to integrate, they do not want to lose their cherished values and cultures. As noted, at the very least to smooth their transition to their new homes, immigrants need to be able to live in communities where many of their familiar ways are maintained. One way in which this has happened for new Muslim children in France has been by attending Catholic schools, which families can do at relatively low cost because government subsidizes the schools. Exact numbers of Muslim students enrolled in French Catholic schools do not exist, but a 2008 *New York Times* article estimated it to be in the hundreds of thousands.

Given centuries of fraught relations between Catholics and Muslims, why the popularity of the Catholic option? As illuminated in this chapter's opening vignette, while Catholics and Muslims have yawning theological differences, they at least share a belief in God.[41] In contrast, echoing concerns of religious Americans since Horace Mann's day, Imam Soheib Bencheikh told the *New York Times*, "*Laïcité* has become the state's religion, and the republican school is its temple." Catholic schools must teach the national curriculum if they receive subsidies, but also allow Muslim students to be openly *Muslim*, enabling more flexible, tolerant integration.

While there is historical evidence that private schooling can help build bridges, the evidence is much more compelling that it helps people avoid cohesion-disintegrating social conflict. School choice, both in America and Europe, has been more of a tunnel for diverse people to escape the gladiatorial arena of winner-takes-all public schooling than a highway to a majestic, social Golden Gate. But that has been important for those it has helped.

In previous chapters, we examined this with regard to the United States, most notably the extensive Roman Catholic schooling system. But it was in Europe that the power of private, chosen schooling to bring peace was most apparent. In many European countries, centuries of political and physical combat eventually made clear that, at least within the realm of education, diverse people must either be given freedom or remain forever on the brink of social war.[42]

Horace Mann drew inspiration, or at least assurance, for his ideas from Europe, especially Prussia, France, and the Netherlands, all of which attempted to promote nationalism through government schooling. State-dominated education remained in force in Prussia, and eventually unified Germany, through the days of the Third Reich. Indeed, authoritarian regimes feel especially compelled to control what their citizens know and feel, and do so in part through public schooling. But even in France, the state had to give in somewhat as regimes after the 1789 Revolution found it impossible to halt people's retreating to the Church for instruction.

Perhaps nowhere has the role of school choice in maintaining peace been better illustrated than the Netherlands. In the early nineteenth century, when Mann approvingly observed Dutch education efforts,[43] it appeared that the Netherlands would have a centralized system of pan-Protestant public schools. The goal was to create unity among the many peoples that had been consolidated into the new country. But like many European countries, the Netherlands was a mix of Catholics and Protestants, as well as classes and regions. Also like many countries, separating people from their religion proved unsustainable.

The first major effort to escape conflict that had been, at the very least, exacerbated by drives to unify through schooling eventually led to national dissolution. Belgium, which had been the southern part of the United Netherlands, declared its independence on October 4, 1830. Writes Charles Glenn, "Belgium has the distinction of being possibly the only country in the world whose very existence resulted in substantial part from controversy over education."[44]

Belgium was more Catholic than the rest of the short-lived United Netherlands, and, hence, more resistant to pan-Protestant schooling. Belgians also wished to continue a tradition of local control over education and other affairs. Like most of Europe, Belgium had its own struggles to reconcile religious and other diversity with unity. In education and elsewhere, this was resolved largely through decentralization. Today, education is governed by the country's distinctive linguistic communities, while the government subsidizes Catholic, Protestant, Muslim, Jewish, and nonsectarian schools, with choice guaranteed in the constitution.[45]

Eventually, the Belgium-less Netherlands resolved its seemingly perpetual struggle between church and state by embracing freedom. It ended its nearly two centuries of *schoolstrijd*—school struggle—largely by attaching funding to children and allowing parents to choose the schools they thought best. As of 1995, there were 17 types of religious schools receiving public subsidies in the Netherlands, including Jewish, Muslim, and Hindu schools, as well as numerous institutions with different pedagogical approaches, including Montessori and Waldorf.[46]

The Netherlands does not have free-market education; the national government creates standards for all publicly supported schools, though in consultation with numerous education groups, religious and otherwise.[47] It also still has social tensions, especially concerning Muslim immigrants. But the historical evidence is that educational freedom helped foster peace. Indeed, in 2017, for the first time a majority of Dutch over age 15 reported having no religious affiliation, and only 16 percent had attended religious services at least monthly, despite high use of religious schools.[48] That should dispel fears that choice creates religious balkanization.

Belgium and the Netherlands are not the only places to see choice as a preserver of peace rather than a threat to unity. Even the Prussians in Horace Mann's time funded separate Protestant and Roman Catholic schools, which taught their own religious tenets. Where students were religiously mixed, they separately received theological instruction.[49] Mann nonetheless reported hearing that children were sometimes subjected to religious instruction to which their families dissented, causing complaints about the system that were otherwise rarely heard.[50]

Today in Germany, private schools represent a small part of overall enrollment. However, most states, which have almost all educational authority, provide some funding for private schooling. The states, though, maintain significant control over programs of instruction, teacher qualifications, and other matters.[51]

Education authority is also vested below the national level in Canada, and publicly funded private schooling is available in several provinces.[52] Additionally, in Alberta, Ontario, and Saskatchewan, Roman Catholic schools are run by separate public school boards and get complete government funding, as do minority language schools in all provinces. The long-standing goal in funding multiple types of schools has been to satisfy diverse groups.[53] However, like elsewhere, Canadian provinces tend to apply regulations to participating schools, including over curricula and teacher qualifications.

Choice-based education exists in much of Europe and North America largely because of social evolution: education systems had to adjust to be sustainable in societies often deeply cleaved by religious differences. They incorporated choice primarily to maintain peace; to forestall the widening of chasms more than to bridge them. Historically, peace seems to have been educational freedom's primary contribution.

WHAT STATISTICAL RESEARCH TELLS US ABOUT SCHOOLING AND BRIDGING CAPITAL

Just as relatively little research has examined how commerce has fostered social capital, while much has tackled how social capital affects commerce, there is an imbalance in the research on social capital and schooling. Many studies have examined the effect of social capital on education outcomes, as well as education levels on social capital, but few have assessed the effects of educational structure on social capital. Researchers have perhaps largely assumed that public schooling unites diverse people, just as it seems the general public has. But history and theory suggest it is an open question whether top-down control or choice better builds bridges.

In part this research dearth is a consequence of real-world decisionmaking and scientific needs not aligning. To obtain a concrete answer about the effect of different educational systems on social cohesion, policies would have to be implemented like clinical drug trials. As mentioned, that would mean random assignment of people to "treatment" and "control" groups, and pre- and post-treatment testing of the different groups to see the effect of the treatment. We have not seen this in education, with even the randomized trials of school voucher programs not drawing on random samples of the population.

Lack of rigor was especially problematic during the period when districts were undergoing the clearest example of top-down control to put different groups together: court-ordered racial desegregation, which peaked between roughly 1968 and 1990. As scholar John B. McConahay stated in a 1978 summary of the research on intergroup bridging through desegregation, "Reading this literature leaves one impressed with how little is known and how much additional research . . . is needed. I begin . . . with such a statement not in obedience to standard academic ritual: the need for more research is truly impressive in this case."[54]

That said, while the quality has been wanting, a lot of research on racial integration in schools has been conducted. Since integration by race has been by far the greatest integration goal of the last 50-plus years, and the subject of the most research, this look at integration research will focus on race. That is not to diminish desires to integrate by religion, native language, or other group dividers, but to deal with the country's biggest divide, and the reality of the existing research.

One last crucial note about the research overall is that much more of it assesses the effects of school-assignment policies on physical integration than bridge building—or decreasing psychological "social distance"—among different groups. That is understandable, because overcoming physically separate schooling was the primary goal of desegregation policies. Assessing the degree to which social distance decreased among groups was at best a secondary concern to achieving initial contact, though as Allport's proviso warns, pushing contact without setting the right conditions can produce negative effects.

Looking first at physical integration, generally, what the research reveals is that within public schooling the more a policy attempts to force people together, the harder people averse to contact will work to escape that compulsion. Conversely, the less compulsion there is, the more likely people are to stand pat rather than integrate. Basically, trying to coerce integration can be like poking your finger in a lake to shove the water down—it just moves somewhere else.

Coerced Integration

At first glance it appears that coerced integration such as busing works, at least for getting students of different races in the same buildings. Analyzing various integration efforts between 1968 and 1991, Christine Rossell and David Armor found that in southern districts with desegregation plans, black students' exposure to whites greatly increased between 1968 and 1972, the peak period of court-ordered integration plans. The average large southern district with a formal desegregation plan saw the average black student's school rise from about 20 percent white to 50 percent white.[55] That said, large southern districts without plans also saw big increases in black students' exposure to whites.

Slicing the data another way—looking at how many black students were in heavily segregated schools—also shows that integration efforts were successful at getting black and white students in the South in the same buildings. According to data from the Civil Rights Project, in the 1968–69 school year 78 percent of African American students in the South attended schools that were 90 to 100 percent minority. By 1980–81, that had dropped to just 23 percent.[56]

Outside of the South integration efforts were not directly tied to de jure segregation, and physical integration came later and was less pronounced. Court orders were allowed by the Supreme Court's 1973 *Keyes v. School District No. 1, Denver* ruling that districts that had implemented policies with segregationist intent, but did not outright require segregation, could be ordered to desegregate. That put districts nationwide in the coerced integration crosshairs, though the courts' reach was curtailed a year later in *Milliken v. Bradley*, which ruled that districts without a history of segregationist policies could not be included in integration orders.

Milliken protected "flight" for millions of white families that moved out of urban areas and into leafy suburbs where houses were expensive and

African Americans were often priced out. Notably, while research suggests that greater school-assignment coercion was associated with faster white flight,[57] it was also clear that white flight was occurring regardless of school integration orders. White families were leaving neighborhoods with increasing minority populations for many reasons.[58]

In the Border states—bordering the old Confederacy, including Kentucky, Maryland, and Oklahoma—the percentage of black students in schools that were 90- to 100-percent minority fell from 60 percent in 1968–69 to 33 percent in 1991–92. In Midwest states, such as Illinois, Kansas, and the Dakotas, the share of blacks in such schools dropped from 58 to 40 percent. In the West, including California, Arizona, and Washington, shares dropped from 51 to 27 percent. However, in the Northeast, which includes Massachusetts, New Jersey, and Vermont and has a tradition of small districts, the share of black students in isolated schools *rose* from 43 to 50 percent.[59]

The broad data can give the impression that coerced integration was highly successful at bringing diverse groups together. And yes, black and white students increasingly shared buildings. But that does not mean a lot of mixing occurred.

Most directly, there was significant segregation by classroom, with white, Asian, and wealthier students disproportionately enrolled in advanced classes, and minority and low-income students in regular or basic. As an African American student remarked in the study of pseudonymous Memphis, Tennessee, "Crossover High," which four years after desegregation had a 60/40 black-to-white mix, "It's possible to go through the years at Crossover and not have a single white person in your class."[60]

The evidence is also increasingly clear that coerced integration is politically unsustainable. After the Supreme Court became more conservative—itself partially a consequence of the public turning against compelled integration—it started winding down courts' power. The final nail in the coffin was *Board of Education of Oklahoma City v. Dowell* in 1991, in which the court ruled that if a district complied with a desegregation decree and was unlikely to return to discriminatory policies, it would cease being subject to the decree even if the schools might again become racially identifiable. Often decrees would be lifted where schools were heavily minority but there were too few white students to change that.

The Civil Rights Project has reported that nationally, in the 1991–92 school year, 33 percent of black students attended schools that were 90- to 100-percent minority. By 2009–10, that had inched back up to 38 percent. In 1991–92, 65 percent of black students attended schools that were 50- to 100-percent minority. By 2009–10, it was 74 percent.[61] Data also show that the white share of students in the average black student's school dropped from 35 percent to 29 percent.[62] Such decreases, though, reflect not just decisions to attend separate schools, but also changing demographics; non-Hispanic white students fell from 66 to 54 percent of all students between 1991–92 and 2009–10.

Public School Choice

Facing sizable public opposition to busing and other aggressive policies, policy makers have looked for less coercive mechanisms to deliver integration. Choice among public schools has gained favor on the sound grounds that school assignments over which parents have some influence are likely to be less objectionable than those that are entirely forced. This has taken numerous shapes, including "controlled choice," public school choice bound by racial or class enrollment targets; open enrollment; and magnet schools, institutions with special focuses, such as the arts or STEM, designed to attract students from around a diverse district.

Research suggests that the more heavy-handed such plans are, the more flight a district will see, but also the greater will be physical integration among remaining students. Basically, those inclined to avoid integration will do so, and those less averse will not. In 1996, Rossell and Armor, analyzing 600 randomly selected districts with desegregation efforts ranging in coercion levels from magnet schools to mandatory assignment, determined that "voluntary plans that emphasize both choice and neighborhood schools can produce as much or more interracial exposure than mandatory reassignment plans."[63]

The worst performer was controlled choice, which Rossell and Armor noted is more "control" than "choice," with policies able to force someone out of their neighborhood school if they would put its racial balance out of the desired range. In a 1995 analysis of 20 districts, Rossell found that controlled choice was almost as unpopular as mandatory assignment, but produced less flight. It produced more flight, though, than magnet schooling, and less interracial contact.[64] Examining various types of public school choice, Rossell found that voluntary majority-to-minority choice was the most effective way to increase interracial exposure.

Charter Schools

Another form of public school choice is charter schooling. Charters are like open-enrollment schools or some magnets—they are required to take all comers and if oversubscribed select entrants by lottery—but they are not district schools. They are schools given a charter by a public entity such as a school district, but run by private groups.

After decades of growth, charter schools had higher enrollment than magnet schools in the 2016–17 school year: 3,010,287 students to 2,537,011.[65] The goal of charter schooling is not racial integration, though some charters take on that mission.[66] By providing chosen schools with unique cultures and focuses, and ostensibly private management free of many regulations governing traditional public schools, chartering is intended to create more innovative and effective schools. That said, those unique focuses—on the arts, "no excuses" cultures, or others—could foster physical integration. There is, however, little evidence of this.

In 2010, the Civil Rights Project found that aggregated at state and sometimes regional levels, charter schools were less diverse than traditional public schools. The average black charter student attended a school that was 73 percent African American, while the average black traditional public school student attended an institution that was half black. The differences for white, Latino, and Asian students were much smaller.[67] A 2017 Associated Press analysis found that in the 2014–15 school year "more than 1,000 of the nation's 6,747 charter schools had minority enrollment of at least 99 percent, and the number has been rising steadily."[68]

That said, comparing enrollment percentages at national, state, or even district levels can be misleading. Charter schools tend to be heavily concentrated in urban districts where the need for options is typically seen as greatest, and population densities enable multiple schools to be within reach of sufficient numbers of students to be viable. To get a better sense of charters' effects on physical integration, they can be compared to traditional schools in their catchment areas, or better yet, researchers can track moves from traditional public schools to charters.

Such better-focused studies have also repeatedly found a stratifying effect for charters,[69] though not as stark as the national numbers. Also, a few studies suggest that that effect might be mixed, with only some groups moving to or attending more racially or economically segregated schools,[70] and only some levels—elementary versus high schools—seeing stratification.[71] That said, the evidence is pretty clear that charter schools overall are not physical integrators.

Private Schools without Choice Programs

In addition to various forms of public school choice there are, of course, private schools. These schools, it is believed by different camps, are either an integration blessing or curse. They are a curse if they allow people to racially, economically, or religiously separate, a blessing if they enable them to overcome segregated public schooling rooted in segregated housing.

It may, at first glance, be difficult to see private schools as furnishing the material necessary for social cohesion. For one thing, in response to deseg-regation orders after *Brown v. Board of Education*, some southern states encouraged private "segregation academies" so white families could dodge integration. Districts basically closed public schools and switched state fund-ing to private schooling.[72] And it is by now crystal clear that people tend to seek others like themselves in housing and schooling.

Contemporary data on private schooling do not make the sector seem like a potentially grand social crossroads. For one thing, as a percentage of elemen-tary and secondary school enrollment, private schooling is small, accounting for approximately 10 percent of all school students as of 2019.[73] By sheer volume, it seems like a weak mechanism for integration.

It also seems like a poor integrator by demographics, too. Minorities, except for Asian Americans, are markedly underrepresented in private schools, with African Americans constituting about 14 percent of the American school-aged population but only 9 percent of private school kids, and Hispanics 25 percent of school-aged children but only 11 percent of private schoolers. Asians are 5 percent of the national population and 7 percent of private school students.[74]

Income differentials are also sizeable. In 2016, 39 percent of students who attended their assigned public schools were from households with incomes below 200 percent of the poverty line, or about $48,000 for a family of four, versus only 21 percent of students in private schools.[75] This income disparity does not mean that most private school families are rich, but it does show that low-income families are underrepresented among private schoolers.

Based on these broad data, it appears that private schools are highly averse to racial or economic mixing. But the status quo does not offer much insight into what is *possible*. Most importantly, the vast majority of private schools must charge tuition, whereas public schools, including magnets and charters, are free from families' perspectives, receiving big subsidies from local, state, and federal sources. In 2018–19, they expended $15,621 per student.[76] Most private schools charge appreciably less than that, with average tuition around $12,000, Catholic schools only clocking in at about $8,000, and other reli-gious around $10,000.[77]

Though many private schools strive to keep their prices low and offer financial assistance, having to charge tuition essentially guarantees student bodies will skew wealthier. And since there are high correlations between income and race, that translates into overrepresentation of white and Asian students. Supporting this, enrollment by race is much less divergent when broken down by income. In 2000, John Yun and Sean Reardon found that while poorer whites were twice as likely as poorer blacks and Hispanics to attend private schools, at the highest income decile private schooling was much higher overall, and whites were only about 20 percent more likely to attend than blacks, and 13 percent more likely than Hispanics.[78]

Several studies have indicated that private schooling is associated with stratification,[79] though sometimes with a twist. Robert Fairlie and Alexandra Resch, for instance, found that in the 1980s there was some evidence that white people would move to private schools to avoid poor black students, but sought out Asians.[80] And John Conlon and Mwangi Kimenyi found that in Mississippi, wealthier white students would attend private schools not to avoid all African Americans, only poor ones.[81] Still, private schools, at least absent access-improving choice programs, are less physically integrated than traditional public schools.

Private Schools with Choice Programs

What is the effect on physical integration of choice programs such as vouchers, scholarship tax credits, and education savings accounts that, by attaching money to students, help mitigate the big cost differentials between public and private schools? As of early 2021 there were 67 choice programs in 29 states, the District of Columbia, and Puerto Rico, assisting approximately 608,000 students. About 41 percent of students were receiving vouchers, 54 percent were using donated scholarship funds or paying tuition for which offsetting tax credits or deductions were provided, and about 5 percent had education savings accounts.[82]

These programs vary in their dollar amounts per recipient and the regulations attached to them, and few supply the full amount that would have been spent in the public school to which a child would have been assigned. Indeed, all are capped in one way or another—maximum voucher size, restricted to just state funding, and more—though some can equal the full cost of tuition. They are also often restricted to particular students, such as low-income or children with disabilities, and some restrict the schools at which they can be used.[83] In other words, they do not provide broad educational freedom, but they get nearer than private schooling without them.

Research in the United States suggests that choice slightly improves physical integration. Several studies have looked at the breakdowns of student bodies in private schools participating in voucher programs and the public schools students might have attended, and have tended to find that while the private schools were stratified, they were somewhat less so than the public schools.[84] Tracking students leaving public for private schools using private scholarships in New York City, Paul Peterson and David Campbell found that the private schools attended by scholarship recipients were less likely to be segregated than the public schools they left.[85]

On the flip side, assessing a voucher program that expanded from just serving New Orleans in 2008 to serving low-income children in poorly graded public schools throughout Louisiana in 2012 suggested students moving out of public schools using vouchers took those districts further from overall district demographic proportions.[86] The study, however, only included districts under long-standing federal desegregation orders, and was unclear what the racial-makeup effect was on the receiving schools, or schools that lost voucher students but were not among those that became less in line with overall district demographics. Did the latter become better integrated?

A more in-depth Louisiana analysis by the Education Research Alliance of New Orleans and the School Choice Demonstration Project at the University of Arkansas suggested the Louisiana program was, on net, integrating students, though hardly in overwhelming ways. They found that 82 percent of voucher transfers rendered their departed public schools less segregated, though 55 percent of transfers made receiving private schools more segregated. They also found that in districts under court desegregation orders, transfers out of the public schools greatly reduced segregation without exacerbating it in the receiving private schools.[87]

One outlier to the findings that U.S. choice programs have had net integrative effects is a 2010 study of Milwaukee's voucher program, which found a wash. While 90-plus percent of students who left public schools rendered their departed schools slightly less segregated, about the same numbers rendered their destination private school more segregated. Essentially, African Americans and some Hispanics were going from public schools in which they were the large majority to private schools in which they were the large majority.[88]

Because private school choice programs in the United States are few and of relatively recent vintage, it is valuable to look at the international research on choice as well. Indeed, much of the research that suggests choice would exacerbate physical separation are analyses of other countries, including the Netherlands and Chile, the latter of which commenced a nationwide transition to school choice in the 1970s. Perhaps the experiences in those countries can tell us something of value.[89]

Typically, international studies have found that choice stratifies, usually along class lines. Chang-Tai Hsieh and Miguel Urquiola found that increasing private school enrollment in a Chilean "commune"—a municipality serving on average 39,000 people—lowered the relative income of parents in the public schools.[90] This is consistent with "revealed preferences"; while parents typically say that academic achievement is their top factor in choosing a school, having a student body socioeconomically similar to themselves swamps it in actual choices made.[91]

Claudio Sapelli suggests that this sorting was a consequence of the voucher program's design, which provided uniform funding for all students even though low-income children needed greater resources to make up for deficits.[92] Research published in 2009 by Gregory Elacqua found that private schools in Chile tended to serve smaller percentages of low-income or indigenous children than publics, and were less internally diverse, but preliminary evidence suggested that a 2008 change to the law furnishing extra funding for low-income students may have helped ease segregation.[93]

How about the Netherlands, with what one might call the world's largest voucher program? With essentially anyone able to take public funds to myriad schools, its reach is very extensive. That said, there are national curriculum standards and teacher salary guidelines, so school autonomy—and thus the degree of choice—is constrained.

There is surprisingly little research on the enrollment effects of Dutch choice. Helen Ladd, Edward Fiske, and Nienke Ruijs, looking at integration by class, chalk that up to choice long having been driven by religious differences, and class-based stratification within religious schools thus being limited. Basically, well-to-do Catholics went to school with poorer Catholics, as did economically different Protestants and nonsectarian Dutch. They write, "The Dutch context of parental choice is that . . . these types of pressures to segregate by socio-economic disadvantage were overwhelmed by a different type of affinity or bond, namely religious."[94]

One last place worth looking is England. The English education system is complicated, with school types ranging from fee-charging privates to locally controlled publics to schools funded by the national government. Also, all state-funded schools must provide religious education and worship opportunities, and there are state-funded schools for various Christian denominations as well as Jews and Muslims.[95]

Research examining economic segregation in England has indicated that choice may have slightly decreased class-based segregation versus assignment to a school by address. But it is very difficult to pin down the effect of choice policies, and any effect was likely marginal. People there, like elsewhere, heavily tend to choose schools based on proximity to their homes, and housing in England is highly segregated.[96]

What can one reasonably conclude from the research on physical integration and private choice? Means-tested or other targeted programs, such as predominate in the United States, may have neutral or slightly integrative effects, perhaps because they help overcome wide disparities between schools wealthier families can afford and what scholarship recipients could have funded on their own. There is also evidence that weighting funding so lower-income children receive more may mitigate stratifying effects of equal funding. To the extent that one can conclude anything, targeted choice slightly decreases physical separation, whereas wide choice exacerbates it.

Bridge Building

The evidence for any school system creating physical integration is not encouraging. While force helps to put black and white students into buildings together, it also fuels, or at best does not abate, white flight. Many "integrated" schools are also highly segregated at the classroom level. Decreasing the amount of coercion via open enrollment and other choice mechanisms within traditional public school systems seems to reduce flight, but also less often result in diverse students in the same schools. And coercive approaches have likely fueled public sentiment heavily against efforts to engineer integration.

Charter schools have proven at best no more effective in fostering physical integration than coercion, though that has not typically been their mission. Private schools are clearly less diverse than public schools, while evidence suggests school choice programs such as vouchers that are means tested could have a small integrative effect. All in all, there seems to be no sustainable way to quickly achieve sustainable, meaningful, large-scale integration.

With sustained physical integration so difficult to achieve, the crucial question is, what school assignment policies best foster bridging capital—affective connections among people of different groups that make integration sustainable? The presence of such capital can be measured in many ways. One is simply to ask people how they feel about members of other groups, ideally including pre- and post-tests before they experience the policy being tested. Researchers can also observe actual social interactions: Do students in chosen schools end up voluntarily socializing more with members of other racial or religious groups than students in assigned institutions?

As mentioned earlier, there is very little random assignment research with pre- and post-testing, and none during the years of peak coerced integration. The studies tend to be much more correlational than causational. Worse, for many types of assignment we have no research on the bridging effects at all, and for others very little. This is perhaps because achieving physical integration was the far more immediate and central concern for most of these efforts.

Looking first at mandatory integration, some studies have attempted to assess whether contact leads to decreases in social distance. Most have found little effect. As Lee Sigelman and co-authors concluded after analyzing "hypersegregation" in Detroit, "integrationist policies can promote interracial contact but can do relatively little to promote close interracial ties."[97]

In 2001, James Moody, using a nationally representative sample of all types of schools—public and private—found that students in more heterogeneous schools tended to have more homogeneous friendships, though the relationship was not strictly linear.[98] Highlighting the hollowness of coerced physical integration, Moody found that schools in the South—the *most* physically integrated region—had the *smallest* degree of interracial friendship. Others have found that intergroup social connections tend to be much lower than would occur were friendships proportionate to group enrollment shares.[99]

Focusing specifically on mandatory integration as it happened—the best way to assess effects—is not encouraging. In 1975, Nancy St. John reviewed 120 studies and reported mixed results concerning interracial attitudes, though they were more often negative than positive. She also noted many flaws in the research.[100] That same year, Walter Stephan found that the research suggested that desegregation generally did not decrease white prejudice against blacks, while leading to increased black prejudice toward whites about as often as decreased.[101]

In a 1986 review, Stephan identified some additional studies that suggested that desegregation decreased black prejudice toward whites and increased white prejudice toward blacks. He also found that the research remained very limited.[102] In 1995, Armor reported that some of the most negative research findings on integration concerned its effect on racial attitudes.[103]

A 2005 study found 1980 graduates of six desegregated high schools felt desegregation made them less prejudiced and more comfortable around other groups, but they also reported little cross-group friendmaking and much segregation, via ability tracking and self-selection. As adults they integrated very little, indicating at best limited integrative effect.[104] In a 2020 study of the long-term impact of court-mandated school desegregation starting in the late 1950s, Chin found that greater exposure to desegregated schools had a negative effect on white people's support for such policies as affirmative action, suggesting forced integration spurred racial resentment.[105]

Overall, the research seems to comport with the historical evidence that compelled integration did a poor job of building bridges. But at least the bridging effects of forced integration have been studied. There is very little research on the effects of magnet schools, open enrollment, controlled choice, or charters.

Robert Bifulco, Christian Buerger, and Casey Cobb tackled bridging in magnet schools, while noting that "within-school, group relations" is an "understudied topic." Their analysis of 10 Connecticut magnet schools found that large majorities of students had at least one friend of a different racial or ethnic group, but they were only able to get two nearby traditional public schools to participate as controls; too few and self-selecting to constitute a useful comparison group. For what it is worth, those schools had appreciably lower rates of intergroup friendships than the magnets.[106]

Beatriz Clewell and Myra Joy examined a move from mandatory busing to magnet schooling in Monclair, New Jersey, and reported that many students said one of their three best friends was of another race. They did not, however, report supporting or comparison data.[107]

For open enrollment, a 1975 study by St. John and Ralph Lewis of 36 sixth-grade classrooms in 1967 Boston—before forced busing—assessed the social status of students based on race, sex, busing status, previous desegregation experience, and other variables. They found that African American children who were bused to schools under a voluntary program were appreciably less popular with white boys than African American children zoned to the school. The finding suggests that even busing under open enrollment could carry a stigma, but not necessarily based directly on race.[108]

Work by Janet Schofield and H. Andrew Sagar looking at seventh and eighth graders in a middle school using open enrollment found that when classes were untracked there were slight upticks in children of different races choosing to sit with each other at lunch. Tracking, however, negated that, suggesting that open enrollment alone, like mandatory assignment, is insufficient to build bridges.[109]

For controlled choice, in 1972 Armor studied Boston's METCO program, which was voluntary for African American children and allowed them to go to suburban schools, but assigned users to certain districts and sometimes used racial balances. Pre- and post-tests indicated that program users saw an increase in "separatist ideology" compared to nonusers who stayed in Boston public schools. However, many in the latter group attended desegregated Boston schools, and Pettigrew and co-authors suggested several problems with the research.[110]

How about charter schools? Surprisingly given their prominence in the national school choice debate, there is not much empirical evidence on their bridging effects. Searches of Google Scholar, ProQuest, and JSTOR coupling "charter schools" with terms such as "social distance," "Gordon Allport," and "intergroup friendship" produced no empirical research, at least not discernable through titles and abstracts.

This leaves private school choice. Perhaps best able to meet Allport's provisos, how does private schooling fare, both on its own and with programs such as vouchers?

Looking broadly, private schools seem to have better climates than public schools. In 2017, the federal government found that roughly 25 percent of public school students ages 12 to 18 reported seeing hate-related graffiti at school, versus only 6 percent of private school students. Seven percent of public school kids reported having been called hate-related words, versus 4 percent of private school students. Finally, 21 percent of public schoolers reported having been bullied, versus 16 percent of private school attendees.[111]

GLSEN, an LGBTQ organization focused on school safety, also found healthier climates in private schools. Both religious and nonreligious private schools outperformed publics on almost every climate measure, from the share of students reporting hearing anti-gay language in school, negative remarks about religion, or even mean comments about body weight.[112] Private schools also tended to have lower incidences of bias-driven bullying, harassment, or assault, and religious schools had the lowest report of race- or ethnicity-driven "victimization."

Nonreligious private schools were also consistently more LGBTQ friendly than traditional public schools when it came to "official" LGBTQ support, such as inclusion of LGBTQ content in curricula and having "supportive staff." Not surprising, religious schools were much less often found to have LGBTQ friendly policies. Overall, though, private schools, especially based on student behavior such as belittling speech or bullying, appeared more welcoming to diversity than in traditional publics, perhaps indicating that private schools are, indeed, able to build identities that at least reduce focus on divisions.

Some research indicates that private school graduates are as likely to have intergroup friendships as public school grads, suggesting private schooling has at least a neutral bridging effect. Cardus, a think tank that explores "social architecture" in the United States and Canada, has found that graduates of public, nonreligious private, Catholic, and evangelical Protestant schools all have close friends of different racial or ethnic backgrounds when between the ages of 24 and 39, including after controlling for numerous variables to more closely pinpoint school effects.[113] A similar effect was found for Catholic schools by researchers in the 1960s.[114]

Jay Greene and Nicole Mellow looked at lunchroom seating selection and found that students in private schools were more likely than public school children to voluntarily sit with members of a different race, though their research was restricted to randomly selected schools in just two unnamed cities.[115] They suspected that this greater integration was a function of private schools drawing students from wider areas than assigned public schools, as well as the attractiveness of religious missions. They also entertained the possibility that student bodies with generally higher social class levels will tend to include families more open to integration.

William Jeynes found that twelfth graders attending religious schools, controlling for variables such as parental education and family income, were much less likely to be in schools that experienced racially motivated fights than were students in nonreligious schools, and were somewhat more likely to have interracial friendships. Note, the comparison group included students in all types of nonreligious schools, including, private. But given public schools' dominance in total enrollment, the large majority of comparison students were likely in such schools, and religion may especially be the tie that can overcome racial divides.[116]

An examination of privately funded vouchers for low-income students found evidence that African American voucher students, but not members of other groups, attending private schools in New York City; Washington, DC; and Dayton, Ohio, had more intergroup friendships than black students in the public schools who applied for vouchers but did not receive them. They were also more likely to eat lunch with a student of another race. These findings were not, however, statistically significant, and Peterson and Campbell found no greater evidence of more powerful intergroup contacts for all—as opposed to just black—voucher users.[117]

Widescale international evidence in countries outside of the United States is limited, and to the extent it tells us anything, it suggests that choice neither greatly exacerbates nor promotes intergroup connections.

Looking *across* countries, the International Organization for the Right to Education and Freedom of Education and the Novae Terrae Foundation created the Freedom of Education Index based on the legality of non-governmental schools, the degree to which public funding can go to such schools, primary-aged children's enrollment in all schools, and non-governmental schools' share of primary enrollment.[118] The index creators correlated freedom to people's stated trust in others and found a slightly positive association.[119]

For his doctoral dissertation, McCluskey created an index of education centralization, including funding and controls for non-governmental schools, and locus of public school control at national or lower levels. He found a correlation associating decentralization with greater trust. However, there was no statistically significant connection after controlling for variables such as income inequality and racial/ethnic diversity.[120]

Both analyses suffer from major shortcomings. It is, for instance, difficult to assess what is in law versus what actually happens. As researcher James Tooley has found, many countries may legally inhibit private schooling, but it may proliferate nonetheless.[121] Gathering data can be difficult—the Freedom Index correlation included only 20 countries due to limited trust data[122]—and indexes often involve subjective component weightings. Generalized trust questions may also do a poor job of capturing broad social cohesion.[123] Finally, both assessments were just snapshots in time, not capturing how cohesion changes as educational choice grows or shrinks.

Combining the bridge-building research on private schooling both in and out of choice programs suggests that private schools might have a small advantage in building bridges. But the evidence overall is very thin, no doubt because very rarely is private schooling an option on even close to a level playing field with public schools. To really determine the potential bridging effect, probably much more choice—and study—is needed. Thankfully, that can be undertaken without too much fear: private school choice is unlikely to make segregation much worse, and the historical evidence is strong that it would at least make education more peaceful.

CIVICS AND PRO-SOCIAL ATTITUDES

Another way education systems might supply bridging material is their inculcation of civic values including community volunteering; tolerance of people with divergent views; and, arguably, knowledge of how one's government works. "Arguably," because high degrees of knowledge do not imply positive interactions with others. Volunteering and tolerance more likely do, though one could volunteer only in one's own, insular community, and one could simply tolerate the beliefs or cultures of others without engaging with them.

Private choice appears to have a clear advantage here. Richard Niemi and Chris Chapman reported that in 1996, private high school students exhibited greater political knowledge, political participation skills, feelings of political efficacy, and tolerance of controversial books in public libraries than did public school students. This held after controlling for student characteristics such as race and gender, and family characteristics such as parents' political knowledge.[124] Belfield and Levin, summarizing two studies on the effects of private schools on community service, civic skills, political tolerance, and more, found typically positive effects for Catholic, non-Catholic religious, and private secular schools.[125]

In 2014, Cardus reported that graduates ages 24 to 39 of public, Roman Catholic, evangelical Protestant, and nonreligious private high schools all had similar levels of civic engagement, rates of taking civics courses, and interest in working for the common good.[126] Cardus's 2016 survey of Canadian graduates had similar results. Except for homeschoolers, graduates ages 23 to 40 from all private sectors were equally connected to society and tolerant of others when compared with public schools, including tolerance of people professing non-Christian religions.[127] Public schoolers exhibited less civic involvement, such as contacting government officials or serving on community boards, than independent private school students.

In 2020, Wolf reviewed 34 quantitative studies, with 86 total findings, on the effects of private choice in the United States on civic values such as political tolerance and voluntarism, and civic skills such as expressing one's opinion. The overwhelming majority of studies with controls for potentially confounding variables yielded either statistically significant or neutral effects for choice, and only three findings indicated a traditional public school advantage. Fourteen findings were of a private school advantage, 12 neutral, and just one a public school advantage.[128]

Looking outside of North America, there is no compelling evidence that private schools are any less likely to promote positive civic values than public schools. That said, while there is often more choice in other countries than the United States, there tends to be more national curricular control as well. That may be why in 2004 Jaap Dronkers of the European University Institute concluded that "it does not seem to be the case that the much greater availability of publicly subsidized parental choice in Europe than in the United States has increased educational inequality or segregation or undermined either student learning or civic socialization."[129]

CONCLUSION

A major assumption on which government-run, free schooling for all has been built is that it will unify diverse people. Whether it is bridging regional divides, as some Founders desired, or shrinking religious, racial, class, philosophical, or political cleavages, public schools have been charged with bringing diverse students into shared physical space and instilling a common identity. As is now increasingly clear, that public schools could accomplish this is questionable at best, dangerously fanciful at worst.

Contrary to the "create common schools and they will bridge" assumption driving public schooling, the evidence suggests that choice may be a better way to foster cohesion than top-down control. Historical evidence strongly suggests that choice beats force when it comes to building social cohesion. Most powerful is its "negative" effect: It enables people to avoid inherently divisive zero-sum clashes, especially those pitting basic values and personal identities against each other. Less intuitive, it might also allow diverse people to come together based on something they share, providing more sustainable bridging material than assigned public schools.

What does statistical research show us? While there are extensive literatures on the effects of social capital on commercial or educational outcomes—people with more social ties tend to do better—there is little going in the other direction: examining how commerce or educational structure impact social capital. In particular, it appears only a handful of studies have attempted to gauge how well different ways of delivering education may help or hinder bridge building among people of socially distant groups.

The research suggests that a system grounded in choice would not greatly exacerbate the physical segregation we have with our housing-based school assignment system, and choice weighted toward lower-income families might shrink it. There is also a bit of research supporting the theory that allowing people to select schools offering specific things—Lutheran theology, Waldorf pedagogy, arts-based curricula—can foster crosscutting identities. These effects are small compared to avoiding unity-smashing conflict, but just as weakling water slowly erodes rock to carve great canyons, choice may, over time, help construct sturdy social bridges.

That said, the education system will *not* be the primary driver of unity. The research strongly suggests that no education policy can move unwilling people, in large numbers, into close physical proximity, or make members of separated groups like each other. Millions of people will, on their own, have to begin to accept integration in their own lives and in society for sustainable integration to occur. But the education system can at least stop forcing divisive conflict, and can shrink barriers that keep families, based largely on their income, from entering schools conducive to building new bridges.

What would such a system look like? The next, and final, chapter lays it out.

NOTES

1. Katrin Benhold, "French Muslims Find Haven in Catholic Schools," *New York Times*, September 28, 2008.

2. Robert D. Putnam, *Bowling Alone: The Collapse and Revival of American Community* (New York: Simon & Schuster, 2000).

3. Katherine W. Phillips, "How Diversity Makes Us Smarter," *Scientific American*, October 1, 2014.

4. Alejandro Portes and Patricia Landolt, "The Downside of Social Capital," *The American Prospect* 26, no. 26, May–June 1996, 18–21.

5. See, for instance, Organization for Economic Cooperation and Development, Table 8.1: Trust, *Society at a Glance 2011: OECD Social Indicators*, http://www.oecd-ilibrary.org/sites/soc_glance-2011-en/08/01/g8_co1-01.html?contentType=%2fns%2fStatisticalPublication%2c%2fns%2fChapter&itemId=%2fcontent%2fchapter%2fsoc_glance-2011-26-en&mimeType=text%2fhtml&containerItemId=%2fcontent%2fserial%2f19991290&accessItemIds=&option6=imprint&value6=http%3a%2f%2foecd.metastore.ingenta.com%2fcontent%2fimprint%2foecd&_csp_=7d6a863ad60f09c08a8e2c78701e4faf.

6. Robert Putnam, "E Pluribus Unum: Diversity and Community in the Twenty-First Century," *Scandinavian Political Studies* 30, no. 2 (2007): 142.

7. Robert Putnam, "Immigration and the E Pluribus Unum Issue," *Wall Street Journal*, March 31, 2017.

8. Dane Stangler and Jason Wiens, "The Economic Case for Welcoming Immigrant Entrepreneurs," Ewing Marion Kauffman Foundation, September 8, 2015, http://www.kauffman.org/what-we-do/resources/entrepreneurship-policy-digest/the-economic-case-for-welcoming-immigrant-entrepreneurs.

9. Francis Fukuyama, *Trust: The Social Virtues and the Creation of Prosperity* (New York: Free Press, 1995), 362.

10. Matthew Diebel, "The Amish: Ten Things You Might Not Know," *USA Today*, August 15, 2014.

11. John Stuart Mill, *Principles of Political Economy with Some of Their Applications to Social Philosophy*, Book III, chapter 17, paragraph 14, http://www. econlib.org/library/Mill/mlP46.html.

12. Ferdinand Tönnies, *Community and Society*, trans. and ed. Charles P. Loomis (Mineola, NY: Dover Publications, 2002), 77.

13. Tönnies, 2002, 78.

14. Peter D. Salins, *Assimilation American Style* (New York: Basic Books, 1997), 53.

15. Robert Putnam, *Making Democracy Work: Civic Traditions in Modern Italy* (Princeton, NJ: Princeton University Press, 1993), 127.

16. For a general discussion of this, see Albert O. Hirschman, "Rival Interpretations of Market Society: Civilizing, Destructive, or Feeble," *Journal of Economic Literature* 20, no. 4 (December 1982): 1463–1484.

17. Montesquieu, *The Spirit of the Laws*, eds. Anne Cohler, Basia Miller, and Harold Stone (Cambridge, UK: Cambridge University Press, 1992), 155.

18. Adam Smith, "Report Dated 1766," in *Lectures on Jurisprudence*, eds. R. L. Meek, D. D. Raphael, and P. G. Stein (Indianapolis: Liberty Classics, 1982), 538.

19. Max Weber quoted in Michael Hechter, *Principles of Group Solidarity* (Berkeley, CA: University of California Press, 1987), 23.

20. Walker Connor, "Nation-Building or Nation-Destroying," *World Politics* 24, no. 3 (April 1972): 319–355.

21. Michael Barone, *The New Americans: How the Melting Pot Can Work Again* (Washington, DC: Regnery, 2001).

22. Edward George Hartmann, *The Movement to Americanize the Immigrant* (New York: Columbia University Press, 1948), 271.

23. Vasiliki Fouka, "Backlash: The Unintended Effects of Language Prohibition in U.S. Schools after World War I," *The Review of Economic Studies* 87, no. 1 (January 2020): 204–239.

24. Robert Wuthnow, *Loose Connections: Joining Together in America's Fragmented Communities* (Cambridge, MA: Harvard University Press, 1998), 31–34.

25. Partha Dasgupta, "Economics of Social Capital," *The Economic Record*, 81 (2005): S2–S21.

26. Simon Szreter, "The State of Social Capital: Bringing Back in Power, Politics, and History," *Theory and Society* 31, no. 5 (October 2002): 588.

27. Cordelia Hebblethwaite, "Who, What, Why: In Which Countries Is Coca-Cola Not Sold?" BBC News, September 11, 2012, http://www.bbc.com/news/magazine-19550067.

28. Mona Chalabi and John Burn-Murdoch, "McDonald's 34,492 Restaurants: Where Are They?" *Guardian*, July 17, 2013, https://www.theguardian.com/news/datablog/2013/jul/17/mcdonalds-restaurants-where-are-they.

29. Tamar Herman, "Why K-Pop Is Finally Breaking into the U.S. Mainstream," *Billboard*, February 28, 2019, https://www.billboard.com/articles/columns/k-town/8500363/k-pop-closer-than-ever-american-pop-mainstream/.

30. Lisa Bisset, "The App Store's Most Downloaded Games of All Time: Angry Birds, Fruit Ninja and Temple Run," PocketGamer.biz,

May 3, 2013, https://www.pocketgamer.biz/news/50604/the-app-stores-most-downloaded-games-of-all-time-angry-birds-fruit-ninja-and-temple-run/.

31. For research on the positive economic effect of bonding capital, see, for instance, James S. Coleman, "Social Capital in the Creation of Human Capital," *American Journal of Sociology*, vol. 94 Supplement, (1988): S95–S120; Putnam, *Making Democracy Work*; Putnam, *Bowling Alone*; Paul F. Whitely, "Economic Growth and Social Capital," *Political Studies* 48, no. 3 (June 2000): 443–466; Jonathan Temple and Paul A. Johnson, "Social Capability and Economic Growth," *Quarterly Journal of Economics* 113, no. 3 (August 1998): 965–990; La Porta et al., 1997; and Stephen Knack and Philip Keefer, "Does Social Capital Have an Economic Payoff? A Cross-Country Investigation," *Quarterly Journal of Economics* 112, no. 4 (November 1997): 1251–1288. For a discussion of negative effects, see Fukuyama, *Trust*, 161–193.

32. Edward L. Glaeser, David Laibson, and Bruce Sacerdote, "An Economic Approach to Social Capital," *The Economic Journal* 112 (November 2002): F437–F458.

33. Simon Ville, "Social Capital Formation in Australian Rural Communities: The Role of Stock and Station Agents," *The Journal of Interdisciplinary History* 36, No. 2 (Autumn 2005): 185–208.

34. Lawrence A. Cremin, *American Education: The Colonial Experience 1607–1783* (New York: Harper Torchbooks, 1970), 309.

35. Christopher Dock, *School Management* (Rise of Douai, 2016).

36. Patrick R. Gibbons, "One Man's War on Florida's Desegregated Schools," redefinED, September 20, 2016, https://www.redefinedonline.org/2016/09/war-florida-desegregated-private-schools/.

37. Tim O'Neil, "Looking back: 1947: Parents Protest after Saint Louis Catholic Schools Are Integrated," *Saint Louis Post-Dispatch*, September 6, 2017.

38. Mira B. Wilson, "Colored Students Are an Asset," cited in Michelle A. Purdy, *Transforming the Elite: Black Students and the Desegregation of Private Schools* (Chapel Hill, NC: The University of North Carolina Press, 2018), 22.

39. North Carolina History Project, "Bishop Vincent S. Waters (1904–1974)," https://northcarolinahistory.org/encyclopedia/bishop-vincent-s-waters-1904-1974/.

40. David Chazan, "France Drops Legal Quota on French Radio Songs as DJs Forced to Play 'Boring Old Ballads,'" *Telegraph*, March 18, 2016; and John Hopewell, "Hollywood Stymied as Europe Sticks with Its Limits on Film and TV," *Variety*, June 14, 2013.

41. Katrin Bennhold, "French Muslims Find Haven in Catholic Schools," *New York Times*, September 29, 2008.

42. See Charles L. Glenn, "Religion and the Adoption of School Choice Policies," *Journal of School Choice* 12, no. 4 (Special issue on religion and school choice): 461–476.

43. Horace Mann, "Report for 1843," in *Life and Works of Horace Mann*, ed. Mary Mann (Boston: Horace B. Fuller, 1868), 230–418.

44. Charles L. Glenn, *Contrasting Models of State and School: A Comparative Historical Study of Parental Choice and State Control* (New York: Continuum, 2011), 73.

45. Robert Maranto and Dirk C. van Raemdonck, "Letting Religion and Education Overlap," *Wall Street Journal*, January 8, 2015.

46. Glenn, *Contrasting Models*, 203–204.

47. Ibid., 203.

48. Statistics Netherlands, "Over Half of the Dutch Population Are Not Religious," October 23, 2018, https://www.cbs.nl/en-gb/news/2018/43/over-half-of-the-dutch-population-are-not-religious.

49. Mann, "Report for 1843," 345.

50. Mann, "Report for 1843," 367.

51. Lutz B. Reuter, "School Choice and Civic Values in Germany," in *Educating Citizens: International Perspectives on Civic Values and School Choice*, eds. Patrick J. Wolf and Stephen Macedo (Washington, DC: Brookings Institution Press, 2004), 224–230.

52. Lynn Bosetti, Deani Van Pelt, and Derek J. Allison, "The Changing Landscape of School Choice in Canada: From Pluralism to Parental Preference?" *Education Policy Analysis Archives*, 25, no. 38 (April 2017).

53. David E. Campbell, "The Civic Implications of Canada's Education System," in *Educating Citizens: International Perspectives on Civic Values and School Choice*, 187–210.

54. John B. McConahay, "The Effects of School Desegregation upon Students' Racial Attitudes and Behavior: A Critical Review of the Literature and a Prolegomenon to Future Research," *Law and Contemporary Problems* 42, no. 3 (Summer 1978): 77–107.

55. Christine H. Rossell and David J. Armor, "The Effectiveness of School Desegregation Plans, 1968–1991," *American Politics Quarterly* 24, no. 3 (July 1996): 276.

56. Gary Orfield, John Kucsera, and Genevieve Siegel-Hawley, "*E Pluribus* . . . Separation? Deepening Double Segregation for Our Students," Civil Rights Project, September 2012, 34.

57. Finis Welch and Audrey Light, "New Evidence on School Desegregation," U.S. Council on Civil Rights, June 1987, https://files.eric.ed.gov/fulltext/ED293936.pdf; Christine H. Rossell, "The Convergence of Black and White Attitudes on School Desegregation Issues during the Four Decade Evolution of the Plans," *William & Mary Law Review* 36, no. 2, (1995): 613–663. A possible dissenter is Mark A. Smylie, who found mandatory desegregation did not increase flight, at least versus voluntary desegregation: "Reducing Racial Isolation in Large School Districts: The Comparative Effectiveness of Mandatory and Voluntary Desegregation," *Urban Education* 17, no. 4 (January 1983): 477–502.

58. Reynolds Farley, Toni Richards, and Clarence Wurdock, "School Desegregation and White Flight: An Investigation of Competing Models and Their Discrepant Findings," *Sociology of Education* 53 (July 1980): 123–139.

59. Orfield, Kucsera, and Siegel-Hawley, "*E Pluribus* . . . Separation?," 44.

60. Thomas W. Collins and George W. Noblit, "Stratification and Resegregation: The Case of Crossover High School, Memphis, Tennessee," National Institute of Education, 1976, 109.

61. Orfield, Kucsera, and Siegel-Hawley, "*E Pluribus* . . . Separation?," 2012.

62. Ibid., 36.

63. Rossell and Armor, "The Effectiveness of School Desegregation Plans, 1968–1991," 298.

64. Christine H. Rossell, "Controlled Choice Desegregation Plans: Not Enough Choice, Too Much Control?" *Urban Affairs Review* 31, no. 1 (1995): 43–76.

65. Digest of Education Statistics, "Number and enrollment of public elementary and secondary schools, by school level, type, and charter, magnet, and virtual status: Selected years, 1990–91 through 2016–17," https://nces.ed.gov/programs/digest/d18/tables/dt18_216.20.asp.

66. Though student body diversity is not a primary goal of charter schooling, many charter operators may seek it, and the National Coalition of Diverse Charter Schools was founded in 2014 "to support the creation and expansion of high-quality, racially and economically diverse public charter schools." As of 2016, the coalition counted 36 charter organizations operating more than 100 schools as members. National Coalition of Diverse Charter Schools, "National Coalition of Diverse Charter Schools Names Dianne M. Piche Founding Executive Director," Press Release, August 10, 2016.

67. Erica Frankenberg et al., "Choice without Equity: Charter School Segregation and the Need for Civil Rights Standards," Civil Rights Project, 2010, 47–48.

68. Ivan Moreno, "US Charter Schools Put Growing Numbers in Isolation," Associated Press, December 3, 2017.

69. For example, Institute on Race and Poverty, "Failed Promises: Assessing Charter Schools in the Twin Cities," University of Minnesota Law School, November 2008; Chad d'Entremont and Charisse Gordon, "Circles of Influence: How Neighborhood Demographics and Charter School Locations Influence Student Enrollments," Working Paper, 2008; Gregory J. Weiher and Kent L. Tedin, "Does Choice Lead to Racially Distinctive Schools? Charter Schools and Household Preferences," *Journal of Policy Analysis and Management* 21, no. 1 (Winter 2002): 79–92; and Robert Bifulco and Helen F. Ladd, "School Choice, Racial Segregation, and Test-Score Gaps: Evidence from North Carolina's Charter School Program," *Journal of Policy Analysis and Management* 26, no. 1 (Winter 2007): 31–56.

70. For instance, John L. Logan and Julia Burdick-Will found charters are more racially isolating for whites and African Americans than traditional public schools, but slightly less so for Asians and neutral for Hispanics. "School Segregation, Charter Schools, and Access to Quality Education," *Journal of Urban Affairs* 38, no. 3 (2016): 323–343. Beryl Nelson et al. found in the 1998–99 school year charters had racial and ethnic shares similar to their surrounding districts, but served higher shares of low-income students, about equal shares of limited-English children, and lower shares of kids with disabilities. "The State of Charter Schools, 2000: National Study of Charter Schools: Fourth-Year Report," U.S. Department of Education, January 2000, https://files.eric.ed.gov/fulltext/ED437724.pdf.

71. David R. Garcia found that students tended to leave more racially integrated elementary schools to attend charters, but charter high schools were equally or less segregated. "The Impact of School Choice on Racial Segregation in Charter Schools," *Educational Policy* 22, no. 6 (October 2008): 805–829.

72. Southern Education Foundation, "Race and Ethnicity in a New Era of Public Funding for Private Schools: Private School Enrollment in the South and the Nation," 2016; Editorial Board, "Segregation Academies and State Action," *Yale Law Journal* 82, no. 7 (June 1973): 1436–1461.

73. Share calculated using U.S. Department of Education, National Center for Education Statistics, *Digest of Education Statistics, 2019*, Table 205.10, https://nces.ed.gov/programs/digest/d19/tables/dt19_205.10.asp?current=yes.

74. Population data from U.S. Department of Education, National Center for Education Statistics, "Indicator 1: Population Distribution," *Status and Trends in the Education of Racial and Ethnic Groups*, February 2019, https://nces.ed.gov/programs/raceindicators/indicator_RAA.asp; private enrollment data from U.S. Department of Education, National Center for Education Statistics, "Indicator 3: Private Schools and Enrollment," *School Choice in the United States: 2019*, https://nces.ed.gov/programs/schoolchoice/ind_03.asp.

75. U.S. Department of Education, National Center for Education Statistics, "Indicator 4: Household Characteristics of Students in Public and Private Schools," *School Choice in the United States: 2019*, https://nces.ed.gov/programs/schoolchoice/ind_04.asp.

76. Inflation-adjusted per student in fall enrollment, U.S. Department of Education, National Center for Education Statistics, *Digest of Education Statistics, 2020*, Table 236.55, https://nces.ed.gov/programs/digest/d20/tables/dt20_236.55.asp?current=yes.

77. U.S. Department of Education, National Center for Education Statistics, *Digest of Education Statistics, 2020*, Table 205.50, https://nces.ed.gov/programs/digest/d20/tables/dt20_205.50.asp.

78. John T. Yun and Sean F. Reardon, "Private School Racial Enrollments and Segregation," in *School Choice and Diversity: What the Evidence Says*, ed. Janelle T. Scott, (New York: Teachers College Press, 2005), 9–26; and Salvatore Saporito and Deenesh Sohoni, "Coloring outside the Lines: Racial Segregation in Public Schools and Their Attendance Boundaries," *Sociology of Education* 79, no. 2 (April 2006): 81–105.

79. See, for instance, Hamilton Lankford and James Wyckoff, "Why Are Schools Racially Segregated? Implications for School Choice Policies," in *School Choice and Diversity: What the Evidence Says*, eds. Janelle T. Scott and Richard F. Elmore, (New York: Teachers College Press, 1996), 95–117;

80. Robert W. Fairlie and Alexandra M. Resch, "Is There 'White Flight' into Private Schools? Evidence from the National Educational Longitudinal Survey," *Review of Economics and Statistics* 84, no. 1 (February 2002): 21–33.

81. John R. Conlon and Mwangi S. Kimenyi, "Attitudes Towards Race and Poverty in the Demand for Private Education: The Case of Mississippi," *Review of Black Political Economy* 20, no. 2 (1991): 5–22.

82. EdChoice, "The ABCs of School Choice: 2021 Edition," https://www.edchoice.org/wp-content/uploads/2021/03/2021-ABCs-of-School-Choice-WEB-2-24.pdf.

83. For a convenient summary of existing programs and their general provisions, see Ibid., 137–149.

84. For a summary of the research see Ed Choice, "The 123s of School Choice: What the Research Says about Private School Choice Programs in America, 2019 Edition," 45–50, https://www.edchoice.org/wp-content/uploads/2019/04/123s-of-School-Choice.pdf#page=26.

85. Paul E. Peterson and David E. Campbell, "An Evaluation of the Children's Scholarship Fund," Working Paper, Program on Education Policy Governance, Harvard University, May 2001.

86. *Brumfield v. Dodd*, Civ. A. No. 71-1316.

87. Anne J. Egalite et al., "The Impact of the Louisiana Scholarship Program on Racial Segregation in Louisiana Schools," Education Research Alliance of New Orleans and the School Choice Demonstration Project, February 26, 2016.

88. Jay P. Greene, Jonathan N. Mills, and Stuart Buck, "The Milwaukee Parental Choice Program's Effect on School Integration," School Choice Demonstration Project Report No. 20, April 2010.

89. Choice critics sometimes also point to New Zealand, but the best-known study of New Zealand was not about private schooling but choice among public schools, accompanied by some devolution of control to the school level, but nothing akin to broad educational freedom. Edward B. Fiske and Helen F. Ladd, *When Schools Compete: A Cautionary Tale* (Washington, DC: Brookings Institution Press, 2000).

90. Chang-Tai Hsieh and Miguel Urquiola, "The Effects of Generalized School Choice on Achievement and Stratification: Evidence from Chile's Voucher Program," *Journal of Public Economics* 90 (2006): 1477–1503.

91. Gregory Elacqua, Mark Schneider, and Jack Buckley, "School Choice in Chile: Is It Class or the Classroom?" *Journal of Policy Analysis and Management* 25, no. 3 (2006): 577–601.

92. Claudio Sapelli, "The Chilean Voucher System: Some New Results and Research Challenges," *Cuadranos de Economia* 40, no. 121 (December 2003): 530–538.

93. Gregory Elacqua, "The Impact of School Choice and Public Policy on Segregation: Evidence from Chile," Documento de Trabajo CPCE No. 10, Centro de Políticas Comparades de Educación, October 2009.

94. Helen F. Ladd, Edward B. Fiske, and Nienke Ruijs, "Parental Choice in the Netherlands: Growing Concerns about Segregation," Working Paper, September 2009, 5.

95. Stephen Gorard, "School Choice Policies and Social Integration: The Experience of England and Wales," in *Educating Citizens: International Perspectives on Civic Values and School Choice*, 136–138; and The Inter Faith Network for the United Kingdom, "Religious Education across the UK," https://www.interfaith.org.uk/activity/religious-education, accessed October 22, 2020.

96. Gorard, "School Choice," 141–145.

97. Lee Sigelman et al., "Making Contact? Black-White Social Interactions in an Urban Setting," *American Journal of Sociology* 101, no. 5 (March 1996): 1326.

98. James Moody, "Race, School Integration, and Friendship Segregation in America," *American Journal of Sociology* 107, no. 1 (November 2001): 679–716.

99. Maureen T. Hallinan and Richard A. Williams, "Interracial Friendship Choices in Secondary Schools," *American Sociological Review* 54, no. 1 (February 1989): 67–78; Kara Joyner and Grace Kao, "School Racial Composition and Adolescent Racial Homophily," *Social Science Quarterly* 81, no. 3 (September 2000): 810–825.

100. Nancy H. St. John, *School Desegregation: Outcomes for Children* (New York: John Wiley and Sons, 1975), 120.

101. Walter G. Stephan, "School Desegregation: An Evaluation of Predictions Made in *Brown v. Board of Education*," *Psychology Bulletin* 85, no. 2 (March 1978): 217–238.

102. Walter G. Stephan, "The Effects of School Desegregation: An Evaluation 30 Years after *Brown*," in *Advances in Applied Social Psychology*, eds. Michael J. Saks and Leonard Saxe (Hillsdale, NJ: Erlbaum, 1986), 183–187.

103. David. J. Armor, *Forced Justice: School Desegregation and the Law* (New York: Oxford University Press, 1995), 71.

104. Amy Stuart Wells et al., "How Desegregation Changed Us: The Effects of Racially Mixed Schools on Students and Society," Teachers College, Columbia University, and University of California at Los Angeles, 2005.

105. Mark J. Chin, "The Impact of School Desegregation on White Individuals' Racial Attitudes and Politics in Adulthood," Ed Working Papers, Annenberg Institute at Brown University, November 2020, https://www.edworkingpapers.com/ai20-318.

106. Robert Bifulco, Christian Buerger, and Casey Cobb, "Intergroup Relations in Integrated Schools: A Glimpse Inside Interdistrict Magnet Schools," *Education Policy Analysis Archives* 20, no. 28 (September 17, 2012): 4, http://epaa.asu.edu/ojs/article/view/1033.

107. Beatriz C. Clewell and Myra F. Joy, "Choice in Montclair, New Jersey: A Policy Information Paper," Education Testing Service, January 1990.

108. Nancy H. St. John and Ralph G. Lewis, "Race and the Social Structure of the Elementary Classroom," *Sociology of Education* 38, no. 3 (Summer 1975): 346–368.

109. Janet W. Schofield and H. Andrew Sagar, "Peer Interaction Patterns in an Integrated Middle School," *Sociometry* 40, no. 2 (June 1977): 130–138; Janet W. Schofield, "The Impact of Positively Structured Contact on Intergroup Behavior: Does It Last Under Adverse Conditions?" *Social Psychology Quarterly* 42, no. 3 (September 1979): 280–284.

110. David J. Armor, "The Evidence on Busing," *The Public Interest*, Summer 1972, https://www.nationalaffairs.com/public_interest/detail/the-evidence-on-busing; and Thomas F. Pettigrew et al., "Busing: A Review of 'The Evidence,'" *The Public Interest*, Winter 1973, https://files.eric.ed.gov/fulltext/ED075535.pdf.

111. U.S. Department of Education, National Center for Education Statistics, "Indicator 7: School Crime and Safety for Public and Private School Students," *School Choice in the United States: 2019*, https://nces.ed.gov/programs/schoolchoice/ind_07.asp.

112. Joseph G. Kosciw et al., "The 2017 National School Climate Survey: The Experiences of Lesbian, Gay, Bisexual, Transgender, and Queer Youth in Our Nation's

Schools," GLSEN, 2018, 163, https://www.glsen.org/sites/default/files/2019-12/Full_NSCS_Report_English_2017.pdf.

113. Ray Pennings et al., "Cardus Education Survey: Private Schools for the Public Good, 2014 Report," https://www.cardus.ca/research/education/reports/cardus-education-survey-2014-private-schools-for-the-public-good/.

114. Andrew M. Greeley and Peter H. Rossi found that while 17-year-old students who went to Catholic school for their entire education were significantly more likely to have more than half of their best friends be Catholic than Catholic students who never attended Catholic school, there was no significant difference in the share saying their three best friends were Catholic as adults. *The Education of Catholic Americans* (Garden City, NY: Anchor Books, 1968), 120–125.

115. Jay P. Greene and Nicole Mellow, "Integration Where It Counts: A Study of Racial Integration in Public and Private School Lunchrooms," paper presented at the American Political Science Association Meeting, Boston, September 1998.

116. William Jeynes, *Religion, Education, and Academic Success* (Greenwich, CT: Information Age Publishing, 2003), 165–178.

117. Peterson and Campbell, "An Evolution of the Children's Scholarship Fund." May 2001.

118. International Organization for the Right to Education and Freedom of Education and Novae Terrae Foundation, "Freedom of Education Index Worldwide Report 2016 on Freedom of Education," https://www.oidel.org/doc/FEI_complet2.pdf.

119. International Organization for the Right to Education and Freedom of Education and Novae Terrae Foundation, "Freedom of Education Index Correlations with Selected Indicators, 2018," 46–47, https://www.oidel.org/wp-content/uploads/2018/07/Version-anglaise_cute_3.pdf.

120. Neal P. McCluskey, "Education and Social Capital Maximization: Does Decentralization Hold the Key?" doctoral dissertation, George Mason University, 2013.

121. James Tooley, *The Beautiful Tree* (Washington, DC: Cato Institute, 2009).

122. International Organization for the Right to Education and Freedom of Education and Novae Terrae Foundation, "Freedom of Education Index Correlations with Selected Indicators, 2018," 46.

123. See, for instance, Patrick Sturgis and Patten Smith, "Assessing the Validity of Generalized Trust Questions: What Kind of Trust Are We Measuring?" *International Journal of Public Opinion Research* 22, no. 1 (Spring 2010): 74–92; and Sebastian Lundmark, Mikael Gilljam, and Stefan Dahlberg, "Measuring Generalized Trust: An Examination of Question Wording and the Number of Scale Points," *Public Opinion Quarterly* 80, no. 1 (Spring 2016): 26–43.

124. Richard G. Niemi and Chris Chapman, "The Civic Development of 9th- through 12th-Grade Students in the United States: 1996," NCES 1999–131, U.S. Department of Education, National Center for Education Statistics, November 1998.

125. Clive R. Belfield and Henry M. Levin, *Privatizing Educational Choice: Consequences for Parents, Schools, and Public Policy* (Boulder, CO: Paradigm, 2005), 51–53.

126. Pennings et al., "Cardus Education Survey."

127. Elizabeth Green et al., "Educating to Love Your Neighbour: The Full Picture of Canadian Graduates," Cardus Education Survey, 2016.

128. Patrick J. Wolf, "Public Schools are Necessary for a Stable Democracy," in *School Choice Myths: Setting the Record Straight on Education Freedom*, eds. Neal McCluskey and Corey DeAngelis (Washington, DC: Cato Institute, 2020), 39–57.

129. Jaap Dronkers, "Do Public and Religious Schools Really Differ? Assessing the European Evidence," in *Educating Citizens: International Perspectives on Civic Values and School Choice*, eds. Patrick J. Wolf and Stephen Macedo (Washington, DC: Brookings Institution Press, 2004), 308.

Chapter 7

For Peace and Cohesion, We Need Educational Liberty

The Bay Area of California is about as diverse a melting pot as anyone could imagine. According to the 2010 federal census, the population of the region including San Francisco, Marin County, Napa County, and a few other juris- dictions, has a population that is 52.5 percent white, 23.3 percent Asian, 6.7 percent Black or African American, 5.4 percent two or more races, and 10.8 percent "some other race." Of course, the area has some intergroup friction, and people do not disperse in perfectly integrated proportions, but generally speaking, folks get along, and do so without being forced to sacrifice what makes their groups distinctive.

What brings so many diverse people to Silicon Valley, and binds them together? A major factor is business—earning a living in the world's tech mecca. Indeed, one study found that slightly more than half of the nation's startup companies valued at $1 billion or more were started by immigrants, many in the Bay Area. People come from all over the planet, and learn to get along, so that they can work together and succeed. Mutual self-interest makes them feel at least like noncombatants, at best like teammates.

In 2013 the Christian Science Monitor *profiled Mohammed Raziuddin, who came from India to attend college in America. He stayed in the United States because "there was so much buzz and excitement in the Valley. I couldn't fathom leaving." But it was on September 11, 2001, that Raziuddin truly felt at home in America. At that point he was working in Boston, and his boss told Raziuddin, a Muslim, not to fear that he would suffer reprisals—the company would take care of him. It was, said Raziuddin, "a moment of great clarity that I had made the right decision to make the US my home."[1]*

We can never know with certainty what other people feel or desire, and there have surely been malignant actors during the centuries of debate—and even armed conflict—that Americans have had over education. But the vast majority of public schooling advocates have no doubt truly sought harmony and cohesion. Nonetheless, history is clear, and the thin statistical evidence suggestive, that forced funding of a single system of government schools is the wrong path to achieve either harmony or cohesion.

In a pluralist nation, populated by sundry races, ethnicities, creeds, and philosophies, such a system entraps all people in the walls of a gladiatorial arena. It forces them to fight to determine who will, and will *not*, have their tax dollars used in accordance with their bedrock values, and affirm their racial, ethnic, gender, or other identities. The outcomes of such a system are often political combat that ends in one side winning and the other rendered unequal under the law, or détente grounded in lowest-common-denominator content that degrades academic value while leaving educators and students tiptoeing across eggshells.

But how can education be within the reach of all children without government supplying schools? And how can we ensure that all children have had basic American values such as civic participation, or tolerance of the rights of others, instilled in them? How can we guarantee that all members of the upcoming generation are prepared to successfully live their own lives while embracing the building blocks of the country that protects them?

The answer is not to maintain an education system that is fundamentally at odds with the most essential of American values: liberty. It is not to keep a system that must first destroy bedrock American values to save them. No, educational freedom, often under the shorthand "school choice," can more peacefully and effectively transmit socially beneficial knowledge and behavior than public schooling, and can do so without sacrificing essential liberty and equality under the law. Broadly speaking, funding can be connected to children, and educators can be unshackled to teach what and how they see fit.

Educational freedom would quickly reduce combat and enable increased rigor. Evangelical Christians could attend evangelical Christian schools without having to sacrifice their taxes to secular public institutions. Parents desiring deep exploration of Mexican history and culture could seek educators who want to provide such instruction. Parents who do not want their 10-year-old reading Harry Potter, or high schooler tackling *The Bluest Eye*, could choose schools where those works are not taught. Meanwhile, teachers could furnish unrepentant evolution, or "great man" history, or social justice theories, rather than diluting to keep peace.

But wouldn't this kind of choice sacrifice academic achievement? And doesn't public schooling guarantee that all children will have access to education, and be held to at least basic standards? The answer is "no" to both concerns.

Just as we have seen superior performance by private schools on civic participation and knowledge, the evidence suggests that public schooling neither provides better academic outcomes nor is necessary for widespread education. People will seek education because it is of great value, and, as James Coleman found, private provision will tend to be superior because it enables like-minded people to work together, maximizing agreement and, in turn, efficiency.[2] It also delivers quick accountability: anyone dissatisfied with their child's school can take their child, and the money attached to her, elsewhere, rather than having to engage in years of political crusading to (hopefully) improve schools quite possibly long after the child has left high school.

As historian Albert Fishlow ascertained, before education was compulsory or government provision widespread, literacy among white adults—people not *barred by government* from attaining an education—approached universality. Indeed, when Union soldiers liberated enslaved African Americans during the Civil War, they were often amazed at how many had illegally learned to read.[3] And literacy was often widespread even in some of the deepest colonial backwaters.[4] Of course, children were also taught trades, whether it was farming with their parents or apprenticeships with master craftsmen.

Traveling much further back, Andrew Coulson has shown that education was widespread in ancient Athens, and primarily sold for profit.[5] Indeed, education—learning things—is a constant and inescapable part of life, and for millennia older generations have instructed the youngest, including inculcating shared values and immersing children in social institutions. Education takes place all the time and, at least partially for all people, without government provision.

Perhaps, though, academic quality is better when government is at the helm. Or perhaps not. This might seem like a clear-cut matter, but it is a difficult question to answer for much the same reason that public schools cannot serve all people equally: there is serious disagreement about what constitutes "academic quality."

As many of the Founding generation—and all generations thereafter—debated, is the purpose of education to shape morals and ground one in the liberal arts, or to furnish practical skills to prepare one to earn a living? Is the right goal to be able to recite and interpret Ovid, or do double-entry bookkeeping? In the modern day, should all students know classic literature, such as Shakespeare or Twain, or score high in standardized tests in science, technology, engineering, and mathematics, the vaunted STEM fields?

And what measures of achievement are the right ones? Are standardized tests of any kind valid measures of education, or only those that measure against specific standards, such as the Common Core? If used, what weight should such tests be given in judging overall academic achievement versus, say, portfolios of student work, or graduation rates?

Questions about the place and value of tests have been hotly debated in American education for decades, and a major change in national emphasis occurred in late 2015 when the test-centric No Child Left Behind Act was replaced with the gentler Every Student Succeeds Act. The latter curbed the former's rigid assessment of schools using student test scores, allowing additional measures of success and targeting only the schools with the poorest outcomes for interventions. The public had increasingly become exhausted with test-as-everything policy, hating the rigidity and seriously doubting standardized tests' value as measures of education.

But assume standardized tests are a good measure of overall achievement. Add high school completion as a second measure. How does choice measure up?

Andrew Coulson examined hundreds of studies assessing the "marketness" of education systems and their academic outcomes. Basically, how freedom correlates with academic performance. What he found clearly favored market provision.

Among studies assessing achievement using test scores, 46 found a statistically significant private school advantage, versus only 10 finding a significant government schooling edge. Twenty-eight had statistically insignificant outcomes. Assessing attainment, measured as high school graduation rates or highest average grades completed, 11 studies with statistically significant findings favored private schooling and none government schooling.[6]

Moving beyond school types to incorporate additional freedom measures—who sets curricula, do parents have some responsibility to help pay for schooling, and so on—systems with more freedom appeared to consistently beat government monopolies. Coulson found that 20 studies reported statistically significant superior free-market results on achievement, versus 7 finding a monopoly advantage. On attainment, eight revealed a market advantage, three a monopoly advantage.

As Coulson conceded, counting studies is not the most rigorous way to determine advantages, but it certainly suggests an academic edge for educational freedom. How have specific programs in the United States done on achievement comparisons, especially the most rigorous, randomized controlled trials? Recall that because students are randomly assigned, hard-to-observe characteristics such as motivation are equally distributed, making it much more likely that observed effects are caused by the treatment than that they reflect preexisting student characteristics.

Choice programs have fared well in these studies, with applicants who randomly received vouchers and attended private schools doing as well as, or better than, recipients who went to public schools. The degree of superior performance has not been overwhelming—no drastically different scores— but as of April 2021, 17 random-assignment studies had been conducted of publicly and privately funded programs, with seven finding the full sample of students benefited from choice.[7] Six studies have found no effect for the full sample, and two negative effects, both assessing the Louisiana Scholarship Program. (One study compared only subgroups.) There were various effects for specific subgroups, the large majority positive or neutral.

The two outliers should be taken with a grain of salt. Louisiana's program had recently had numerous rules placed on it when it was first assessed, including requirements to administer state tests that would determine if a school could stay in the program. The new regulatory scheme likely encouraged many top-performing private schools to stay out of the program, lest they be forced to significantly alter their academic focus and curricular goals. There is evidence of this participation deterrent effect not just in Louisiana, but also Wisconsin, New York, California, Indiana, the District of Columbia, North Carolina, and Ohio.[8]

The District of Columbia Opportunity Scholarship Program has also been targeted for producing poor test scores. Prior to the most recent set of evaluations, the program had been assessed over several years, culminating in a 2010 evaluation that found no statistically significant difference in math and reading scores for voucher winners who attended private schools and those who applied but did not win the lottery. That said, the reading results suggesting better outcomes for voucher users missed statistical significance by a sliver: a p-value of .06 instead of .05 or smaller.[9]

The more recent set of studies started with an evaluation published in 2017. It assessed the performance of students in their first year in the program and found statistically significant negative effects for voucher users on math but not reading.[10] But this was far from a conviction of school choice.

Washington, DC, has a huge amount of choice. Not only can parents who work in the district choose to live in Maryland or Virginia, but 42 percent of control group students attended charter schools, and 10 percent private schools. And while money has limited effects on student achievement, some parity is necessary for schools to compete and survive. Relatively speaking, the DC voucher program provides very little: the maximum voucher was roughly $8,500 for grades K–8, and $12,500 for 9–12,[11] while traditional public schools spent a whopping $30,000 per pupil, and charters received about $17,500.[12]

While negative effects persisted into year two, in 2019 the third study in the series was released. It found no significant difference in test scores between voucher users and students who applied for a voucher and did not receive one.[13] So even with major competition, greatly unequal funding, and likely lesser private school emphasis on standardized tests than public schools, vouchers produced the same test results.

One reason for DC public schools' later, at-first somewhat superior performance against private schools may be that competition spurred them to improve. Indeed, this might be the most frequently documented effect of choice. As of early 2021, of the 27 studies that have analyzed the effect of private school choice on public school test scores, 25 have found positive impacts, 1 neutral, and 1 negative.[14] Choice, it strongly appears, catalyzes system-wide improvement.

How about attainment? This has been less studied than test scores, but the choice impact appears to be much greater. In their official evaluation of DC's program, Patrick Wolf and co-investigators found that being offered a voucher raised students' high school graduation rate by 12 percentage points, and using one to attend a private school boosted it 21 points.[15] While not random assignment, Joshua Cowen and co-authors controlled for many student characteristics and found that students in Milwaukee's voucher program were more likely to graduate from high school, and enroll and persist in college, than students in Milwaukee public schools.[16]

The empirical evidence should allay fears that absent a government schooling monopoly children go uneducated. Historically it has not been the case, even with incentives to pursue education far weaker than they are in the post-industrial world. Nor do modern choice programs indicate that private schools will supply worse academic experiences than public, even using standardized tests to which public schools are more geared and accustomed. Indeed, even without playing-field-leveling choice programs there is evidence that private, including for-profit, schools will exist, work with the poor, and outperform government schools.

Researcher James Tooley has spent decades unearthing evidence about elementary and secondary education in many of the world's poorest places. From the urban slums of Lagos, Nigeria, to the mountain villages of China, he has found almost ubiquitous for-profit schooling, with parents often paying unaided by government. Administering tests to public and private students and adjusting for student characteristics such as family income, Tooley has found that the private school children outperform students in government schools.[17]

How could this be? The answer is that private schools, dependent on customers freely choosing their services, must perform well lest their customers take their extremely precious money elsewhere. In addition to social capital and other somewhat intangible benefits that private schooling might supply, Tooley has found basic accountability for academic outcomes, proceeding from the inescapable need to attract paying customers, is huge.

Of course, in-school social capital matters. Researching Catholic schools to ascertain why they seem to get better results for comparable kids with far less generous resources than public schools, James Coleman and Thomas Hoffer determined that they succeed due to high degrees of bonding capital. By forming enclosed communities in which all members agree on norms and, to a large extent, keep tabs on each other's children, Catholic schools have strong bonds that enable them to work efficiently and effectively. They are a single unit, not an assemblage of students, teachers, and administrators held together by the wispy threads of zip codes and regulations.[18]

As discussed in the previous chapter, one of the upshots of voluntary association is that schools can teach more content-rich, coherent lessons. Among other factors, that appears to produce better civic outcomes. Far from balkanizing, even the bonding capital of private schooling has potentially strong bridging benefits.

OUTLINE OF PROGRESS: HOW CAN WE GET THE FREEDOM WE NEED?

It is easy to imagine the education system that would be most consistent with a nation based in liberty and equality: it would consist of whatever people freely chose. Millions of individual educators and families would agree on what would be taught, when, how, and at what price, in myriad arrangements. And though decisions would be made by individuals, it would likely be anything but hyperindividualistic, as is often the knock on such a vision. Instead, it would create more *true* communities: *voluntary* groupings bonded by shared norms, desires, and beliefs.

That said, there is a crucial consideration that complicates matters. While total educational freedom would maximize liberty, true liberty is something that exists only for people capable of self-government. We typically call these people "adults," excluding those with impairments preventing them from competently making decisions for themselves. By definition, "children" are not "adults." That means, contra a fully laissez faire system, someone other than the person to be educated will be making decisions for them, whether parents or government. Children will not, because they presumably *cannot*, make such decisions for themselves.

What does this mean for the role of government? Should it be, as Durkheim, Gutmann, and others have argued, that children should be put into government institutions in part to free them of their parents' prejudices? Certainly parental control is no more freeing than governmental. From the child's perspective, control is control, right?

Children are, indeed, subject to someone else's rule no matter what, though the older children get the more they tend to buck any such dominion. That said, the consequences of defying government tend to be more dire than blowing off a parent-imposed curfew, or trombone practice. Being grounded by parents can mean loss of allowance or texting privileges for a week. Being grounded by government can mean imprisonment, often for much longer than a week. For this reason alone, parental decision-making ought to be preferred to governmental: the potential negative consequences of government control are much more dire.

At least as important as the wide gulf in potential severity between parental and governmental justice is that parental control, even if it confines a child's experience to one religious tradition or ethnic group, helps to preserve distinctive, emotionally powerful communities; groupings of people along ethnic, religious, or other lines that are rich in social capital. If government homogenizes children in such communities, it de facto *curbs freedom* by stifling these communities' reproduction. Pluralism is hurt if we undermine the distinctive communities in which people live, and from which they draw meaning and fulfillment.[19]

Public schooling must also be secular—it would violate the First Amendment's establishment clause were government schools to teach devotional religion—but that means public schooling inherently elevates the secular over the religious, rendering religious Americans unequal under the law.[20] Beyond the Constitutional violation, the societal message that attends to that is religion is for the margins and secularism is "mainstream," rendering religious people second class. Choice would be neutral; government supporting neither religion nor non-religion. Free people's decisions would decide what is mainstream.

It is also inherently dangerous to empower government to decide what are "right" and "wrong" worldviews and ways of living. Not only is government not omniscient—no human being nor group of people is even close to all-knowing—judgments about the right values or beliefs are inherently subjective. In light of these massive limits, it is far better to let conceptions of the good freely coexist and compete than have government take a side.

It should also be noted that parents are much more likely to care about their children than politicians or bureaucrats. Indeed, parents are biologically compelled to care about their children.[21] Of course there are outliers, but the average parent is essentially chemically invested in their child.

Education must be based in freedom, even if it is largely freedom for parents, not only because liberty is the fundamental building block of American society and a good in and of itself, but because it is key to preserving the communities in which people find their psychological place—their homes. Meanwhile, empowering government to decide what all children will learn empowers the greatest threat to liberty: government, the institution with a legal monopoly on the use of force.

That said, just as the state steps in when parents neglect their children— they hurt them by failing to feed or clothe them—government should intervene if there is reasonable suspicion that parents are not providing their children with the basics they need to become self-governing adults. Arguably, those are literacy and numeracy, the foundational skills necessary to access subjects that are also important, such as history and biology, but that involve beliefs and political issues on which government should not tread.[22] And even in suspected cases of neglect, due process should be followed, with parents presumed innocent until proven guilty in court.

But how can educational freedom be realized, especially given the current reality that for the vast majority of Americans education is supplied directly by government? The solution—at least the beginning of it—is to do as Nobel laureate economist Milton Friedman proposed in 1955: separate the funding of education from its provision.[23] Government can, and many would argue *should*, pay for all or part of a child's education. But it should not supply the education itself. It would be a system of public *education*, not public *schooling*.

Such a separation would be a leap in the direction of liberty and equality. But as great an advancement as it would be, some compulsion would remain. A voucher, or government-funded education savings account that could be used for various expenses, takes money from a taxpayer and gives it to parents to use as they see fit. Should religious parents take an atheist's tax dollars to a Lutheran school, or atheists take a Lutheran's money to an atheist school, Thomas Jefferson's dictum would still apply: "to compel a man to furnish contributions of money for the propagation of opinions which he disbelieves and abhors, is sinful and tyrannical."[24]

Avoiding such compulsion is the ostensible justification for the "Blaine" or "compelled support" amendments in many state constitutions. James G. Blaine, recall, was a U.S. senator who in the 1870s proposed an amendment to the U.S. Constitution barring public money—federal, state, or local—from flowing to "sectarian" schools. At the time, "sectarian" was a euphemism for "Roman Catholic," while the public schools were de facto Protestant. Though Blaine's effort failed, many states adopted his idea for their own constitutions, and it was a required component for some western territories to be admitted to the union.[25]

Blaine's goal appeared to be to keep public funding for Protestants, which gives the amendments named after him an anti-Catholic taint. Today, however, the provisions are obstacles to government funding flowing to *any* religious institution, even by individual choice, making them discriminatory against religion generally. But they are slowly disintegrating.

In its 2017 *Trinity Lutheran Church of Columbia, Inc. v. Comer* decision, the U.S. Supreme Court came close to declaring unconstitutional policies that allow the use of taxpayer funds for anything as long as the recipient is *not* religious. It ruled that it is unconstitutional to deny a church access to playground improvement funds solely on the grounds that it is a religious institution.[26]

The court came even closer to requiring true religious neutrality in 2020's *Espinoza v. Montana Department of Revenue* decision, holding that the Montana Supreme Court erred in striking down a scholarship tax credit program on the grounds that parents could use scholarship funds at religious schools.[27] Chief Justice John Roberts wrote that striking down a choice program because religious schools could participate was unconstitutional, but stopped short of saying choice was *necessary*: "A State need not subsidize private education. But once a State decides to do so, it cannot disqualify some private schools solely because they are religious."

There has been significant progress toward full religious liberty and equality under the law in education, but more needs to be done. For one, the 2004 *Locke v. Davey* Supreme Court decision upholding Washington State's decision to bar a graduate student from receiving a generally available state grant because he was going to study for the ministry needs to be overturned.[28] Government should neither act for nor against freely chosen religious uses of funds.

At the time of this writing, the court had just accepted a case that could upend *Locke. Carson v. Makin* involves "town-tuitioning" in the state of Maine, where districts unable to support public schools give money to parents to access private institutions.[29] The state allows such funding to be used at a private school as long as it does not provide religious instruction. Technically, then, a family can choose a religious school, but not if it teaches religion, which would be a religious use of the funds. Plaintiffs argue, correctly, the discriminating against "use" is discriminating against religion.

Beyond allowing religion within choice programs, courts need to recognize that forcing religious Americans to pay for secular public schools inherently discriminates against religion. This is legally untested, but it has received scholarly attention.[30] Justice Stephen Breyer also grasped it in his *Espinoza* dissent, though he did not like the expansive choice it portended: "If making scholarships available to only secular nonpublic schools exerts 'coercive' pressure on parents whose faith impels them to enroll their children in religious schools, then how is a State's decision to fund only secular public schools any less coercive?"

All this said, the broad idea captured by Blaine amendments, even if not originally intended by them, is just: Government should not compel you to support someone else's decisions if you find them objectionable, much less abhorrent or immoral. But if government pays for education, government money *will* fund values-laden decisions. Must we simply accept that some amount of compulsion must occur?

The answer is close to "no," and that is good news for advocates of liberty of all stripes, not just school choice advocates. By allowing individuals to receive credits on their taxes for money they spend on private schooling or homeschooling, public policy can essentially just stop people from having to pay twice for education: once for the public schools they do not use, again for private education they do.

For families with too small a tax liability for a credit to meaningfully defray private schooling costs, individuals and corporations could receive tax credits for donations they make to groups that furnish scholarships, or that put money into education savings accounts, for children in such families. To maximize freedom, donors should be able to choose to whom they donate, including religious scholarship programs, arts-based schools, Montessori institutions . . . whatever. Liberty is maximized when families receive funds they can direct to the educational arrangements of their choice, and taxpayers choose whether to donate, and to whom.

Such credits, of course, exist. As of January 2021, tax credits and deductions were being utilized to help fund nearly 330,000 private school scholarships, and had grown faster and more numerous than vouchers.[31] It seems likely that tax credits have surpassed vouchers at least in part because they do not take a dollar from a taxpayer and give it to someone else, but instead just make whole, or partially whole, people who *choose* to direct their own funds to the education of others. They also tend to be less regulated, likely because the funders themselves have more direct control over their money.[32]

Vouchers, and even more donation tax credits, are huge advances for liberty in education. But even tax credits involve a small amount of coercion, albeit indirectly. Credits can and often do save the taxpaying public money if they move students from more expensive public to less expensive private schools. But if programs cost more than they save, which is rare but possible, taxpayers could end up paying for government functions that would otherwise have been covered by funds from tax credit claimants.[33] This substitution effect—taxpayers having to cover other expenses so donors can fund choice—could be perceived as coercion to fund private schools.

Even this could be avoided, but it would require moving to a system that we could not realize right away: no government involvement in education. The reality is that roughly 90 percent of school-aged children attend public schools, and Americans have little experience obtaining K–12 education on their own. There are also far-insufficient private school seats to accommodate all students were there suddenly an education free market. And because the norm has for so long been that children are assigned to schools, there are few guides to help people choose, though websites such as GreatSchools.org and Niche.com have begun to fill that void.

In the long run, once choice is expanded, a free market would absolutely be possible. American history attests to it—education was widespread long before public schooling—and in the poorest parts of the world, as Tooley has found, for-profit schooling is serving many of humanity's most destitute young members. There would also be help for consumers: American higher education, grounded in tuition-paying students, features guides aplenty, including the *U.S. News & World Report's* "Best Colleges" issue; the Princeton Review's rankings of party schools, happiest students, and so on; the *Forbes* ranking of schools' value propositions; and the *Washington Monthly* assessment of contributions to upward mobility.

That said, in a free market there would probably be a relative handful of parents who would do nothing to educate their children. The group would indeed be small—as discussed, human beings are biologically driven to care for their young—but they would exist. Of course, their children would almost certainly face crippling neglect *well before they were school aged*, and suffer in ways that any school would struggle to ameliorate. In such cases the state has a duty to intervene, perhaps even removing a child from a home. But that should be a last resort, and the existence of such families in no way justifies blocking freedom as the education norm.

CONCLUSION

To see all Americans—indeed, all people—live as a harmonious, unified whole is, hopefully, a universal desire. For many, it is the primary goal of public schooling. But that system is doomed to fail, not just because at its very core it is incompatible with bedrock liberty and equality under the law, but because it is virtually guaranteed to foster social fabric–ripping, zero-sum conflict over people's most basic values and identities.

To break free of public schooling we must first awaken from our ignorance about it. We must know and acknowledge its true history: how it often served mainly homogeneous communities, excluded large swaths of humanity thought unassimilable or perhaps naturally unequal, and tried to transform through humiliating processes those considered too different from the "American" norm. We must acknowledge that imagery of the public school as the great American unifier, or "bedrock of our democracy," is rhetoric, not reality.

Once Americans absorb the truth, we can move to a system that is consistent with liberty and equality; that is far less likely to spark social war; and that furnishes sustainable, social-bridging material—voluntary attraction. A system that can, over time, help to surmount the distance between long disconnected groups and build new, common identities. That begins with what we call "school choice," but is far better described as "educational freedom." It is the only system of education fit for a nation of free and equal people.

NOTES

1. Bay Area Census, "San Francisco Bay Area," http://www.bayareacensus.ca.gov/bayarea.htm, accessed January 24, 2019; Stuart Anderson, "Immigrants and Billion Dollar Startups," *NFAP Policy Brief*, National Foundation for American Policy, March 2016; Stephanie Hanes, Immigration and Assimilation: Feeling Global, but Being an American," *Christian Science Monitor*, July 7, 2013.

2. James S. Coleman, "Social Capital in the Creation of Human Capital," *American Journal of Sociology*, vol. 94 Supplement (1988): S95–S120.

3. Derek W. Black, *Schoolhouse Burning: Public Education and the Assault on American Democracy* (New York: Public Affairs, 2020), 88.

4. Robert E. Gallman, "Changes in the Level of Literacy in a New Community of Early America," *Journal of Economic History* 48, no. 3 (1988): 567–582.

5. Andrew J. Coulson, *Market Education: The Unknown History* (New Brunswick, NJ: Transaction Publishers, 1999), 40–49.

6. Andrew J. Coulson, "Comparing Public, Private, and Market Schools: The International Evidence," *Journal of School Choice 3, n*o. 3 (2009): 31–54.

7. EdChoice, *The 123s of School Choice: What the Research Says about Private School Choice Programs in America*, 2021 Edition, 25–30, April 14, 2021, https://www.edchoice.org/wp-content/uploads/2021/04/2021-123s-SlideShare-1.pdf#page=25.

8. Corey A. DeAngelis, Lindsey M. Burke, and Patrick J. Wolf, "The Effects of Regulations on Private School Choice Program Participation: Experimental Evidence from California and New York," EDRE Working Paper 2019-07, March 12, 2019; Corey A. DeAngelis and Blake Hoarty, "Who Participates? An Analysis of School Participation Decisions in Two Voucher Programs in the United States," Cato Institute Policy Analysis no. 848, September 17, 2018; Corey A. DeAngelis, "Regulatory Compliance Costs and Private School Participation in Voucher Programs," *Journal of School Choice* 14, no. 1 (October 2019): 95–121.

9. Patrick Wolf, et al., "Evaluation of the DC Opportunity Scholarship Program: Final Report," NCEE 2010–4018, U.S. Department of Education, June 2010.

10. Mark Dynarski et al., "Evaluation of the DC Opportunity Scholarship Program: Impacts after One Year," NCEE 2017–4022, U.S. Department of Education, April 2017.

11. Serving Our Children, "For Parents," http://servingourchildrendc.org/our-program/.

12. DC Charter Public School Board, "National Report Finds Funding Inequities for D.C. Charter Schools," press release, May 17, 2010.

13. Ann Weber et al., "Evaluation of the DC Opportunity Scholarship Program: Impacts Three Years after Students Applied," NCEE 2019-4006, U.S. Department of Education, May 2019.

14. EdChoice, *The 123s of School Choice*, 25–30.

15. Patrick Wolf et al., "Evaluation of the DC Opportunity Scholarship Program: Final Report," 35.

16. Joshua M. Cowen, et al., "School Vouchers and Student Attainment: Evidence from a State-Mandated Study of Milwaukee's Parental Choice Program," *Policy Studies Journal* 41, no. 1 (February 2013): 147–168.

17. James Tooley, *The Beautiful Tree* (Washington, DC: Cato Institute, 2009).

18. James S. Coleman and Thomas Hoffer, *Public and Private High Schools: The Impact of Communities* (New York: Basic Books, 1987).

19. For a good discussion of education and pluralism, see Ashley Rogers-Berner, *No One Way to School: Pluralism and American Public Education* (New York: Palgrave Macmillan, 2017).

20. To see the many ways public schools must make decisions with serious religious implications, see Neal McCluskey, "Toward Conceptual and Concrete Understanding of the Impossibility of Religiously Neutral Public Schooling," *Journal of School Choice* 12, no. 4 (2018): 477–505.

21. See, for instance, James K. Rilling and Larry J. Young, "The Biology of Mammalian Parenting and Its Effect on Offspring Social Development," *Science* 345, no. 6198 (August 15, 2014): 771–776. Also Adrienne LaFrance, "What Happens to a Woman's Brain When She Becomes a Mother?" *Atlantic*, January 8, 2015, https://www.theatlantic.com/health/archive/2015/01/what-happens-to-a-womans-brain-when-she-becomes-a-mother/384179/.

22. What children should be taught to become self-governing adults is subject to debate. See, for instance, Meira Levinson, The Demands of Liberal Education (Oxford, UK: Oxford University Press, 1999). Levinson argues that children need to be exposed to diverse people and ways of thinking in school to become autonomous adults. For the argument that children benefit from being educated in communities with strong norms, see Rita Koganzon, "Pork Eating Is Not a Reasonable Way of Life: Yeshiva Education vs. Liberal Educational Theory," in *Religious Liberty and Education: A Case Study of Yeshivas vs. New York*, eds. Jason Bedrick, Jay P. Greene, and Matthew H. Lee (Lanham, MD: Rowman & Littlefield, 2020), 31–45.

23. Milton Friedman, "The Role of Government in Education," in *Economics and the Public Interest*, ed. Robert A. Solo (New Brunswick, NJ: Rutgers University Press, 1955).

24. "Virginia Statute for Religious Freedom," Thomas Jefferson Foundation, https://www.monticello.org/site/research-and-collections/virginia-statute-religious-freedom, accessed December 12, 2019.

25. Richard D. Komer and Clark Neily, "School Choice and State Constitutions: A Guide to Designing School Choice Programs," Institute for Justice and American Legislative Exchange Council, April 2007, 4.

26. *Trinity Lutheran Church of Columbia, Inc. v. Comer*, 582 U.S. ___ (2017).

27. *Espinoza v. Montana Department of Revenue*, 591 U.S. ___ (2020).

28. *Locke v. Davey*, 540 U.S. 712 (2004).

29. Alexa Lardieri, "Supreme Court to Hear Maine Religious School Tuition Case," *U.S. News & World Report*, July 2, 2021, https://www.usnews.com/news/education-news/articles/2021-07-02/supreme-court-to-hear-maine-religious-school-tuition-case.

30. See, for instance, Michael W. McConnell, "Unconstitutional Conditions: Unrecognized Implications for the Establishment Clause," *San Diego Law Review*

26 (1989): 255–275; and Steven G. Calabresi and Abe Salander, "Religion and the Equal Protection Clause: Why the Constitution Requires School Vouchers," *Florida Law Review* 65, no. 4 (2013): 909–1087.

31. EdChoice, *The ABCs of School Choice: 2021 Edition*, January 2021, 7–8, https://www.edchoice.org/wp-content/uploads/2021/03/2021-ABCs-of-School-Choice-WEB-2-24.pdf.

32. Andrew J. Coulson, "Do Vouchers and Tax Credits Increase Private School Regulation? A Statistical Analysis," *Journal of School Choice* 5, no. 2 (2011): 224–251.

33. Of 70 private school choice fiscal effect studies, 65 have found positive effects for taxpayers and public schools, and only 4 a negative effect. EdChoice, *The 123s of School Choice*, 41–48.

Selected Bibliography

Adams, John and Thomas Jefferson. *The Adams-Jefferson Letters: The Complete Correspondence between Thomas Jefferson and Abigail and John Adams*, edited by Lester J. Capon. Chapel Hill, NC: The University of North Carolina Press, 1987.

Allport, Gordon W. *The Nature of Prejudice*. Boston: Beacon Press, 1954.

Aristotle. *The Politics of Aristotle*, translated by Peter L. Phillips Simpson. Chapel Hill, NC: The University of North Carolina Press, 1997.

Armor, David. J. *Forced Justice: School Desegregation and the Law*. New York: Oxford University Press, 1995.

Arons, Stephen. *Compelling Belief: The Culture of American Schooling*. Amherst, MA: University of Massachusetts Press, 1983.

Arons, Stephen. *Short Route to Chaos: Conscience, Community, and the Re-constitution of American Schooling*. Amherst, MA: University of Massachusetts Press, 1997.

Bailyn, Bernard. *Education in the Forming of American Society*. New York: W. W. Norton and Company, 1960.

Banks, James A. and Cherry A. McGee Banks, eds. *Handbook of Research on Multicultural Education*. New York: Macmillan Library Reference, 1995.

Barone, Michael. *The New Americans: How the Melting Pot Can Work Again*. Washington, DC: Regnery, 2001.

Bedrick, Jason, Jay P. Greene, and Matthew H. Lee, eds. *Religious Liberty and Education: A Case Study of Yeshivas vs. New York*. Lanham, MD: Rowman & Littlefield, 2020.

Belfield, Clive R. and Henry M. Levin. *Privatizing Educational Choice: Consequences for Parents, Schools, and Public Policy*. Boulder, CO: Paradigm, 2005.

Berkman, Michael and Eric Plutzer. *Evolution, Creationism, and the Battle to Control America's Classrooms*. New York: Cambridge University Press, 2010.

Black, Derek W. *Schoolhouse Burning: Public Education and the Assault on American Democracy*. New York: Public Affairs, 2020.

Bourdieu, Pierre and Jean-Claude Passeron. *Reproduction in Education, Society, and Culture*, 2nd ed. Translated by Richard Nice. Thousand Oaks, CA: SAGE Publications, 2000.

Coleman, James S. "Social Capital in the Creation of Human Capital." *American Journal of Sociology* 94, supplement (1988): S95–S120.

Coulson, Andrew J. *Market Education: The Unknown History*. New Brunswick, NJ: Transaction Publishers, 1999.

Counts, George S. *Dare the School Build a New Social Order?* Carbondale, IL: Southern Illinois University Press, 1978.

Cremin, Lawrence. *American Education: The Colonial Experience, 1607–1783*. New York: Harper Torchbooks, 1970.

Cremin, Lawrence. *American Education: The National Experience, 1783–1876*. New York: Harper Colophon Books, 1980.

Cubberley, Ellwood. *Changing Conceptions of Education*. Boston, MA: Houghton Mifflin Company, 1909.

Cubberley, Ellwood. *The History of Education*. New York: Kessinger Publishing, 1920.

DeAngelis, Corey A. and Neal P. McCluskey, eds. *School Choice Myths: Setting the Record Straight on Education Freedom*. Washington, DC: Cato Institute, 2020.

Delmont, Matthew F. *Why Busing Failed: Race, Media, and the National Resistance to School Desegregation*. Oakland, CA: University of California Press, 2016.

Dewey, John. *Democracy and Education*. New York: Barnes & Noble Books, 2005.

Dovidio, John F., Peter Glick, and Laurie A. Rudman, eds. *On the Nature of Prejudice: Fifty Years after Allport*. Malden, MA: Blackwell Publishing, 2005.

EdChoice. *The 123s of School Choice: What the Research Says about Private School Choice Programs in America*.

Friedman, Milton. "The Role of Government in Education," in *Economics and the Public Interest*, ed. Robert A. Solo. New Brunswick, NJ: Rutgers University Press, 1955.

Fukuyama, Francis. *Trust: The Social Virtues and the Creation of Prosperity*. New York: Free Press, 1995.

Glenn, Charles L. *Contrasting Models of State and School: A Comparative Historical Study of Parental Choice and State Control*. New York: Continuum, 2011

Glenn, Charles L. *The Myth of the Common School*. Amherst, MA: University of Massachusetts Press, 1987.

Glenn, Charles L. "Religion and the Adoption of School Choice Policies." *Journal of School Choice* 12, no. 4 (Special issue on religion and school choice): 461–476.

Goodlad, John I. and Timothy J. McMannon, eds. *The Public Purpose of Education and Schooling*. San Francisco, CA: Jossey-Bass, 1997.

Gordon, Milton M. *Assimilation in American Life: The Role of Race, Religion, and National Origins*. New York: Oxford University Press, 1964.

Green, Steven K. *The Bible, the School, and the Constitution: The Clash That Shaped Modern Church-State Doctrine*. New York: Oxford University Press, 2012.

Gutmann, Amy. *Democratic Education*. Princeton, NJ: Princeton Paperbacks, 1999.

Haidt, Jonathan. *The Righteous Mind: Why Good People Are Divided by Politics and Religion*. New York: Vintage Books, 2013.

Hartmann, Edward George. *The Movement to Americanize the Immigrant*. New York: Columbia University Press, 1948.

Henig, Jeffrey R. *Rethinking School Choice: Limits of the Market Metaphor*. Princeton, NJ: Princeton University Press, 1994.

Hobbes, Thomas. *Leviathan*, edited by Crawford B. Macpherson. London, UK: Penguin Books, 1968.

Herberg, Will. *Protestant-Catholic-Jew*. Chicago: The University of Chicago Press, 1983.

Hirsch, E. D. Jr. *Cultural Literacy: What Every American Needs to Know*. New York: Vintage Books, 1988.

Hirsch, E. D. Jr. *The Making of Americans: Democracy and Our Schools*. New Haven, CT: Yale University Press, 2009.

Jefferson, Thomas. *Jefferson: Writings*. Compiled by Merrill D. Peterson. New York: Literary Classics of the U.S., 1984.

Jeynes, William. *Religion, Education, and Academic Success*. Greenwich, CT: Information Age Publishing, 2003.

Jorgenson, Lloyd P. *The State and the Non-Public Schools: 1825–1925*. Columbia, MO: University of Missouri Press.

Justice, Benjamin. *The War That Wasn't: Religious Conflict and Compromise in the Common Schools of New York State, 1865–1900*. Albany, NY: State University of New York Press, 2005.

Kaestle, Carl F. *Pillars of the Republic: Common Schools and American Society, 1780–1860*. New York: Hill & Wang, 1983.

Kahlenberg, Richard D. *All Together Now: Creating Middle-Class Schools through Public School Choice*. Washington, DC: Brookings Institution Press, 2001.

Kilpatrick, William H., et al. *The Educational Frontier*. New York: Century Company, 1933.

Levinson, Meira. *The Demands of Liberal Education*. Oxford, UK: Oxford University Press, 1999.

Locke, John. *Two Treatises of Government*, edited by Peter Laslett. New York: Cambridge University Press, 1994.

Lucas, J. Anthony. *Common Ground: A Turbulent Decade in the Lives of Three American Families*. New York: Vintage Press, 1986.

Mann, Mary, ed. *Life and Works of Horace Mann*. Boston: Horace B. Fuller, 1868.

Mathews, David. *Reclaiming Public Education by Reclaiming Our Democracy*. Dayton, OH: Kettering Foundation Press, 2006.

McClellan, B. Edward and William J. Reese, eds. *The Social History of American Education*. Urbana: University of Illinois Press, 1988.

Meier, Deborah. *In Schools We Trust: Creating Communities of Learning in an Era of Testing and Standardization*. Boston: Beacon Press, 2002.

Montesquieu, *The Spirit of the Laws*, edited by Anne Cohler, Basia Miller, and Harold Stone. Cambridge, UK: Cambridge University Press, 1992.

Neem, Johann M. *Democracy's Schools: The Rise of Public Education in America*. Baltimore: Johns Hopkins University Press, 2017.

Orfield, Gary, John Kucsera, and Genevieve Siegel-Hawley. "E Pluribus . . . Separation? Deepening Double Segregation for Our Students." Civil Rights Project. September 2012.

Pangle, Lorraine Smith and Thomas L. Pangle. *The Learning of Liberty: The Educational Ideas of the American Founders*. Lawrence, KS: University of Kansas Press, 1993.

Petrilli, Michael J. *The Diverse Schools Dilemma: A Parent's Guide to Socioeconomically Mixed Public Schools*. Washington, DC: Thomas B. Fordham Institute, 2012.

Pettigrew, Thomas F. and Linda R. Tropp. "The Meta-Analytic Test of Intergroup Contact Theory." *Journal of Personality and Social Psychology* 90, no. 5 (2006): 751–783.

Plato. *The Republic*, translated by Desmond Lee. London, Penguin Books, 1987.

Putnam, Robert D. *Bowling Alone: The Collapse and Revival of American Community*. New York: Simon & Schuster, 2000.

Putnam, Robert. "E Pluribus Unum: Diversity and Community in the Twenty-First Century." *Scandinavian Political Studies* 30, no. 2 (2007): 142.

Ravitch, Diane. *The Death and Life of the Great American School System: How Testing and Choice Are Undermining Education*. New York: Basic Books, 2010.

Ravitch, Diane. *The Great School Wars: A History of the New York City Public Schools*. Baltimore: Johns Hopkins University Press, 2000.

Ravitch, Diane. *The Language Police: How Pressure Groups Restrict What Students Learn*. New York: Alfred A. Knopf, 2003.

Ravitch, Diane. *Left Back: A Century of Battles Over School Reform*. New York: Touchstone, 2000.

Rogers Berner, Ashley. *No One Way to School: Pluralism and American Public Education*. New York: Palgrave Macmillan, 2017.

Rossell, Christine H. and David J. Armor. "The Effectiveness of School Desegregation Plans, 1968-1991." *American Politics Quarterly* 24, no. 3 (July 1996): 276.

Rossiter, Clinton, ed. *The Federalist Papers*. New York: Mentor Books, 1961.

Rothstein, Richard. *The Color of Law: A Forgotten History of How Our Government Segregated America*. New York: W. W. Norton & Company, 2017.

Rudolph, Frederick, ed. *Essays on Education in the Early Republic*. Cambridge, MA: The Belknap Press of Harvard University Press, 1965.

Salins, Peter D. *Assimilation American Style*. New York: Basic Books, 1997.

Scott, Janelle T. and Richard F. Elmore, eds. *School Choice and Diversity: What the Evidence Says*. New York: Teachers College Press, 1996.

Seybolt, Robert F. *Source Studies in American Colonial Education: The Private School*. Urbana, IL: University of Illinois, 1925.

Sherrill, Lewis J. *Presbyterian Parochial Schools: 1846–1870*. New Haven, CT: Yale University Press, 1932.

Tönnies, Ferdinand. *Community and Society*. Charles P. Loomis, trans. and ed. Mineola, NY: Dover Publications, 2002.

Tooley, James. *The Beautiful Tree*. Washington, DC: Cato Institute, 2009.

Tyack, David B. *The One Best System: A History of American Urban Education*. Cambridge, MA: Harvard University Press, 1974.

Tyack, David. *Seeking Common Ground: Public Schools in Diverse Society*. Cambridge, MA: Harvard University Press, 2003.

Urban, Wayne J. and Jennings L. Waggoner Jr. *American Education: A History*. 3rd ed. Boston: McGraw-Hill, 2004.

Washington, George. *Washington: Writings*. Compiled by John Rhodehamel. New York: Literary Classics of the U.S., 1997.

Wiebe, Robert H. *The Segmented Society: An Introduction to the Meaning of America*. New York: Oxford University Press, 1979.

Wolf, Patrick J. and Stephen Macedo, eds. *Educating Citizens: International Perspectives on Civic Values and School Choice*. Washington, DC: Brookings Institution Press, 2004.

Zimmerman, Jonathan. *Small Wonder: The Little Red Schoolhouse in History and Memory*. New Haven, CT: Yale University Press, 2009.

Zimmerman, Jonathan. *Whose America: Culture Wars in the Public Schools*. Cambridge, MA: Harvard University Press, 2002.

Index

About the Author

Neal P. McCluskey is the director of the Cato Institute's Center for Educational Freedom. He is the author of *Feds in the Classroom: How Big Government Corrupts, Cripples, and Compromises American Education* and is coeditor of several books, including *School Choice Myths: Setting the Record Straight on Education Freedom*. He maintains Cato's Public Schooling Battle Map, an interactive database of values and identity-based conflicts in public schools; is on the editorial board of the *Journal of School Choice*; and is on the editorial advisory board of *The Line*, a journal promoting civil discourse in K–12 policy debates.

Prior to joining Cato in 2003, McCluskey worked at the Center for Education Reform, taught high school English, was a freelance reporter covering municipal government and education, and served in the U.S. Army. McCluskey holds an undergraduate degree from Georgetown University, where he double majored in government and English; a master's degree in political science from Rutgers University, Newark; and a PhD in public policy from George Mason University.